Camps, Cottages and Cabins

Gift from

Joanne Palmisano

Camps, Cottages and Cabins

Tips and Ideas for Getting the Most Out of Your Seasonal Home

Joanne Palmisano

HAPPY HOLLOW
P R O M O T I O N S
Burlington, Vermont

Camps, Cottages and Cabins
Tips and Ideas for Getting the Most Out of Your Seasonal Home

Book Edited by Lyle Nelson
Cover Copy Edited by David Cleveland
Book Layout by Michele Fairchild

ISBN: 0-9657890-9-8

Printed and Bound in the United States of America

For Mom and Dad,

All my love,
Joanne

So many people to thank!

A big hug and kiss for...

Lyle Nelson, a dear friend and fabulous editor, played a key role in making the words in this book flow like a river. I cannot thank him enough for his generosity and friendship.

Also special thanks goes to my family, Stephen Booth, Charlie Palmisano, Julie Anderson, Yvonne Palmisano, Charles Palmisano, Rosanne Palmisano, Brenda Palmisano and Curtis Anderson, for their encouragement and the key roles they played in putting together the contents of this book.

Michelle Quinlan and Meghan Scalley, my college interns, are also to be thanked profusely for their hard work in creating a marketing plan and helping in photo shoots, editing and information gathering.

Many thanks go to Kim Moran, my research assistant, Michele Fairchild for her incredible design work and Jeanette DiScala, Joanne LaBrake, Marty Rudolph, Shannon Quimby, Holly and Dan Boardman and Elizabeth Boardman-Davis for their support and the wisdom they impart to my life.

I also want to thank the following individuals and cottage owners for all the hard-to-find information they provided: Debbie and Eric Hanley, Julie Myers, Bob Smith, David Cleveland, Amy Africa, Carmone Austin, Celine Teeson, Liz Neeld, Barbara Harrington, Karen Edgerly, Dan Lewitt, Stuart Close, Kristin Brown, Chris Moran, Becky Angelone, Jana Singer, Rock Benoit, Emily Cassani, Robin and Greg Rabideau, Suzie Petrie, Carol Lee Mason, Peggy and Jesse Anderson, Barry Genzlinger and Timna Genzlinger Dulmer, Bob Hill, Laury Shea, John Frieke, Warren and Kathy Miller, the staff at the Pearson Library, South Burlington Library, Lake Champlain Basin Program, and Fletcher Free Library. Also, thank you to Sherri and Jessica, at Heartworks Preschool, for taking such good care of Gabrielle, three mornings a week.

About the Author

Fisher Photography

Joanne Palmisano is the author of the book, *The Vermont Wedding & Event Resource Guide*. Before Joanne became an author, she spent twelve years in executive positions for non-profit organizations. With over twenty years experience as a camp, cottage and cabin owner and renter, Joanne has put together this handy book for other cottage owners. She, her husband, Stephen, and their little girl, Gabrielle, spend a lot of time on the beach of their lakefront home looking for sea glass, sunken treasures and fishing with a stick, string and paper clip.

Table of Contents

"Our 'getaway' provides us with a delightful vacation spot for the entire summer. It's a different atmosphere—less household cleaning and fussing—and an opportunity to relax and enjoy the outdoors. It's a special lifestyle and we've always been grateful that we have this to share with our children and now our grandchildren. It is a family tradition loved by all."

—Celine, Lake Champlain, Vermont

chapter one

Introduction

When my husband and I first met, he was in the middle of building a cabin on his thirteen wooded acres of land in Vermont. Trees, native flowers, a stream and wildlife surrounded the cabin. When finished, it was an adorable seven hundred square foot, cedar shingled, wind powered cabin with a loft bedroom, marble tiled bath, antique filled kitchen and cozy living room. Heat came from a woodstove and sunbeams streaming through the antique French paned windows. Each pane created its own kaleidoscope of rainbows that danced on the walls.

When we drove to the cabin, even though it was only thirty minutes from town, we felt as though we had entered a different world. In reflection, it is easy to see how we fell in love and why we continue to share the love of the lifestyle a cabin in the woods can bring.

For several years, we spent almost every

weekend there reading books, snowshoeing through the woods, watching stars from the porch and listening to the total stillness. The dirt road leading to the small cabin was named, Happy Hollow Road (hence the name of my company).

Later, we traded our snowshoes for water wings and purchased a fairy tale cottage on beautiful Lake Champlain in Vermont. We now spend our evenings with friends and family on our beach watching the sunset.

Why This Book?

My desire to write this book stems from the rich experiences acquired over twenty years of renting and owning a variety of camps, cottages and cabins.

It is easy to believe that 1 out of 10 families in the United States owns a second home, when we, owners of a camp, cottage or cabin, understand the importance they play in our lives. I have put this book together for everyone who wants to get away and yet understands that it takes time, energy and sometimes hard work to make our getaway places stay simple and fun.

The words camp, cottage and cabin, have different meanings to most people you ask, depending on where they are from. In Seattle, cabin is the most heard name for personal getaways. In New England, most people think of cabins as small abodes on a mountainside, deep in the forest. Cottages, too many, conjure up an image of a Maine ocean front home or a lake side dwelling. Whatever you call your retreat, one thing is

for sure, it is your own "little peace of heaven." (We will use words camp, cottage or cabin interchangeably throughout this book.)

Whether you are close to the clouds in your mountain retreat or hear water lapping at the shore, your instincts to get back to nature and the simpler things of life are embedded in human nature. Your special place will keep families together and bring friends closer, providing many wonderful memories for you to cherish throughout your lifetime. It is important that your second residence remains a pleasant stress free area. You will find this book filled with time and energy saving ideas regarding the upkeep of your cottage. Whether it is decorating, cleaning, fun things to do with the kids or quick meals for large groups, this book is designed to help you enjoy your special getaway place.

Know Why You Own a Cottage

You should have a basic understanding of why you own or want to buy a camp. Is it for you and your buddies to go fishing and hunting? Is it for your family and the dozens of grandchildren you now have? Or is it a romantic getaway for two? By knowing its purpose, you can make your dreams come true, by creating the right environment for you. Are you looking to update that primitive cabin from backwoods living to modern day comforts? Or do you want to transform your modern day cottage back into the simplicity of life fifty years ago? Whatever your intent, a cabin requires regular maintenance and daily routines to keep them ship-shape for you and your guests.

What's in a Name?

As I walk along the road to my parent's camp (lakehouse to them), there is always a smile on my face as I read the names of each camp; Camp Friday, Sunshine Knoll, the Sugar Shack, the Lake House, Camp Run-A-Muck, Smith's Cubbyhole, the Nip and Nap Shack, Camp Overflow, Big Pine Retreat and Trade Winds, just to name a few. A name helps transition you to another place and mindset when you arrive at your cottage.

Having a name for your place is both fun and practical. Cottage roads along the lake and ocean can be difficult to navigate due to the natural contours of the land and gobs of off shooting no-named roads. Who hasn't been lost when following "perfectly clear" directions provided by the camp owner? Columbus found the new world without any signs, but it took him one hundred and fifty days to do it. Name your place and post a sign at the intersections and your friends will be sure to arrive on time at your Columbus Day party!

Help your family and friends find you by also placing your sign on the side of the house that is nearest to the road or the end of your driveway. Remember to tell them the name of your special place before they head out to find you! See the Decorating chapter for how to make a sign or where to acquire one.

Picking a Name

Choosing a name can be a lot of fun. One family we spoke with related how they made a game out of choosing a name. Each family member was given a sheet of paper and asked to write down eight names or phrases that had special significance for their family. They were surprised at the diversity of the names and laughed for an hour before a friendly consensus was reach. Remember to stick the sheets of rejected names into your camp journal.

Your Surroundings and Activities Checklist

- ☐ National parks
- ☐ State parks
- ☐ Hiking, fishing and boating spots
- ☐ Other sporting activities allowed in your area
- ☐ Harvest suppers, church bazaars and fire department barbeques
- ☐ Beach days
- ☐ Clean up days
- ☐ Concerts
- ☐ Car shows, antique and craft fair
- ☐ Holiday rituals
- ☐ Neighborhood parties
- ☐ Neighborhood sporting events
- ☐ Tennis tournaments
- ☐ Seasonal events
- ☐ Music, food and wine festivals
- ☐ Mini golf, golf and driving ranges
- ☐ Sleigh rides and horse trails
- ☐ Coffee shops and book stores
- ☐ Open studio day for artisans
- ☐ Fundraising events
- ☐ Kid's centers and parks

Get to Know the Area

Safety first. Whether your cabin is miles from the nearest neighbor or so snug you could reach out your window and touch your neighbor's house, you should get to know your surroundings. More than one happy camper have gotten lost in their backyard. I remember venturing forth on cross country skis with friends from our cabin in the woods. We were soon disoriented and then totally lost. Without food, we started to panic. Fortunately, we happened upon a road and managed to catch a ride home. We avoided disaster and we learned not to leave home again without a map, water, food and a basic understanding of the forest around us.

Fun second. Knowing your surroundings is important not only for safety reasons; it also helps you get the most enjoyment out of your cottage life. Near my parent's lakehouse is a small historic community that has an outdoor antique fair every spring. We bring our blankets and picnic and listen to the band in the town's gazebo. The fireman's charity supper is a community must, and watching the annual "swim the length of the lake" is a hoot, especially when gripping a cool drink in our pontoon boat. There are similar special occasions to be enjoyed in your surroundings. Make a list of all the things you can do in your area, the special events (days may change but if you have a basic time of year, just call later for the exact date), sporting activities, parades, church suppers, volunteer fire department meals and more.

Be a Part of Your Seasonal Community

The joy and comfort of knowing your surroundings extends to knowing your neighbors. My sister, who married the boy from the camp down the street, can attest to the benefits of knowing your neighbors.

If there isn't anything that brings your neighbors together create the occasion. A block party, a street clean up day including a picnic for all, apple pie bingo (where all you have to do to join in is bring a dessert, which the winners get to choose as prizes), or even a night time bonfire. Some of your life long friends may come from your seasonal neighbors, maybe even your new son-in-law.

Even if your getaway is designed to provide quiet and personal time, attend a few community events to show your support of the area.

Keep a Family Journal and a Guest Book

Generation to generation, cousin to aunt, family to family, week to week, whatever your situation, keeping a camp journal will preserve your memories for years to come. Your family will laugh once when a humorous event occurs, and then a dozen times again revisiting the event in the journal. You may choose to place a guest book in the entryway for visitor's comments and keep a journal just for the family. Whether you write in them weekly, monthly or even daily, they will be keepsakes you and your descendants will cherish. We would love to hear your humorous stories and cabin tips, please email them to us at our web site at www.loveyourcottage.com.

"*The history at our cottage is rich with memories. My father grew up opening the cabin with his father and now the whole family helps. Then we spend our days exploring the beach together.*"

—Julie, Cape Cod, Massachusetts

chapter two
Opening Your Place

I still remember the first weekend at the camp that my family rented for six summers. My mom was so organized and I had never in my life witnessed a station wagon so full of kid's clothes, toys, cleaning supplies and sporting equipment. A family of six and everything we needed for the entire summer in one trip. Aren't mom's incredible! It took a full day to clean, unload and get organized, but after that it was all fun and games.

The Surprises That Await You

Many people come back to their cottage with a sense of excitement and apprehension of facing the unknown. The unknown comes in a variety of shapes and sizes: a burst pipe and a couple inches of water covering the floor, a family of raccoons who are not paying rent, or the loss of several bottles of liquor and a broken backdoor. Return to your cottage each year with more joy and less trepidation by following the closing tips in our Closing chapter.

When we read the surveys returned from camp and cottage owners, we hear every imaginable story: caved in roofs from snow,

the stolen wicker furniture, the aroused hornets nest, and driving around the lake looking for a missing dock. These war stories (which later become humorous) are part of owning a private haven. Know they will happen and take them in good spirit. Now let's clean up and get ready for another joy-packed season.

Gathering the Troops

It is best if every family (and users) feels as though she or he are part owner of the cottage and for this to happen everyone must pitch in

general store, your neighbor's, and look in the telephone book under electrical, plumbing, camps, etc. Your local handyman may also be interested in helping open or close your place. Just be sure you have a list of exactly what you want them to do. The advantages of hiring professionals include knowing the job is done right, not needing all the tools yourself, and in some families, worth the money in terms of stopping the family bickering before it begins. Many professional specialize in opening and closing seasonal homes and the convenience is well worth the nominal charge.

The Mechanics

Turning things on will be the first thing to do with your cottage, you can't clean or do much else without water, electricity and heat. Follow the guidelines in the back of the book in the Water, Sewer, Heating chapter. You will want to be sure there are no burst pipes, broken lines or other surprises before you continue with the list of opening up projects. Don't forget reconnecting the phone and plug in all the appliances and inspect the cords for frayed wires or unwanted nibbles.

Cleaning

Cleaning up during the opening always appealed to me, it always feels like we are scrubbing away thoughts of our daily troubles and creating a shiny new beginning. Depending on your area, the opening of camp requires a variety of projects. Keep a complete selection of essential cleaning

to maintain it. Who is everyone? That is up to you. If it is a shared family cottage, then all those who enjoy it should carry their share of the load. At the first of the year identify all the tasks that need to be done and assign them appropriately.

As for having others help, that can be just as fun. Promise them a great meal and a cool dip in the lake. Just a word of caution: Some people, who feel ownership in the opening process, may be around a lot throughout the season. Choose your friends wisely.

Hiring It Out

There are a variety of services in your area that will open and close camps. Ask at your

materials at your camp. Being organized maximizes play time and minimizes schlepping or dashes to the store for cleaning products. If guests use your cabin in your absence, explain where the cleaning materials are and announce the cabin rules that it to be left as they found it (spotless) for other visitors or for your arrival.

Check for Unwanted Creatures

Getting out the bugs, quite literally, is one of the first jobs. You may also notice that other unwanted creatures are around. Snoop out signs of them. Read the chapter on Pets, Pests and Other Critters for ideas about evicting them. Depending on your budget, level of squeamishness, and the type of rodent, you can decide if you should call in the experts or

eliminate them yourself. Once you are rid of the creatures, close up any holes they may have created and then begin the cleaning process.

Airing it Out

The best way to start is to air the place out. Open all the windows and doors and let the place breath. Not only to get the mold and musty smell out but there may have been a build up of propane or argon or other types of gases.

Drying in Out

If your camp is in a damp area, some wizened old-timers suggest starting a woodstove or fireplace (after they are sure there is no blockage in the stove and chimney) and let

What to Bring (or Stock) List:

- [ ] Cleaning products
- [ ] Trash bags
- [ ] Vacuum, broom, mop and bucket
- [ ] Dishwasher soap, dish soap, towels and scrub pads
- [ ] Towels: beach, bathroom, kitchen
- [ ] Linens: bedroom, dining room, curtains
- [ ] Blankets: picnic, bedroom, couch throws
- [ ] Clothes: a variety for every type of weather
- [ ] Games: cards, games, videos
- [ ] Books
- [ ] Kid's craft box (Family Fun chapter)
- [ ] Kitchenware: pots, pans, silverware, dishes, glasses
- [ ] Serving items: trays, pitchers, serving spoons
- [ ] Grill and all accessories
- [ ] Safety and emergency equipment (Safety chapter)
- [ ] Fire extinguisher
- [ ] Lawn furniture and games
- [ ] Water and boating items (On the Water chapter)
- [ ] Food and drinks (Feeding the Gang chapter)
- [ ] Drinking water
- [ ] Toilet paper, tissue paper, paper towels
- [ ] Basic tool kit
- [ ] Basic lawn tools

the fire get really hot for a day or two. Wood rot is a serious source of structural damage for many cottages. During the summer you should also have a way to let your foundation breath, such as opening air vents to let the sub floor dry out.

Linens and Curtains

If you leave your linens and curtains up over the winter to serve as vision barriers, now is the time to take them down for a washing, dry cleaning or to be aired out. Check for holes, stains or discoloration from the sun and care for appropriately. If your curtains are fading from the sun be sure to rotate the curtains to different windows. Linens that do have moth holes in them can be reused as pillow covers, place mats, napkins, appliance covers and other interesting camp items.

Other Fabric Items

Next come the pillows and cushions. Use a fabric spray or wash them with a damp sponge with a diluted soap mixture. Wool blankets should be aired out or dry cleaned. You might as well get it all done at once and clean the slip covers on the couches and chairs, along with your picnic cloth and table linens.

Clothes

Open up the storage boxes and cedar chests full of clothes and once again check them for moth holes and the like. Wash them if you see any sign of rodents, otherwise airing them out is fine. Take this opportunity to

wash and/or reline the dresser drawers as well. Wash the inside with a diluted solution of water and vinegar. Let them dry completely before you return the clothes. It is best to replace the cedar blocks or balls in the drawers every season. You can find these at any home goods store. Keep some extra sweatshirts and hats for your guests who forget the evenings can be chilly.

Walls and Ceilings

Washing the walls will make the air even fresher (dust collects on the walls). For sheetrock use a dry or mist sprayed cloth and move in sections. For a paneled wood wall, you can use a wood soap, such as *Murphy Oil Soap*. Take down the wall hangings and clean

them thoroughly too. This may be the time to simplify your cottage and pack away the things you don't use. Use a duster to get rid of all the corners and ceilings of cob webs. An old t-shirt wrapped around the end of the broom stick works just as well.

Windows and Screens

Choose an inside person and an outside person to clean the windows. Try and do the same window simultaneously so you are sure to get all the spots. Use newspaper instead of paper towels for no streak results. Screens can be pulled down and pressure washed and scrubbed with a plastic bristled brush with a mild soap mixture. Be sure to dry completely before returning to the window.

Furniture, Bookshelves and Storage Units

Take it one room at a time and wipe down all the furniture, repair wobbly legs, oil squeaky doors, remove books from the shelves and air them outside by fanning each book, wipe down the shelves and then replace the books.

Bathroom and Kitchens

Turn the water on, open the taps of each faucet and let the water drain for several minutes until the water has run clean. If you drink the water, especially from a well, we recommend getting the water tested before drinking. If your kitchen counters and drawers seem clean, don't assume it. Be sure to wipe them down with a disinfectant. Then clean the kitchen to your standards.

Floors and Carpets

Unroll the rug and let them air outside while you quickly go over the floors with the proper cleaner, then flop them in place. Throw rugs can be brought outside and beat with a stick or bat to remove the majority of the dust that may have collected on them.

Hose it Down

The easiest way to clean the outside of your house and your outside furniture is to simply hose it down. Wipe the furniture down with soap and water first.

Trees, Shrubs and Driveway Matters

Overgrown or downed trees and branches need to be trimmed and removed. This is the right time to trim your shrubs, bushes and prune any fruit trees before they bud. Take care of any driveway holes; fill the pothole with gravel (create a mound that will later compress) and level off the frost heaves with a shovel.

Take a Closer Look

While you clean up around the outside of the house, you will see the things that need attention. A loose front door, a wobbly walking stone, a ripped screen, missing shingles on the roof, all can be easily repaired over the weekends. This is also a good time to search for small holes that you will need to close to keep critters out.

One Thing at a Time

Opening up can sound like a lot of work but it can be fun if you make a party out of it. Be sure to check your lists so that you have everything on hand and everyone has an assignment. Assigning tasks can be as easy as picking a name out of a hat. Take one task at a time! If you work efficiently, you may finish before the drinks are cold in the refrigerator you just plugged in.

Associations

Many camps belong to an association that set the days in which you can live at your camp, when the water is turned on (and off), or even other utilities. One great thing about associations is many of them have opening days which groups of people put in all the docks or help take down all the plywood from the windows. If you don't have a day like this, talk to your neighbors about any interest in creating one. As a group, you may have better leverage (and possible discounts) with garbage, recycling, lawn services and or even talking to the town about a speed limit or street lights.

"After the sun has gone down and the fire is in the woodstove, we spend hours together playing games, making crafts, or building a puzzle, really, the games are just a way we learned to enjoy and understand each other."

—Mark, White Mountains, New Hampshire

chapter three
Family Fun

The experiences of life at a cottage are a gift that can forever shape and embellish the life of a child. The love of the outdoors, the family time, the pure enjoyment of getting away together, will bring your family closer than you might have ever thought possible. Whether it is day with grandpa on the dock learning to fish, a day inside watching a storm go by, or collecting fireflies for your own lamp, each experience teaches us the wonders of family and nature. Today, my siblings and I still act like children when we arrive at our parents' cottage. I remember how it all got started…

When the four of us became teenagers, my parents started to fear we were going our own separate ways and leaving the family concept behind. Wisely, they decided to rent a lakefront cottage. After thirteen years of renting different cottages, my parents bought a year round cottage on Lake Elmore in Vermont. For twenty years we have enjoyed a close knit family relationship, thanks to the insight of our very special parents. We still enjoy watching a really good water ski fall of a sibling, but the majority of our time is spent teaching our babies how to swim and sitting by the bonfire and talking until the fire dims to embers. Generation to generation, our family's cottage has been and will be a big part of who we are as we move from one stage of life to another. Each stage, bring a variety of activities into our cottage life.

Whatever the age, there is always something to do for kids. You should never hear "I'm bored," but if you do, you can be prepared with a list of fun activities. Remember, part of the fun is to doing things together. As many parents know, a special connection, if not nurtured, can fade away as children get older. Fortunately, special places play a key role in keeping us all together and keeping us young at heart.

When Friends Stay Over

If you are like most cottage owners, you will have lots of visiting kids. Over a twenty year period, my parents have had hundreds of our friends stay at their place. Once we set a record of twenty-seven people sleeping over at the cottage we were renting (you must read Feeding the Gang chapter to handle that). Most of time things stay under control, but for the periodic episode, it is best to be prepared. When a child stays over you should know about existing medical conditions, such as allergies, diabetes and asthma. The child should have necessary medications with them at all times, and you should have a signed form to seek medical attention

if necessary. We have put one as a guideline in the back of the book for you, but please create your own that will suit your individual situations.

Camp Rules Game

Vacation is a blast at the cottage and you can make the rules fun to learn. Your children and their friends can appreciate nature and respect the rules of the cottage through a game. Only you will know the hazards of your getaway place: water's edge, poison ivy nearby, a busy street, a dilapidated barn. What are the most important rules to abide by? List them. Now what are some of the things kids can do? Where are the areas they can play in? Have a same amount of "can do" as "don't." Cut them all into squares and put them in a can. Have each child take one out and read it (if they can't read, you can read it for them), then ask them if it should be taped to the paper with the smiling face (can do page) or the frowning face (can't do page). Make sure they understand why they can or can't and the consequences for breaking the rules. Be sure to reward them for playing the game. Repeat this game often!

The Play Area(s)

It is always great to have an area or two that are specifically designed for kids' enjoyment. Whether it is a sand box, a small wooded area or a fenced-in swing set. A picnic table in the area is great for outdoor craft projects and a picnic lunch. Get an outdoor storage box to enable kids to get their own toys. If you have a big enough area for badminton, volleyball or crochet, set them up! They will provide you with hours of fun and great exercise. They are also wonderful spectator sports, so if some of the adults or grandparents can't play, they can be cheerleaders. (Be sure to have plenty of Adirondack chairs available for the spectators.)

Scavenger Hunt

A scavenger hunt is an exceptional game that will delight both children and adults. It is a wonderful way for children to learn more about their surroundings.

Prepare a list (with copies) of twelve to sixteen things that children might find in your area. Depending on the age of the children, depends on how difficult the objects to find will be. Remember, children don't have to bring it back, they can just check it off their list that they saw it (especially if that object is a bird, fish, or some other object they should not touch).

Examples of Scavenger Items

A pine cone, a four leave clover, a flower, a penny, an oak leaf, a round stone, see a duck, a shell with a hole in it, a small piece of drift wood, a bottle cap, the neighbor's signature, see a sign with the word "lake" in it, an acorn, dog tracks, see a blueberry bush, and other exciting items that are unique to your area.

Be sure the children are in teams of two, three or four and give each team a copy of the list. Be sure to let the kids know where they can go and cannot go. Give them a time

limit. A prize will be given to the first team that brings back (or sees) all of the items on the list. If they do not find everything, the team with the largest number found wins. (You can also pair up an adult and child to make it a fun family outing).

A Bingo Walk

Get the kids out walking with you and help them to enjoy their surroundings with the Bingo Walk Game. Keep the walkman's at home and enjoy the sights and sounds of nature. It is similar to a scavenger hunt, except you don't have to bring anything back and everyone's bingo card has different items on them.

Each player has a page with twenty-five 1-1/2 inch squares of drawings of items that you will probably see on your walk. Be sure to draw or put the pictures in different locations on the bingo sheets. (Paste the page to cardboard with a string so they can hang them from their necks for ease during the walk.) They each get a crayon to mark off the items they see (or hear). To make the cards reusable cover them with clear self-adhesive vinyl and use grease pencils (items found at office supply store).

Marching Band

Get all the neighborhood kids together to create a marching band. On rainy days you can make your instruments. A drum out of an

oatmeal can, a tambourine out of a tin pie plate with tassels, morocco's, and more! Then have everyone create a camp song that is unique to your area! What fun to pass that song on from generation to generation!

Keep a kazoo, wood flute, old bugle, drum in the toy closet. Friends of mine, the Rudolph family of Chicago, while attending a family reunion at a Vermont cabin, formed a spontaneous marching band one morning that caused John Phillips Sousa to cover his ears. Documented by photos, this family still laughs at the thought.

Rainy Days

Whether donning a raincoat and rubber boots to splash in puddles, or inside playing a game or making crafts, rainy days can be just as fun as sunny days. For many of us, it forces us to relax, curl up with a book, or play a family game that was long forgotten.

You can use these days (or at least a few hours) as an opportunity to strengthen your relationship with your children. Be sure to stock up on a few basic supplies that you can choose from for your fun.

Craft Ideas

There is a huge selection of activity books for young children, such as *Parents, Play and Learn*, by the editors of *Parents Magazine*, the *Preschooler's Busy Book* and even a few which are geared towards older kids. All are filled with crafts, games, outdoor and indoor activates that you can do together for hours. These books also have a list of suggested

items to have around for your crafts. Crafts are great gift ideas for kids to make for the owners of the camp or relatives.

Birds Treats

For this easy bird treat all you need are pinecones, lard (shortening), peanut butter, birdseeds and string. Kids love to make these treats because they get messy. Be prepared for the mess with an easy to clean surface. Mix the lard and peanut butter together then add half of the birdseed (keep other half in a pan for rolling after). Take a pinecone that has a string tied around the top and start spreading the mixture on it with a spoon. Be sure to get in between all the pieces of the pinecone.

Once the cone is covered in the mixture, then roll the cone in birdseed for the final step. You can place these cones in the refrigerator for a few hours to harden before you hang it outside for the birds. Be sure to have your binoculars and bird book close by after a day of putting out the treat. This makes a great gift for a neighbor's birthday or a take home gift from a kid's party.

Wind Chime

Sea shells, sea glass, spoons, and other interesting items can make wonderful music if you put them together in a wind chime. All you need is a pie tin, string, a pointed tool and the items that will make music (for some

items you may want to hot glue onto the string). Have two holes in the middle of the pie tin to put string through so you can hang your wind chime. Poke holes along the side of the pie tin. Cut your string in a variety of lengths and attach your items, spoons you can tie, sea shells with holes in them are also easy to tie, you may want to tie and glue the sea glass, and other items like sticks also make interesting sounds. Give them all a try! (Don't have a pie tin available? Use two pieces of sticks and make a cross to hang the strings from.)

Edible Necklaces

Diamonds may be a woman's best friend but an edible necklace can be just as priceless to a child. Make an edible necklace for a hike or make a bunch and put them in a jar for an entire weekend of fun. Every time you and the kids head out for a walk, hike, a boat ride, or car ride, you can each grab a necklace and go! Some of the best ingredients you can have for necklaces are *Cheerios*, raisins, cranraisins, marshmallows, dried fruit, chocolate chips, or other favorite foods that are easy to put a needle through to string. Be cautious of children

A Few Craft Items

- ☐ Recyclable Items (aluminum foil, jars, coffee cans, paper towel rolls, toilet paper rolls, egg cartons, cereal boxes, cardboard, brown paper bags, plastic jugs and more)
- ☐ Glue
- ☐ String and needles
- ☐ Card stock paper
- ☐ Self-adhesive clear laminate paper
- ☐ Crayons
- ☐ Children's safety scissors
- ☐ Paper plates/bowls/cups
- ☐ Dried beans
- ☐ Old t-shirts
- ☐ Children's paints
- ☐ Construction paper
- ☐ Felt squares
- ☐ Pie tins
- ☐ Yarn scraps
- ☐ Box of dress up clothes, hats, jewelry, shoes

using a needle. If the child is too young, have them pick out what the next item will go on the necklace while you thread it.

Memory Placemats

Homemade memory placemats make great gifts for a cottage owner. If you are like our family, you always get doubles when you develop your pictures. Take the pile of doubles and spread them on the table. Allow the kids to cut out the pictures and create a collage on an 8-1/2 x 11 piece of construction paper. Once the photos are glued on the paper, you can use clear self-adhesive paper (purchased from an office supply store) to cover both sides and seal. You can also bring the placemats to a local copy center where they can laminate or make numerous copies for you. This way you will always have conversation piece during dinner.

Personalized Greeting Cards

You can purchase a box of blank white cards and envelopes at any office/craft store. Make a bunch of copies of your favorite photos of

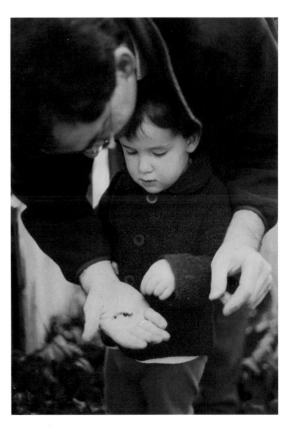

the kids playing at your cottage. Let the kids color, paint, decorate the outside of the folded card. Once they are decorated, glue their favorite photo onto the center of the card. Leave the inside blank but have them autograph the back of the cards. Package ten

homemade cards together and bundle them with ribbons. They can give these packages of cards to their grandparents for them to use to write letters on—maybe even letters back to the kids!

Musical Instruments

Tambourine

Put one or all of these items: dried beans, corn, pasta or cereal, in between two paper plates. Glue or staple the plates together and decorate with crayons, ribbons, stickers, markers or paint. You can also use tin pie plates for your tambourines and bottle caps for the inside or around the edge. Use a variety of stickers for decorations.

Drum

Use coffee cans or oatmeal cans with their lids as drums. Cut to holes in the side to pull a string through to hang the drum around your neck. Decorate the cans with construction paper, crayons, markers or stickers. You can use sticks are drumsticks or spoons.

Morocco

You can use paper towel cardboard rolls as morocco. Close up one end and fill with dried beans or something similar. Close the other end and decorate. Hold in the middle and shake for lots of fun.

Your Game Collection

My family grew up playing games. We spent hours playing cards together, then the game *Aggravation,*® next it was *Pictionary,*® followed by *Trivia Pursuit*® and now our fix is *Sequence.*®

Basic Game Collection

Basic playing cards (at least two decks)

Go Fish cards

Uno® cards

Twister® (great for all ages)

Aggravation®

Monopoly®

Puzzles

Trivia Pursuit®

Pictionary®

Scrabble®

Chess

Checkers

And a few of your own favorites

We still enjoy playing cards a lot. There are dozens of family games to choose from. We listed a few basic games that many children know how to play or that are easy to learn. Be sure to have a least one game for every age group.

Your Own Olympics

Whether you are inside during a thunderstorm or it's a gorgeous sunny day, you can create a unique family day by having your own Olympics. Who can carry a bean in a spoon (held on by their teeth) the longest? Who can recite the "Pledge of Allegiance" with the most facial expressions? Who can waterski for the longest amount of time? These ideas, and many more that you create, will give you hours and days of fun. Decorate jar lids for your medals and pass them out after dessert. Whatever you choose to do, doing it together is the most fun of all.

Families build cottages and cottages build families.

"One of our favorite cottage memories was when we kids canoed to the end of the lake to pick wild blueberries. Then we would canoe home and Mom would make us blueberry cobbler."

—Chris and Becky, Coxton Lake, Pennsylvania

chapter four
On the Water and In Your Boat

Many cabins are so close to a body of water that you could toss a stone in to it. We have spent years swimming, boating, and fishing on our lake and the pleasure of it never seems to end. Now we have added cruising in our pontoon boat, sipping lemonade and talking about teaching our children to waterski, fish and swim.

Water is serene, water is picturesque, water is a play site and water brings a special set of safety concerns. As a waterfront cottage owner, you inherit a practical responsibility for the safety of others. Here are some safety rules that will allow you and your family to enjoy the water while respecting it.

Water Safety Rules

- Be sure the life jacket is the correct one for the age and size of the wearer. Non-swimmers and infants should always use flotation devices when they are near or enter the water.
- Avoid entering the water alone, try to have at least three people with you.
- Abide by all signs regarding swimming, wildlife, warning hazards, and private property.

- If you pass through a gate to get to the water, for the safety of others, be sure to close it behind you.
- Don't wear heavy packs or carry heavy equipment in your pockets or around your neck while boating.
- Only swim in areas that are safe and properly supervised.
- Respect the community you live in. Follow the swimming, fishing and boating rules and keep noise to a minimum.
- Carry your garbage out and don't feed the wildlife.
- Have fun!

With Your Kids

If properly introduced to it, kids love the water! Show your children that you are having fun too as you teach them to swim. No matter what level of swimming ability your child has, watch them in the water until they are older and stronger. One of the first things you should teach your children is the back float—it is a life saving skill! Many camp owners don't let their children play near water without a life vest on until they can swim at least 50 yards without a vest. Small children should never be left alone to play in ocean waves. They don't have the judgment to gage the force of the waves and the strength of an undertow. Judgment is the first part of safety.

Know where your kids are at all times. There are many excellent kids' books at the library that together you can read regarding swimming, the ocean, and boating safety.

Personal Flotation Devices (life jackets to most of us)

Personal Flotation Devices (PFD's) have come a long way from the basic off-white ones seen on the movie "Titanic." Besides the exciting new colors (including the infamous bright orange), their level of safety and specialty is highly developed.

No matter what level swimmer you are, please wear your PFD on your boat. Write, display and enforce boating rules at your camp. Your rules should look something like this: all children under 12 and any adult who cannot swim must wear PFD's, and we highly recommend all individuals wear one while on their boat. Everyone must wear one at night and while tying up the boat or doing other difficult tasks. Just like seat belts, they do save lives!

There are five types of PFD's approved by the Coast Guard, Types I-V. Jackets exist for every type of sport: sailing vest, three belt, fishing vest, waterskiing vest and many more. *West Marine's Master Catalog* offers a variety of PFDs, and includes pages on safety and coast guard regulations. We highly recommend this catalog for most of your boating needs (see Resource List).

PFD Regulations for Boats

- Boats under 16 feet. You must have a Type I, II, III or V for every person on board.
- Boats between 16 feet and 65 feet. You must have a Type I, II, III or V for every person on board, plus a Type IV that can be tossed.
- Type I, II and III PFDs must be accessible and suitable for every person, while Type IV must be immediately available. Type V hybrid PFD's must be worn to be counted as part of the PFD's on the boat.
- Know and follow your state's boating regulations as well as those of the U.S. Coast Guard's.

Boating Fun

The varieties and sizes of boats are endless: rowboats, sailboats, kayaks, powerboats, pontoon boats, canoes and more. Novices can operate some, while others take years of experience. School courses can quickly elevate the skill level of a boat operator. A variety of day courses teach canoeing, kayaking, small boat sailing. Take a lesson; it's fun and will make you a safer boater.

Boating courses are one of the best ways to learn about larger boats and ones with engines. Select courses approved by the U.S. Coast Guard. In many places, you cannot operate a powerboat without having a certificate from a boating course.

Over the years, I have seen several alarming boating incidences. Luckily they consisted of a few torn props and broken egos—nothing too serious. What we find to be the most frequent cases of accidents are: a boat not properly tied to a mooring, boaters driving too fast near docks and swimmers, waterski boats and waterskiers too close to shore, and improper boat maintenance. Follow the boating rules and use common sense and you will have fun boating, as well as a safe ride.

Boating With Kids

We highly recommend you call the U.S. Coast Guard and the National Safe Boating

Council and ask for copies of their kid's boating safety booklets. They are filled with fun games and safety information.

Waypoints, *A Guide to Boating Safely*, U.S. Coast Guard at 800-368-5647, B*oating Fun—Adventure on the Water*, U.S. Coast Guard at 800-368-5647, B*oating Safety "Side-Kicks,"* National Safe Boating Council at 800-336-2628.

Some Nautical Language

Sometimes when people talk about boats they seem to be speaking a different language. Learn a few basic terms and you will better understand them. Many boaters use these terms, so it is important to memorize them, especially in a quick maneuvering situation.

Terms

The bow, stern, port and starboard: The bow is the front of the boat (the pointed side), the stern is the back, and port is the left side (when facing the bow) and starboard is the right side.

Lines are the ropes on sailboats and other boats.

Rudder is the blade that helps steer a sailboat. It is in the stern of the boat.

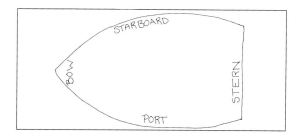

Tiller is the handle that moves the rudder.

Oarlock is where you attach your oar (paddle).

Tack is the word used when you change direction in a sailboat.

Reach is when the wind comes over the side of the boat.

Moor is the action of tying your boat to a location on land, a mooring ball or stake in the water.

Sounding is a measurement that indicates the depth of the water.

Boating Rules

Boaters must follow the rules of the water just like car drivers. The Coast Guard and Marine Patrol watch the waterways as the Highway Patrol watches the roads. They will occasionally stop your boat to ensure that you are properly equipped. Thank them for their hard work and concern. Remember, they are looking out for you and your family.

Call 1-800-368-5647 or get on the web www.uscgboating.org for a copy of *Federal Requirements and Safety Tips for Recreational*

Boating Checklist

- [ ] Have a copy of your state's boat safety handbook readily available.
- [ ] Know and follow your state and local area's water rules and regulations.
- [ ] If you are boating, be aware of the other boats around you.
- [ ] If you have a powerboat, please know that wind powered boats have the right of way.
- [ ] Know which is give way boat and who the stay boat is.
- [ ] When out boating, be sure to bring water and a snack.
- [ ] Wear sunscreen and sunglasses.
- [ ] Maintain the speed limit and be sure to slow down when warning signs say "no wake."
- [ ] Monitor the weather at all times.
- [ ] Always have a spotter (additional person) in the boat when waterskiing.
- [ ] Be sure to know the laws of your waterway.
- [ ] Always have the proper type and amount of PFDs on board.
- [ ] Be sure your engine, or craft, is running properly.
- [ ] Don't steer the boat too close to the shore.
- [ ] Watch for swimmers, docks, and small crafts near the waters edge.
- [ ] Be sure to let someone know where you are going and when you expect to be back.
- [ ] If you are fishing off of your boat, be sure to have the proper licenses.
- [ ] Think twice before bringing a baby onto the boat.
- [ ] If you have toddlers, be sure you have PFDs specific for toddlers.
- [ ] Just like the road, do not drink and drive.
- [ ] And finally be sure your boat is tied up properly to the dock, mooring or land.

Dock Checklist

- Use waders when putting in or taking out your dock
- Never try to remove the dock alone
- Check the cleats on the dock for tightness on a regular basis
- Watch for wood rot and loose boards
- If using your dock at night, have proper lighting nearby
- Have extra buoys nearby for other boats owners who may want to tie up.
- Use gritty paint if you are going to paint your dock to reduce slipperiness
- In flooding conditions, tie your dock, and boats with ropes to other locations, such as trees so your dock does not float away unexpectedly.
- Have a throwing type of PFD near the dock

Boats and Boating & Safety. Both are a must have for everyone who owns a boat.

Tidbit

If you are looking for a boat to buy, check out *Soundings, The Nation's Boating Newspaper.* It lists over 9,000 boats for sale, plus hundreds of waterfront properties (see Resource List).

Docks

If you choose to make or repair your own dock, then we highly recommend you purchase a copy of the book, *The Dock Manual,* by Max Burns. It is the ultimate source for every type of dock (floating, concrete piers, permanent pilings, cantilever and suspension), every shoreline, and every situation out there. Plus it has many sources that will build or supply you with a dock. We can't say enough about this book. If you feel confident without the book, then be sure to review the dock checklist.

Stop the Spread of Zebra Mussels by Cleaning Your Boat

As a cottage owner on Lake Champlain, I am well aware of Zebra Mussels, (small, dark and light colored, stripped mussels, the size of a thumbnail) that have invaded our beautiful lake and part of my beach. Since 1988, Zebra Mussels have been identified throughout many of North America's interconnected waterways and the Mississippi and Ohio river systems. The mussels continue to spread to other waterways, challenging scientist throughout the United States to slow their invasion.

The negative impact spans from the individual cottage owner's lake-feed water system to multibillion dollar industrial facilities. They harm tourism by covering beaches and historic artifacts with their sharp shells (and bad odor when decaying). There are several fact sheets available through many science centers, including online at Lake Champlain Basin Program, www.lcbp.org, to help you understand the Zebra Mussel's impact and learn what you can do to stop the spreading.

Here is a list, provided by the Lake Champlain Basin Program, of a few precautionary steps for you to take after boating or fishing. It is important that cottage owners, boat owners, and avid water users, play a role in stopping the spread of Zebra Mussels or other opportunistic plants and species by properly caring for your boat and equipment before entering another waterway.

Important Precautionary Steps

- ☐ Inspect your boat and trailer carefully for mussels and aquatic vegetation. Remove any mussels or vegetation and discard in the trash.

- ☐ Drain all water from the boat, including the bilge, live well, and engine cooling system.

- ☐ Dry the boat and trailer in the sun for at least 5 days or if you use your boat sooner, rinse off the boat, trailer, anchor, anchor line, bumpers, engine, etc. with hot water or at a car wash.

- ☐ Leave live aquatic bait behind—either give it to someone using the same water body, or discard it in the trash.

"Fishing in the river behind our cabin is loads of fun, but I'm still not sure which activity the kids like better — the fishing or searching for the worms."

—Christi
Boulder, Colorado

chapter five
Fish Stories

I've been waiting to tell this story for years, ever since we started planning this book. My brother and my father went out on the pontoon boat to fish one day. My brother had just purchased a new fly fishing rod and was extremely excited to practice. The next thing we know they are heading back to the house pretty fast. Well, it turns out my brother caught himself in the throat with the hook. Off to the emergency room they went—they should have a room reserved for him on a 24 basis, he is there so much! It is funny now because he was fine after they removed the hook—and we all agree it was worth all the trouble because we get an immeasurable amount of pleasure telling that story.

Now that I totally humiliated my brother, I hope you are thinking of a few of your own fun fish stories. Fishing is a huge pastime for many people during all seasons. Local laws determine what types of fish you can catch, and also, those that you can keep. For your local rules and regulations, pick up your state's booklet on Fish and Wildlife Regulations. For your convenience, we have listed all the states numbers in our Resource List.

Who Fishes?

People young and old enjoy fishing, over 60 million to be exact! It's relaxing and a wonderful way to be in the great outdoors, alone

or with family and friends. Adults should take the time to teach children how to fish properly and understand the importance of the laws. Take a class with your siblings, friends or kids or just ask a neighbor who has been fishing for a lifetime to take you out and show you the ropes. Casting, removing a hook (out of yourself and the fish), cleaning and cooking a fish, selecting a lure, catch and release: enjoy learning how to do these things right, so you may pass down these skills to the next generation.

The Basics

People who fish are called anglers, because sport fishing is called angling. There are two basic categories of fishing, fresh water and salt water. The five major types of fishing are still-fishing, fly-fishing, trolling, spin-fishing and bait-fishing. The number and types of fish in both fresh and salt, and the ways you catch them depends on where you are. Check your local fishing charts to learn the types of fish that you can eat, those that must be released and the species you should avoid. Numerous fishing books and magazines are fun to read and promise to guide you to that big catch. Whenever possible, please catch and release.

Fishing Language

Still Fishing

In this type of fishing you usually stand (or sit) on the shore and cast a bobber into the water. Then you wait for the fish to come to you. Be careful a fish doesn't take your fishing pole if you set it down for a little while. (Yes, there is another fishing story behind that comment.)

Fly Fishing

If you've seen the movie, *A River Runs Through It*, you've seen fly fishing. The angler uses a long, light-weight rod and with a whipping action sails the hook across the stream or lake. The hook is camouflaged to look like an insect on the water.

Bait Fishing

This style of fishing resembles still-fishing, but it is usually done from a boat in the ocean. The gear is more heavy duty because (hopefully) the fish are bigger.

Trolling

This is when you let your line drag behind a boat as it slowly moves forward. (This is my father's favorite type of fishing from the pontoon boat.)

Spin Fishing

This is when you cast your line and immediately begin turning your reel to bring in your line. This type of fishing usually uses a special lure, called a spinner.

Rod

A rod and fishing pole are interchangeable terms. Some rods are heavy-duty which are

Basic Fishing Equipment

- ☐ Fishing rod and reel
- ☐ Well-stocked tackle box
- ☐ Bait
- ☐ Net
- ☐ Life jacket
- ☐ Cooler for fish you keep
- ☐ Food and water for yourself
- ☐ Waders (if necessary)
- ☐ Sunglasses, hat and sunscreen

made for ocean fishing and others are small which work well for freshwater fish. You can also make your own rod out of a branch or a stick.

Reel

The Reel is the device that winds in the fishing line. It is attached to the rod close to the handle. There are a variety of types of reels, again it depends on the type of fishing you are doing.

Tackle

Tackle means your rod and reel.

Tackle Box

This is a box or tool-like kit that holds all your supplies for your tackle. You should have your hooks, lures, extra line, bait, bobbers, a small safety kit, pliers, sunscreen, insect repellent, a small jackknife or *Leatherman*, small net, sinkers, measuring tape (unless you want to lie about the size of the fish), and a camera (again, depends on the honesty factor).

Hooks

These are the items that are tied to the end of your line and are used to hold the bait and hopefully catch a fish.

Lures

It is exactly how it sounds; lures are man-made items that will lure the fish to bite the hook.

Bait

Bait is used to attract the fish and it can be natural or man-made. Natural bait includes worms, minnows, flies, shrimp, crab, grasshoppers, crayfish and fish eggs. Common man-made bait includes jigs (instead of minnows), imitation flies and plastic worms.

Line

This is the very strong thread made out of nylon that you use to reel in fish. There are lightweight and heavy weight lines, each specific for the type of rod and fishing you do.

Bobber

A bobber is a small plastic ball that you attach to your line and floats on the surface of the water. The hook and bait extend below the bobber into the water. When a

A Few Helpful Fishing Tips

Purchase a fishing license if necessary.

Know the game laws where you are fishing.

Always tell someone where you are going.

Always wear your safety gear.

Never go on private land without permission.

Never fish during a thunderstorm.

Carry food and water with you if you are fishing for a long time.

Novices should consider joining a local fishing club or take a lesson.

Keep a fishing journal about the great spots you have found.

Be careful when handling fishing equipment (and fish) and always carry pliers.

Many fish have sharp spines and teeth, so know your fish!

Fish have a protective slime along their bodies; be careful not to rub it off, if you are returning them to the water.

Be careful when casting a fishing line near others.

Always look around before you cast.

Never leave trash behind or throw it into the water.

Enjoy yourself, fishing is a fun and relaxing sport.

And always have a good fish story, even if you have to make it up!

fish nibbles at your bait the bobber will move up and down. This type of fishing delights kids, beginners, and those who fish periodically and want to keep it simple. (Or for those, like me, who just like to watch the bobber go up and down.)

Sinker

A sinker is a weight that helps pull the line under the water. The weights of sinkers vary so you can choose the right one for the water current and the type of bait you use. Lead sinkers are the most common, but others are available.

Catch and Release

This requires that when you catch a fish, you will then release it gently back into the water. This has become a rule in many locations and it's essential that you know how to gently remove the hook and release your fish back into the water in a timely manner, because it will die if you do not do it properly.

Game Laws

These are the rules for your area that governs fishing, specifically where you can fish and what you can keep. Contact the Fish and Wildlife Department of your state (see Resource List).

Homemade Kid's Fishing Stick

My siblings and I spent hours behind Grandmother's house trying to catch fish in the river with a stick, string and safety pin. We could occupy ourselves forever and still not come home with a single fish. Going fishing with kids with homemade fishing poles is extremely rewarding. Even if you don't catch a thing, you will certainly come back with great stories!

Find an old-fashioned clothespin (craft stores) and attach fishing line to it (kite string will do). Add a hook, bobber and sinkers to the fishing line. Put bait on your hook, hang your clothespin stick over the edge the dock or from the shore and wait. Use rolled up balls of bread, they work well to catch perch and sunfish. If you catch something, just wind the fishing line around the clothespin to bring it up! This is a good way to learn catch and release, and yak away with your grandpa while you wait—even if it scares the fish away.

"My family has a farm in rural West Virginia, where we spend hours exploring the one hundred and eighty acres of land surrounding it. Here we have time to walk to the general store, which is over a mile away. The kids play cowboy games in the fields on the way. I am always pleasantly surprised how peaceful it is here and how time appears to slow down."

—Liz, Moyers, West Virginia

chapter six

Walking and Hiking

Gorgeous countryside, majestic mountains and exceptional parks surround many cottages. One of the joys of walking and hiking from your cottage is the luxury of returning to it for a tasty meal, a warm shower and a comfortable bed.

Whether you are going for a short walk with the family or a long hike with friends, you should be prepared for a variety of situations. There are many guidebooks for each region of the country, check your local bookstore. We also recommend the book, *The 2 oz. Backpacker, A Problem Solving Manual for Use in the Wilds,* by Robert S. Wood. This is a perfect pocket size book for all hikers.

The Basics

Always have water and a snack with you. Be sure to have a water bottle per person for a short walk and two for longer walks. Have a snack that will give you energy, such as *gorp* (trail mix), and a peanut butter and jelly or a cheese sandwich for ease.

Individuals hike at different speeds. Be aware of your group's ability and fitness level. It is not rude to hike in two separate groups and then meet at a designated spot; lunch is a

good time to stop and regroup. Hiking is not a race or a contest; remember to allow time to smell the roses along the way.

It is wise for at least one member of the group to be familiar with the trail. Familiarizing yourself with the level of difficulty, the length (round trip), the fauna and wildlife should be part of your preparation. If this is a new adventure for everyone, be sure to get as much information from a local, a hiking club or the parks service.

Make sure you let those who are staying behind know where you are going and how long you think you will be gone.

Seasons and Temperatures

No matter what the temperature or season, always dress in layers and bring plenty of

Footwear

It is important that you are comfortable in your footwear and you break in any shoes before any long walks or hikes. Wear shoes with gripping treads and high sides for traction and ankle support. Be sure to bring extra socks on the trip. Have extra shoes in the car if you had to drive to your hiking trail to put on after the trip.

Wet and Cool Season

When hiking during the spring, it is important to walk along the path so you do not ruin the trails. Many locations ask you not to hike during certain seasons to ensure the trail is not ruined. Also be careful to try and keep you feet dry. Waterproof hiking boots and extra socks go a long way in comfort. Bring an extra sweater and a wind/water proof parka.

water. Hypothermia can happen in all seasons and it is a serious condition. Proper clothing, food, water and pacing are important to preventing hypothermia and its opposite cousin, heat exhaustion, which is equally debilitating. Keep the pace reasonable and water supply plentiful.

Medical Conditions

Be sure to know about any allergies, diabetic situations or heart conditions of those people hiking with you. Is anyone allergic to bee stings? Ask...that way you can be prepared with a bee kits, other shots and medication if necessary.

Dry and Hot Season

Be extra cautious regarding fires in dry seasons. Be sure fires are permitted in the area if you plan on making one. And know your fire hazard level in the area and if there are any forest fires nearby. Also be sure to bring extra water and sun protection, including a breathable hat.

Cold Season

Check weather forecast for snow accumulations or storms. Be sure to dress in many layers that are made for winter weather as well as wicking sweat away from your skin. Hats and mittens are a must.

Hunting Season Precautions

Be sure to know your seasons, whether you are a hunter or not, it is best to respect the seasons and not go in the woods during hunting seasons in your area. If you are hiking on a marked trail during hunting season, be sure to dress in bright colors and keep your dog on a leash. You can easily find out hunting seasons by calling your Fish and Wildlife Department and asking for a copy of hunting, fishing and trapping laws booklet. See our Resource List for contact information.

Hiking with Children

This is a perfect time to relax and slow your pace. Never be in a hurry when hiking with children, they have their own schedule. It is important for them to be able to stop and look around, point out rocks, look at worms and slugs and just enjoy their surroundings. A great kid's reading book about hiking is, *Buck Wilder's Small Twig Hiking & Camping Guide*, by Tim Smith and Mark Herrick. It is a wonderful fun book for kids about our National Parks, hiking, equipment, safety and more.

Try to keep hikes short and allow the children to lead whenever safely possible. Never let a child out of your sight and always have an adult bringing up the rear. Once the children get comfortable with short hikes, then you can start trying harder ones.

Be sure children drink plenty of water (not juice, which causes dehydration) and eat a snack. Also watch for early signs of hypothermia, such as listless or cranky complaints of feeling cold.

How much fun to stop and enjoy your surroundings! You will see a variety of mushrooms, flowers, birds and leaves. Bring an identification book with you for fun and a better appreciation for the natural surroundings.

Keeping children interested and excited in hiking now will keep them hiking for a lifetime. Just know that it will take you twice as long to finish a hike with kids and enjoy watching their excitement.

Checklist for Day Hikes

- ☐ Check into hunting season
- ☐ Map and/or directions for hike
- ☐ Tell someone trip information
- ☐ Backpack or fanny pack
- ☐ Water and snacks (sandwiches)
- ☐ Sunscreen and insect repellent
- ☐ Jacket (wind breaker, rain coat)
- ☐ Layer (warm sweater for winter, over shirt for summer)
- ☐ Extra socks
- ☐ Summer hat (winter hats and mittens)
- ☐ Matches (waterproof or in plastic bag)
- ☐ Toilet paper and small shovel
- ☐ First aid kit (with whistle)
- ☐ Individual medical prescriptions/shots
- ☐ Compass
- ☐ *Swiss Army Knife* or *Leatherman*
- ☐ Flashlight
- ☐ Camera
- ☐ Cell phone (optional for emergency only)
- ☐ Extra shoes and clothes in car
- ☐ Dogs allowed? Add leash, water and bowl

Snowshoeing

It is true, snowshoeing is just like walking, and with just a little effort, and you can be enjoying the countryside like you've never seen it. If your cabin is anywhere near snow, or you visit it periodically during the winter, you should have some snowshoes. In this case, the right equipment can be the difference between a love of the sport and a one time deal. The old-fashioned wooden shoes with leather straps are great as wall hangings, but for slapping them on and going, it's another story. You can get basic snowshoes for a decent price so take some time to research the variety of snowshoes that are good quality but easy to use. Then all you need are good winter boots or a sturdy pair of hiking boots (in milder climates) and head out the door. Remember to write the cabin's name on the snowshoes, so all visitors can enjoy them. Ski poles are also great to have around. Poles are wonderful for those who are beginning and would like the security of additional balance. For those who want an extra workout, poles do the trick.

Other Sports

There are dozens of other sports you may enjoy at your special getaway place. Whether you are mountain biking, snowshoeing, cross-country skiing or snowmobiling, you must respect nature and prepare properly. The above information for hiking and walking can be used for all sports. Be sure to remember any additional things you may need for your specific sport, such as, bike tire repair kit, wax for your cross country skis, helmets for snowmobiling, etc. Enjoy your sports and play safe!

"For Mother's and Father's Day, my husband and I planted apple trees and blueberry bushes at my parent's lakehouse. Now, when we visit, we pick our own blueberries for breakfast and enjoy apple pies in the fall."

—Joanne, Vermont

chapter seven

Weekend Gardening

At their homes, most people find little time for playing in the dirt. But at your cottage, all you need is a few minutes and a little space with some sun. It is a joy to come back after a long week to see how much more your flowers, herbs and vegetables grew. Setting up a low-maintenance garden at your getaway helps to keep it carefree and manageable. Focus on plants that enhance your cottage experience such as vegetables and herbs for cooking, fruits for snacks, and cutting flowers for decorating inside.

Raised beds and containers dry out much faster than the ground, so we suggest you plant directly in the ground and consider using several inches of bark mulch around the plants to keep moisture in and to help cut down on weeds.

Vegetables

Choose vegetables that naturally do well in your climate and are easily maintained. It is a good idea when first planting your garden that you spend extra time watering it, or ask someone to water it a little while you are away. Even so, young plants need consistent watering. (If you don't have a neighbor who can water during your absence, timed watering systems have gotten much cheaper and can be installed by the homeowner.)

WEEKEND-GARDENING

Think simple. Radishes and Carrots can be planted together because you will harvest the radishes at the beginning of the summer and carrots can grow until the first frost. Radishes are done when you can see the red tops coming out of the ground.

Greens can be planted early in the season. Use mesclan lettuce instead of heads of lettuce and cut the greens with scissors so they can grow back. Remember, greens do not like hot weather, so plant them early and late in the season.

Scallions and garlic require little space and are tasty when grilled.

Potatoes of all varieties can be planted in a mound. Be patriotic; plant red, white and blue potatoes. These potatoes are great for salads or roasting.

Tomatoes can work if you buy plants and water them well when they are first put in the ground. Planting a couple of cherry tomatoes, a beefsteak, and a roma, will give you choices for snacking, slicing and dicing.

Peppers, just like tomatoes, will need to be planted and watered well when first put into the ground. There are a variety of peppers; look at the packages for hardy brands.

Herbs

Fresh herbs can change the entire taste of a meal, drink or dessert. Throwing some fresh basil in your spaghetti sauce can make you feel like a true Italian cook (or least closer to one). Great weekend gardening herbs are parsley, basil, chives and mint. If you do have them in pots, you can plant the pots directly into the garden by cutting out the bottom. Chives and mint are perennials, so plant them in the ground at the end of the season and they will come back next year. Nasturtiums flowers are a fun addition because they are edible and eye catching in a salad.

A Garden Recipe: Chive Blossom Vinegar

Put chive blossoms in the bottom of a mason jar and fill it with white vinegar. Place the jar in the sun for an afternoon and the vinegar will turn pink. Remove the blossoms from the jar (straining works best) and use for salads, marinades or as a gift.

Flowers

Flowers bring beauty to the world and lift our attitudes. A cutting garden is one of the best property improvements you can make. If your soil is not naturally rich, all the department stores carry peat moss and top soil that you can mix in. You can mix and match your flowers for a variety of colors, textures and height. Be sure to get varieties of flowers that are hardy and don't need regular watering (check with your local gardening shop if you are unsure).

Use wildflower mixes too. Go to your local gardening store for a variety of native wildflowers. Every spring my friend Marty plants a field of wildflowers in front of her mountainside cabin and it is stunning to see the flowers against the base of Mount Hood.

Flower Arrangements

It is best to cut flowers in the early morning or late afternoon and place them immediately in deep water. Use a sharp, clean tool to cut them. Strip the stems of leaves below the water line. To help the flowers stay fresh longer, use a clean vase and add a teaspoon of sugar and an aspirin.

Fruits Trees, Berries and Shrubs

So many hybrids and options exist today. You should pull into a local nursery and inquire about what grows best in your area. Once you

get a berry patch started, it can produce for several years with very little care. And the right fruit tree, well, your grandkids could be picking fruit from it for decades to come. For immediate fruit, the dwarf varieties produce fruit the quickest.

Lawn Art

Can you think of a better place to let your creative side out? I can't. At home, lawn art might raise an eyebrow, but at your cottage, whimsical and interesting lawn art is a joy for you, your family and those who pass by. My friend Shannon, has fabulous lawn art,

she made a plant holder out of a chandelier and a still-life from an old bicycle and some salvage pieces. Have fun with your lawn— let those creative juices flow!

Another wonderful piece of lawn art can be an old wicker chair with a garden in its' seat. Instead of throwing away old lawn chairs use them to create a whimsical flower pot. Just place a plastic bag on the seat of the chair, add some stones, then topsoil. Surround the edge with moss or ground cover and then add some annuals into the middle to create your masterpiece. The old chair and the fresh flowers create an eye catching

Great annual cutting flowers

- Achillea (yarrow)
- Anemone japonica (Japanese anemone)
- Campanula (bellflower)
- Carnation
- Coreopsis (cosmos)
- Echincea purpurea (purple cornflower)
- Gaillardia (blanket flower)
- Hibiscus moscheutos (rose mallow)
- Iris
- Liatris (gay-feather)
- Monarda (bee balm)
- Paeonia (peony)
- Phlox
- Rosa (Rose)
- Rudbeckia hirta (black-eyed Susan)
- Salvia
- Veronica (speed well)

Perennial best sellers

- Ageratum (floss flower)
- Calendula (pot marigold)
- Centaurea cyanus (bachelor's button)
- Consolida (larkspur)
- Dianthus caryophyllus 'Clove Pink'
- Gladiolus biennial
- Helianthus (sunflower)
- Zinnia (make sure you buy the cutting variety)

contrast. You can even hang your cottage sign from the top of the chair—this is sure to make a great landmark for your guests.

Seating Areas

Now that you have this fabulous garden, you need to find a place to sit and admire it. Look around your garden and see what would work best for your space. Do you have two strong trees to hang a hammock? Is there plenty of room for a French café table and two chairs? Is there a part of the space for a sandy beach for your umbrella and beach chairs? Whether it is a homemade swing, two wicker chairs or tree stumps that are painted in a wildflower theme, make sure you create a cozy space for you to read in, for a romantic conversation or even to sip a tall glass of lemonade and just relax.

chapter eight
Around the Campfire

For our family, building campfires began long before we rented our first camp. Dad built a cinderblock campfire pit in the backyard at our home. It was not the prettiest setting of stones, but no one noticed as we spent hour after hour by the fire. The first lakefront cottage my family rented did not allow campfires. Therefore we improvised and made S'mores over our charcoal grill. Today, at my parent's lakefront home we have a permanent fire pit. Built of beautiful stones we found around the property, it serves again and again as a gathering place for our family and friends. We spent hours talking, cooking and singing until the last spark of fire had died. So many other cottage owners related similar stories centered around their fire pit.

Fire Safety and Permission

First and foremost is safety. Follow the tips in this chapter to keep your fire safe for yourself, the neighbors and property around you. Check at your local fire department to see if open fires are allowed and if they require a permit. Be aware, the fire rules can change due to dryness or seasonal and climactic changes in your area. Please respect the law and find an alternative way to gather the gang around a grill or some other alternative fire that the town allows.

Selecting Your Spot

After you have confirmed that campfires are allowed or have received your permit, be sure you have enough space between you and your neighbors. You want to make sure that the smoke of your fire is not going to go directly on their porch, in their kitchen window or become bothersome to them. Then select a spot at least fifteen feet from trees. Be sure there are no hanging branches or dry grass anywhere near your site. Do not build over roots because the fire can follow the root through the ground. Make sure to know the wind speed and direction, sparks and smoke can travel a long way.

Building a Fire Pit

You may want to use an existing fire pit if it meets the criteria above. Otherwise, you can create one in a flat place that has ample space for the fire and the size of your gatherings. Clear the space of dry grass, leaves, and all other cumbustables that could be ignited by a

spark. Next circle the fire pit with large stones. Think smaller at first, if need be you can expand it later. You may also use cinderblocks or bricks in a crisscross pattern for your circle.

Wood Fires

Tinder

The first thing you put at the bottom of your fire pit is tinder. Tinder is a combination of things such as dry grass, pinecones, newspaper, and small twigs. Place these items in the middle of your fire pit.

Kindling

Kindling is made up of small pieces of wood or dry sticks that will light easily and burn longer than tinder in order to help the larger pieces of wood burn. You can purchase kindling at a home goods store, but it is more fun to find it by scouring the beach or woods. Place the kindling around and on top of the tinder, leaning in towards the middle almost like a tepee.

Logs

Add several small dry logs to the top portion of the tepee. Maple and oak wood burn longest but as long as the wood is dry all types work fine. Green logs will smoke, so be sure to use only dry woods.

CAUTION:

Do not pour gasoline or other flammables liquids on a campfire.

Attending to Your Fire

Before you start your fire, be sure you have prepared the area completely and gathered all the items needed to put a fire out quickly. *Never* leave the fire unattended and when you are finished, always fully extinguish the fire. Be sure to have a large bucket of water nearby (at least 10 gallon bucket), a bucket of sand and a long handled shovel. The easy solution is to have the water hose stretched out to the fire pit.

Putting the Fire Out

When the fire burns down, all that will remain are hot coals. Use a stick to spread the coals so they burn out faster. Then slowly sprinkle water over *all* the coals. You can use sand or water if that is what you have on hand. When the coals are cool enough to touch you can rest assured. For extra precaution, layer the fire pit with sand. Before your next fire, dispose of the ashes and start at the bottom of the fire pit again.

Alternative Fires and Charcoal Fires

Most people prefer wood for fires, but if wood is scarce, illegal, or unsafe, you can use charcoal instead. Pile it in a pyramid and follow the instructions on the charcoal bag very carefully. Lighter fluid is a serious hazard when used improperly. Be sure to follow instructions and *never* have it in reach of children or let them light a fire with it. Many types of enclosed barbeque fire pits are sold through mail-order catalogs, such as *Waterfront Living* and *Restoration Hardware* or you can check out your local camping and hardware store to purchase one.

Campfires with Kids

Teaching children the dangers of fire is as important as teaching them how much fun a campfire can be. For very young children whose level of comprehension is just not there, it is best to keep them away from campfires all together. We have found a book called, *The Kids Campfire Book*, by Jane Drake & Ann Love, a great book to have when creating a fun atmosphere for kids. It teaches them safety tips, how to build fires, collect wood, cook food, sing songs and much more. We highly recommend adding this to your resource collection. See our Resource List for this book and other campfire resources.

Campfire Gatherings

My friend Marty has a permanent campfire location behind her secluded cabin in the woods of Oregon. Surrounding the fire pit are the four symbols representing wind, water, fire, and earth. She is renowned for her solstice parties around the campfire, filled with song, dance and wine. Even her shyest friends do not mind belting out a campfire tune. Seeing everyone sitting around the fire singing songs with wildflowers in their hair is a sight to behold.

Create your own lifelong memories. There are many types of campfire parties you can have, a solstice party, a ghost story party, and a nighttime beach party, or even a neighborhood campfire party that combines an association meeting.

Fire-Side Songs

There are a variety of campfire songs books, including a cute, hand-sized one called, *A Little Book of Camp Fire Songs*, from Chronicle Books. We have listed a few songbooks in our Resource List. You can also download songs from the Internet. Compose a unique song for your own place. Jot down the verses while you sit around the fire making up your own campfire song. It can be the theme song for your cabin for generations to come.

A Few of Our Favorites . . .

This Land Is Your Land

This land is your land, this land is my land,
From California, to the New York Island,
From the redwood forest, to the Gulf Stream
　　Water,
This land was made for you and me.

As I went walking, that ribbon of highway,
I saw above me, that endless skyway,
I saw below me, that golden valley,
This land was made for you and me.
This land is your land, this land is my land,
From California, to the New York Island,
From the redwood forest, to the Gulf Stream
　　Water,
This land was made for you and me.

I roamed and I rambled and I followed my
　　footsteps,
To the sparkling sands of her diamond
　　deserts,
While all around me a voice was sound,
Saying "This land was made for you and me."

This land is your land, this land is my land,
From California, to the New York Island,
　　From the redwood forest, to the Gulf
Stream Water,
　　This land was made for you and me.

The sun came shining and I was strolling,
And the wheat fields waving and the dust
　　clouds roiling,
As the fog was lifting, a voice was chanting,
"This land was made for you and me."

This land is your land, this land is my land,
From California, to the New York Island,

From the redwood forest, to the Gulf Stream
    Water,
This land was made for you and me.
This land was made for you and me.

Home on the Range
Oh, give me a home, where the buffalo roam,
Where the deer and the antelope play,
Where seldom is heard a discouraging word,
And the sky is not cloudy or gray.
Home, home on the range!

Oh, give me a land where the bright
    diamond sands,
Lie awash in the glittering stream,
Where days glide along in pleasure and song,
And afternoons pass as a dream.
Home, home on the range…

Oh, give me a home, where the buffalo roam,
Where the deer and the antelope play,
Where seldom is heard a discouraging word,
And the sky is not cloudy or gray.
Home, home on the range!

Someone's in the Kitchen with Dinah
I've been working on the railroad all the live
    long day.
I've been working on the railroad just to pass
    the time away.
Can't your hear the whistle blowing, rise up
    early in the morn?
Can't you hear the Captain shouting, Dinah
    blow your horn?
Dinah will you blow, Dinah will you blow,
    Dinah will you blow your horn.
Dinah will you blow, Dinah you blow, Dinah
    will you blow your horn.

Someone's in the kitchen with Dinah,
    someone's in the kitchen ah know.
Someone's in the kitchen with Dinah, play-
    ing on de 'ole banjo and singing,
Fee-fie - fidly-i-o, Fee-fie – fidly-i-o,
    Fee-fie – fidly-i-o,
Playing on de 'ole banjo.

America (My country 'tis of thee)
My country 'tis of thee, Sweet land of liberty,
Of thee I sing.
Land where my fathers died,
Land of the pilgrim's pride.
From every mountainside let freedom ring.

My native country, thee,
Land of the noble free,
They name I love,
I love thy rocks and rills,
They woods and templed hills;
My heart with rapture thrills
Like that above.

Let music swell the breeze,
And ring from all the trees
Sweet freedom's song'
Let mortal tongues awake,
Let all that breathe partake,
Let rocks their silence break,
The sound prolongs.

Our father's God! To thee,
Author of liberty,
To Thee we sign;
Long may our land be bright
With freedom's holy light;
Protect us with Thy might,
Great God, our King.

Your Campfire Checklist

- [ ] Permission from town and/or permit
- [ ] Safe location for fire
- [ ] Large stones (concrete blocks) for circle
- [ ] Bucket of water
- [ ] Bucket of sand
- [ ] Shovel with long handle
- [ ] Tinder (small twigs, pine cones, newspaper)
- [ ] Kindling (larger twigs, small sticks)
- [ ] Small logs
- [ ] Long safety matches
- [ ] Sticks for cooking
- [ ] Chairs (or stump stools)
- [ ] Song book
- [ ] Ghost stories
- [ ] S'mores (chocolate, marshmallows, graham crackers)
- [ ] Hot dogs
- [ ] Camera
- [ ] Have fire safety rules for kids

Fireside Stories

Storytelling is an entertaining art practiced in all cultures of the world. You can become a master storyteller and mesmerize your audiences. One of the best neighborhood or family activities to do at night, sitting by firelight, listening to the crackle of the logs, is to tell a story. What better type than a scary one? Whether you make up your own scary tale, embellish a true story that happened in your own area long ago, or read from one of the books of campfire tales, be sure to get into character.

When telling the story, your voice, tone, pausing, and facial expressions play a large part of the tale. If you choose to become the regional maestro, "how to" books are available. Consider the ages and disposition of your guests when choosing your story topic.

Cooking on the Fire

Cooking Sticks

For the ever popular basics like hot dogs and marshmallows, roasting sticks are a must. The stick can be a sprig from a nearby willow, a coat hanger cut in two, or even grilling skewers you find at an outdoor equipment store. Whichever you choose, be cautious: metal sticks can get very hot, wood sticks can catch on fire, and all skewers have a sharp point that can cause an accident. Be sure your roasting stick is long. You don't want to be bending over too close to the fire. You can easily cook your food on the edge of the heat; you do not need to place it over the middle to cook. For campfire cooking books, check out the campfire section in our Resource List.

S'mores

What is a campfire without S'mores? Anyone who has cooked on a campfire knows that S'mores, the taste-dazzling sandwich of graham crackers, marshmallow and chocolate, is the best open-air dessert possible. Put two marshmallows on your roasting stick and heat them all the way through, until golden brown on the outside. Place two chocolate squares on two graham crackers and slide the heated marshmallows between them. The challenge of S'more is to make sure the chocolate is not too cold, but not too soft. Give the marshmallows time to warm up the chocolate before you take a bite.

To create a unique and tasty S'more, make your own sugar cookies, roll, cut and bake them into squares and use a small cookie cutter to create a design in half of them. This will allow the marshmallow to show through the design. Use good milk chocolate bars and it's a piece of heaven.

Another S'more idea: My friend, Holly, uses *Ritz* crackers because she likes the combined taste of sweet and salt. Give it a try!

There is something magical and
mythical about fire;
your campfire location will become
hallowed ground.

"One of our evening joys, is bringing our dessert and coffee onto our pontoon boat. We pick up our friends from a few camps down shore and we circle the lake and talk until the sun goes down."

—Yvonne, Naples, Florida

chapter nine

Feeding the Gang

Is it just me or does food taste better at your cottage? There is nothing like corn on the cob at the lakehouse cooked on the grill. After a long snowshoe in the winter, a steaming bowl of chili with grated cheese will instantly melt away any body chill. Enjoying meals at camp does not necessary mean more work. By keeping your meals simple, you can leave your cottage feeling relaxed and pampered. We have a few strategies and recipes for those who are looking to keep things simple but tasty.

My mother has been feeding large groups ever since she and Dad rented their first camp on Joe's Pond, twenty years ago. I have a new appreciation for the time and energy my mother has put into cooking for so many visitors. After a short time of owning my own cottage and faced with growing crowds, I gathered feeding tips from my mother, my sister and other cottage owners. Now ten late-shows for lunch or dinner is not a panic.

Your Kitchen

First survey what you have in your kitchen and what you use on a daily basis. Avoid carrying items repeatedly from your home kitchen to the cottage. Think about the best use of your energy, maybe it is worth buying utensils for the cottage that stay there. Garage sales and recycle shops are great ways to get the equipment you need without spending a fortune.

If you don't have a lot of room, think about multi-purposing your equipment. If I had to, I could live with three pans: a wok shaped pan, a pot for boiling pasta and an iron skillet.

Dull knives are not only irritating but also time consuming; they keep you in the kitchen longer. Be sure that your equipment is in working order.

bring, it makes them feel part of the cottage experience and more at ease. Let them know how many guests will be there, so everyone can plan appropriately.

Across the lake from us, cottage owners have barbeques every weekend. They ask their guests to bring whatever they would like to grill such as steak, chicken, fish and their own beverages. The cottage owners provide a variety of side dishes, such as potato salad, chips and salsa, corn on the cob and a dessert. Everyone has a great time and the cottage owners can to afford to have

Instead of having a slew of dinnerware, china, and plastic picnic ware, choose good looking heavy plastic dinnerware that you can use inside or out. Make sure that it is heavy enough so it does not blow over in a swift wind. This way you can have one table service for all your dining needs. If you are fortunate enough to have a dishwasher and microwave, be sure these plates are usable in both.

"What Can We Bring?"

You may hear this question a lot when friends come to visit. When we first moved in, I would always say, "Just you!" After we had guests almost daily for five months, I suggest specific items for them to bring. Feeding large groups on a regular basis is expensive. Even if you can afford it, feel comfortable asking guests to chip in. Most guests appreciate when you recommend a specific item to

Basic Spices and Condiments

- ☐ Drinking and cooking water (if you can't drink the water at your cottage)
- ☐ Salt
- ☐ Pepper
- ☐ Chili powder
- ☐ Ground cumin
- ☐ Garlic powder
- ☐ Cinnamon
- ☐ Nutmeg
- ☐ Italian spices
- ☐ Vanilla extract
- ☐ Baking soda
- ☐ Baking powder
- ☐ Relish, ketchup, mustard, barbeque sauce
- ☐ Mayonnaise
- ☐ Olive oil and vegetable oil

Kitchen Recommended Equipment

- ☐ 3 sturdy mixing bowls (all fairly large)
- ☐ 3 sharp knives—varying sizes
- ☐ Iron skillet
- ☐ 3-5 gallon pot with cover
- ☐ Wok shaped pan with cover
- ☐ 2 smaller pots with cover
- ☐ Baking sheet
- ☐ Rectangle baking pan
- ☐ Cutting board
- ☐ Garbage can with secure lid
- ☐ Glass storage containers
- ☐ Coffee thermos and coffee pot
- ☐ 2-3 trays
- ☐ Plastic storage containers
- ☐ Measuring cups and spoons
- ☐ Drinking glasses (you may want to consider plastic)
- ☐ Paper plate, napkin, and cup supply
- ☐ Pasta strainer (use for all straining and washing needs)
- ☐ 15 forks, knives, spoons
- ☐ 2 ladles, serving spoons, wooden spoons and spatulas
- ☐ One whisk and set of barbeque tools
- ☐ 3-4 baskets for bread, fruit and other serving needs
- ☐ Corkscrew, bottle opener and can opener

guests on a regular basis. Find what works for you and it will allow everyone to enjoy your cottage, including you!

Important Note

Please be aware of any special dietary needs, allergies, vegetarian, lactose intolerant of your guests or any allergies they may have. If others are bringing food items, let them know what not to bring.

Packing It In

Many cottage owners, including my brother-in-law's family, pack in complete meals every weekend. His mother prepares meals and packs them in coolers so when they arrive they can prepare a meal with the limited kitchen facilities on hand. This also saves her a lot of time in the kitchen, allowing her more time to ski, walk and boat with her family.

Packing it in Suggestions and Tips

Frozen water bottles can be the ice for the cooler and then you have water to drink when they thaw out. Prep most of your food in advance and pack them into reusable plastic bags or storage containers. When you want grated cheese, all you have to do is pull out the bag. Sliced veggies, cheeses, cubed ham and turkey snack for kids and just a few suggestions for prep work. We have also put together some recipes that are easy to pack in.

Grilling It

Tin foil and cooking spray are my best friends, and they will be yours too if you want

We are not going to labor you with the basics, such as hot dogs, hamburgers, steaks and the like; we figured if you don't have those down yet… well…you get the point.

A Big Pot of Chili

Planning on spending a weekend at the cabin skiing, snowshoeing and sledding? What better way to enjoy it than having a steaming pot of chili ready for when you come in to warm up? This popular meal can be planned ahead and either frozen or refrigerated. All you need to do when you arrive at the cabin is let it unthaw and heat. Shredded cheese and great bread are all the condiments you will need for this meal. Besides being an inexpensive meal to make, chili will feed a large gang for a night or a small one for a few days!

to create some easy one dish meals. Wholesale grocery stores can be your friend if you want to buy items in large quantities. Bags of frozen chicken breasts, salmon, corn on the cob can easily be put in your cooler and brought to the cottage. Unthaw and you are ready to grill a tinfoil bag of vegetables, potatoes or a fillet of salmon.

A Few of Our Own

Many of you are geniuses in the kitchen and already have your own favorite cookbooks and recipes. But for those days you don't feel like making an elaborate meal, we compiled a few recipes that are camp friendly and inexpensive to make. Some of these recipes can be made in advance and packed into a cooler.

Ingredients
2 tablespoons Olive Oil
2 garlic cloves
1 teaspoon of salt
1 teaspoon of pepper
1 teaspoon of chili powder
1 teaspoon of ground cumin
1 large onion (or two medium sized ones)
1 red pepper
1 green pepper
1 pound hamburger (or ground turkey)
1 28 oz of crushed tomatoes
1 28 oz of diced Fire Roasted tomatoes
2 19 oz cans of black beans (drained)
2 19 oz cans of red kidney beans (drained)
2 cups shredded cheddar cheese or sour cream
2 loaves of freshly baked bread

Pour the olive oil into a large soup pan. Add the chopped onions, red pepper and green pepper. Cook on medium heat for 5-10 minutes, stirring frequently. Add the hamburger and spices and cook till brown (another 5-10 minutes). Add all the other ingredients; be sure to drain the beans before adding to the pot. (Fire Roasted diced tomatoes are recommended—they make the flavor. Look for them at your local grocery store or health food store.) Simmer on low, stirring frequently for an hour. It's ready to serve or let it cool completely before you freeze or refrigerate.

When serving, add a handful of shredded cheddar cheese or a spoonful of sour cream. Cut up a few pieces of bread and enjoy an easy, inexpensive and delicious meal.

Strata — A Breakfast Delight

Going for a long hike or spending the day on the water, start it with this very hearty breakfast. It is simple, filling and easy to throw in the oven while you get ready for the day. If you want, you can substitute the sausage for vegetarian sausage or even spinach.

Ingredients

1 8oz package maple flavored brown and serve sausage sliced nickel size
5 slices white or wheat bread
1 cup of shredded sharp cheddar cheese
5 eggs
2 cup milk (1 or 2 percent)
1 tsp dry mustard
Salt and pepper to taste
Optional (Tabasco to taste)
Butter

Butter a round or square casserole dish then layer the bottom with bread and next the sausage. In separate bowl combine eggs, milk, dry mustard and pour mixture over the bread and sausage. Sprinkle the shredded cheese on top. Bake at 350 degrees for 35-45 minutes.

Ricotta Cakes

This is truly a "campy" dessert not to mention totally decadent. This dessert is not only easy to make, but tons of fun for the whole family. We make this at our family's camp all the time and everyone gets involved. The older kids roll out the dough while the younger kids spoon on the Ricotta cheese and place the chocolate. The cooking is up to the adults and then everyone gets to eat these fun, yummy desserts!

Ingredients

1 15 oz container of Part Skim Ricotta Cheese
2 containers of pop-open biscuits (or dough that can be rolled)
3 chocolate bars (break into very small pieces)
1 cup of sugar (2 tablespoons for the Ricotta Cheese – put the rest in a plate)
3/4 cup of vegetable oil

Mix two tablespoons of sugar into the Ricotta Cheese and set aside. Then pop open the dough containers and roll out the dough until they each become five inch circles (give or take an inch). Place two tablespoons of the Ricotta Cheese mix in the middle of the dough. Then place 1-1/2 tablespoons of chocolate pieces on top of the Ricotta Cheese. Fold the dough in half and seal the edges. Place the sealed half moon shaped desserts into a frying pan with the vegetable oil. Be sure the vegetable oil has had a

chance to warm up so it can fry them properly. Medium heat works best. Cook on each side till the dessert is well browned. Take out and drain the desserts onto paper towels, then immediately roll them in a plate of sugar to coat. Eat warm! This recipe makes about 12 cakes.

Date Bread Pudding

For those of you who couldn't even think of frying a dessert, bread date pudding is a little more on the conservative side of desserts (and less, shall we say, fat gram content). This dessert can be easily turned into the traditional bread pudding by substituting the dates for raisins. But give the dates a try—they add a nice touch and a little extra sweetness.

Ingredients
4 cups of cut up day old Italian, French bread or
*   white bread*
2 eggs (or egg substitute for 4 eggs)
2 egg whites
2 cups of skim milk
1/2 cup of packed brown sugar
1-1/2 teaspoon of vanilla
1 cup of dates
Sprinkling of cinnamon

Place milk, eggs, brown sugar, and vanilla in a greased casserole dish. Take the cut up (or ripped) bread and put into the wet mixture enough to cover it, not too firm. Then mix the dates into the mixture. Then sprinkle the top with cinnamon. Cook at 325 degrees until it is firm (not wiggly in the middle) about 45

minutes to an hour. Eat warm. Give it a try with a little milk and maple syrup. Serves six.

Pasta Special

When friends drop by, I throw something together representing a pasta dish such as the recipe below. A jar of sun dried tomatoes, garlic, feta cheese and some frozen vegetables always get us by. Remember, you can always substitute your favorite vegetable, cheese, or fish.

Ingredients
1 box of pasta (rotini works best)
1 clove garlic
1 small onion
1/2 cup of sun dried tomatoes in olive oil
2 cups baby spinach
2 tablespoons of extra virgin olive oil
1 cup of feta cheese
1/2 of shredded parmesan cheese
1 cup of Greek olives
Optional: 1 cup of small pieces of grilled chicken
*   or pieces of grilled salmon*
Salt and pepper to taste

Cook the pasta according the directions on the box. Set aside. In a large wok-shaped pan, put in olive oil, sun dried tomatoes, garlic, chopped onion and cook till onions are slightly brown. Stir in the baby spinach and olives (chicken or salmon) and then cook for two minutes, remove from heat and add the pasta, feta cheese, parmesan cheese and salt and pepper to taste. Serve with some fresh French bread and garlic infused olive oil and a salad.

"When I arrive at my cottage I want to feel as though I just entered another world, one filled with sun, bright colors and comfortable furnishings, that is why our cottage looks like it bloomed from a flower garden."
— Marylee, Outer Banks, North Carolina

chapter ten

Decorating Made Simple

The first cottage my family rented had an old picnic table in the middle of the kitchen. We spent hundreds of hours preparing meals, eating and playing games on that table. Our second cottage had four bedrooms with only half walls, making the upstairs seem like community living. Now my parents own their lakeside camp. It has hardwood floors, a separate dining room and bedrooms with complete walls. Their camp is beautiful, but there are moments I long for the picnic table and the slumber party feel. Whatever your budget and type of place, you can create an atmosphere that suits your family.

Make a List

List the major interests you want your cabin to support and see if the décor and furnishings reflect these interests. List the conveniences you want, and what you would need to do to get these conveniences. What's your particular pleasure? Maybe it takes only a few minor changes to make your place what you want it to be.

Basically, ask yourself, how many people will stay here, what will they do, and how much money can you spend on changes? Be realistic about the number of guests you have on a regular basis and be sure you, your cottage, your sleeping areas, the sewer system and the well can handle them. Do you like your privacy? Is a reading corner a must? A screened-in porch off the kitchen, more lawn furniture, sports equipment, new paint, are ways you can design to fit the function.

Each place comes with its own character, history and quirks; try to retain the original charm of your place. Grandma's rocking chair and the bright blue couch may be easily updated, but are they part of the ambiance of the place? If not, by all means, a quick fix is in order. There are dozens of interior decorating books and magazines geared towards the camp, cottage or cabin. They are full of wonderful ideas and solutions to your decorating needs. Below are a few ideas we discovered in a variety of cabins that are easy and inexpensive. You can find hundreds of other ideas in the decorating books and magazines listed in our Resource List. Plan first, it's part of the fun.

Paring Down

One of the simplest ways to make your cottage more comfortable is to pare down your

things. Over the years, we accumulate things which start to take over our homes. Look at all the knick-knacks, photographs, trophies, books and see if they add—or distract—from charm of your place. It may be hard to box them up, but just think of the simplicity of your place after and reduced cleaning time.

Whiten Up

One of the first things I did when we moved into our lakefront cottage was paint the living room a "cottage" white. The dark paneled walls made me feel like I was in a hunting cabin (there was even an outline of a gun on the wall from the darkening of the sun). Go to a paint store and describe your walls before you paint. The type of primer and paint you use will depend whether there are knots in the wood and other sub-surface conditions. Be sure to use the right kind or all your hard work with be for "knot."

Brighten Up

Using bright colors, such as sea blue, pastel pink, or moss green, depends upon the type of cottage look you want to achieve. If you want a restful room, light moss green or a morning sky blue are good choices. Bright Caribbean colors are in at the moment and make for fun rooms. Paint is an easy and inexpensive way to change the entire look of a room or furniture. (Remember, a good paint job can make the difference between "shabby chic" or just plain shabby.) I used a bright pink on all the Adirondack chairs that came with our cottage (which everyone loves). They look great against the grey stones of the beach, plus no one can miss our cottage from the water—we are the interesting family with the pink chairs!

Slipcovers

Throwing a bedspread or flannel sheet over a chair or couch can give it that relaxed shabby chic look. You can learn to sew a slipcover for your chairs by following instructions on a sewing package or by forming the fabric, pinning it and then hand sewing it one piece at a time. This may take a little longer but you will get more of a form-fitting slipcover.

Cover it with Rugs

Instead of replacing a carpet, or sanding a scratched up floor, you can purchase a throw rug or a carpet remnant and improve the look of a room. The great thing about throw rugs is you can easily take them outside and clean them. Go to your local carpet store and ask them about their remnants. You might be able to cover the entire floor or carpeted area

with one solid carpet piece, or your could get a variety of colors and sizes of carpets or throw rugs to scatter around the cottage. Ask the carpet store to cut the carpet or remnant to the size you desire and have them finish the edges (sometimes edging will be done for free or for a nominal fee). Look for some fun colors in the remnants. If your walls are white and your furniture with a flower motif, then call around to the carpet stores and ask if they have any bright blue carpet remnants or inexpensive complementary carpet they can cut for you.

Copper Top Table

I found an old worktable at a recycle shop. No matter how hard I tried I could not get the top to look good. We gave the legs a distressed look and I called my local plumbing store (or a sheet metal contractor) and asked for a sheet of copper. (Give the supplier the exact dimensions, including the lip, so they can bend the metal for you.) I slipped the copper over the top, and used small copper nails to

ing barbeques and use it as the buffet table. We get tons of compliments! (Other friends have used sheet metal for a cool outdoor table and even cut a hole in an old table to add a sink, great for ice and beers!

Decoupage Bureau

If you have tons of magazines that are just sitting around, start cutting out the flowers and collect them in a box for a decoupage project. My husband had an old white bureau (sometimes you have to take the stuff with the man) that I gave a totally new look. With some decoupage glue (craft store) I covered the entire bureau with flowers. Then I coated it a few times with shellac to protect it against wear and tear. You can also decoupage old tin cans and use them for storage containers in the kitchen or bathroom. Glue a colorful ribbon around the edge to give it a finished look. This is a fun project to do with kids.

Old Window Frame

Do you have an old window frame leaning against the side of the house or inside the barn? If so, it can become part of a great family art project. We have an old window frame (purchased for pennies at a salvage shop) filled with family pictures. The matting is a brown paper bag! Add a hook (an old door hinge works well) at the top of the frame and hang it on your wall. You can find a variety of colors and sizes of window frames and create a whole wall of fun family photos. We varnished our window because the paint was chipping and we did not want paint chips all

nail it to the bottom edge. You can leave it untreated for a more distressed look, or you can coat the top (polyurethane, varnish or shellac, depending on the use) to keep that gleaming copper look. Wear gloves when working with the sharp edged metal for safety and to keep from smudging the top with finger prints. If you do get spots on the table, use a metal cleaner to remove them. This is great for a kitchen island, counter tops, coffee tables. We bring our copper table outside dur-

over the place. You can use varnish, polyurethane or shellac. If you tape off the glass before you seal the wood it will go faster. You can change the pictures regularly to include everyone who comes to the cottage!

Corkboard Memory Display

When my guests arrive at my house, they spend a lot of time in the entranceway. It is not because they are unsure if they want to stay, it is because of my memory board on the wall. I purchased a corkboard and clear push pins from an office supply shop and made an entire wall of photographs. Guests looks for their photograph and comment about all the others. It is a one-of-a-kind conversation piece and not one person has walked by it without stopping to look. Spruce up the edges of the corkboard with a little paint, decoupage, glued on pinecones, buttons, or for a nautical theme, hot glue on some rope. Kids will love to help decorate the sides and pick out the pictures that will go on your memory board. Pushpins make it easy to rotate the pictures on a regular basis. (If your friend's boyfriend becomes an ex, he is easy to remove.)

Memory Duvet Cover

You can also create a memory duvet cover. Purchase a couple of sheets; if you select white, then purchase a black fabric pen; for bright sheets, use a white fabric pen. Wash the sheets and iron them. Spread one out evenly and put heavy items on the corners to keep it taut. Start up at the left hand corner and begin writing. You can write a love letter to your spouse, words that describe your kids (all good!) or sentences that evoke wonderful cottage memories. This is a whimsical and inexpensive way to cover your beds. Make one for each room, unique to each person. You only need to decorate one sheet, sew the other sheet to it and leave a small opening to slip the comforter into. You can seal the opening with some Velcro or buttons. Be careful when you work, the fabric pen can mark through the sheet.

Shutter Magazine Stand

Have any old shutters lying around? And some time-enduring, interesting magazines? Making a stand for them with an old shutter is clever. Simply lean a shutter against a wall, the couch or hang it on the wall of your bathroom. It makes for an easy and creative way to display your magazines. Open the magazines and slide them over the slates in the shutter as pictured.

Make Your Own Sign

My friend, Shannon Quimby, owner of *Arts & Antique's*, in Portland, Oregon, has been featured in a variety of magazines, including *Country Living*, and *Country Accents*. She has wonderful taste in cottage decorating and is known for her signs. We copied her style and made a few signs of our own; if you are unsure about the type of paint to use, whether to prep the wood, or if you need to topcoat the sign with sealer, call your local paint or hardware store.

Often simpler is better. For fun indoor signs, look for old farm signs, you see along side of roads or in antique shops. Old wooden signs like, Apples, Cider, Cabins for Rent, Vacancy, Fruit and Vegetable Stand, Hay for Sale, remind us of the good 'ol days. Think of your own fun saying, or your camp's name and have it made for you (see Resource List) or make it yourself.

"Apples" Sign

We used an old floor board (1880's) from a previous house we remodeled. You can purchase old boards at a recycle/salvage yard/ antique shops or ask you neighbor for the old board leaning against his barn. Clean up the old board with either steel wool or a sander. If you want to lighten it or clean it, use 3/4 water and 1/4 bleach mixture. Use acrylic paint to paint your sign. We wanted it to look weathered so we didn't mind if we missed spots and we hand painted it for the older look. We then slightly sanded it again. Varnish it if you want a more finished look.

"Sugar Shack" Sign

We used an old barn board bought at a salvage shop, we cleaned it up and slightly sanded it. We washed the board and let it dry before lightly outlining our words with pencil. After the paint dried we applied three coats of polyurethane because the sign was going to hang outside. Follow the instructions on all your paint products. For an added touch you can white-wash (use watered-down paint) before painting the letters on. This will make the colorful paints stand out.

"Stay Long" Sign

I found a plywood cabinet door in the basement of our cottage; I have no idea where it belonged. It already was painted white, so we cleaned it up and applied a crackle inducing coat and then green paint. The crackle agent caused the newly applied paint to crack and appear aged. Next we painted on our words "Stay Long, Talk Much," and design (flower and vase) and sanded the whole thing, especially so around the edges to give it that worn look. It will stay inside so we did not put a finish over the top. We used old door hinges to hang it.

Folding Chairs

Space is sometimes an issue at cottages. That is why Chris, one cottage owner, uses unique folding metal chairs at his place. Purchased from a used office furniture store, he lightly sanded the chairs and then painted them bright colors. He brought them outside and splatter painted them with a variety of colors. Choose your own unique paint design— paint them with red, white and blue stripes or green with lemons and oranges or another design that matches your decor. Need some space? Just fold them up!

Chalk Boards

Have some wall space in your kitchen or entrance way? A great cottage decorating idea is to cover the space with an old school chalk board. If you purchase a new one, just add old trim around the edges. This way you can always have a place to put the neighbor's numbers, the grocery list or a place to let your guests know you are down at the beach! My friends always have a great time reading the messages and coloring on our chalk board. Keep a basket of colored chalk nearby by for your artist friends who want to make a masterpiece. (It is also a great kid occupier.)

Concrete Patio Floors

You can make your own floor cloth on your concrete patio floor. Pull out your kid's

crayons one night and design a rug that will match your patio furniture and cottage style. Once you have a design on paper that you like, you can use it as a pattern. Get the concrete paint in the colors that you need and go to town! Over time, your rug will fade and wear adding to the charm of your concrete rug!

Just Relax

Don't worry about keeping up with the Jones with the decorating of your camp. It is your getaway place and even though it is fun to putz around, you should not stress yourself out by the number of decorating projects that could be done. Decorating is as much for fun as for aesthetics.

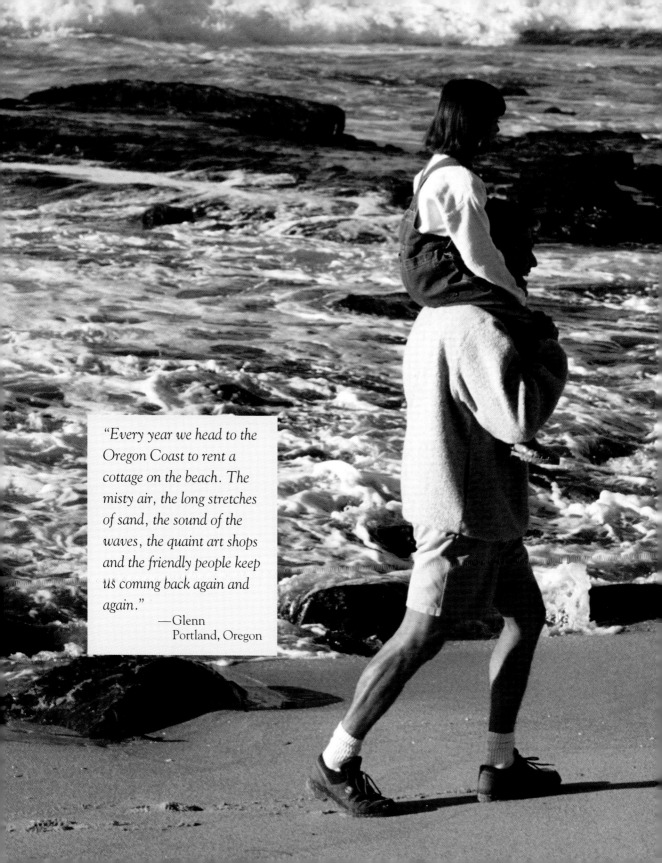

"*Every year we head to the Oregon Coast to rent a cottage on the beach. The misty air, the long stretches of sand, the sound of the waves, the quaint art shops and the friendly people keep us coming back again and again.*"
—Glenn
  Portland, Oregon

chapter eleven

Rental Considerations

tarting in the mid-90s, a new trend in vacationing began. People preferred renting a cottage, villa, cabin, or second home to traveling to hotels and motels. This way, it is possible to vacation all over the world and still have the luxuries you would have at home. And in some cases, it is less expensive to rent a cottage than other types of lodging.

The Pros and Cons

Those of you who rent out your cottage, or are considering it, need to know all the pros and cons of renting. It can be a good source of extra income, some owners like knowing someone is there, and others use it to pay the mortgage and taxes. For many owners renting is not practical because the camp is owned by several families, and someone is there all summer, or they cannot stand the thought of careless renters in their special place. If you do choose to rent, we have put together some information to make renting as smooth as possible.

If you choose to rent, be sure you understand all owner liabilities. A variety of renting/landlord books are available and you should talk to other owners that rent for their advice. Browse the Internet for sample leases and see which ones best match your situation. Know the local laws and regulations regarding renting and incorporate these into your rental lease.

What Can You Offer?

Inform potential renters of exactly what you are offering—with no exaggerations. Are

Your Rental Checklist

- [ ] The responsible person(s) contact information (local plumber, hospital...)
- [ ] Inventory and description of what you are renting
- [ ] When is the place available
- [ ] Where to list rentals
- [ ] Interview the renters
- [ ] Checking references
- [ ] Directions and entry
- [ ] Ensuring the clean-up

you offering a fully furnished cabin with cleaning services and a long list of amenities? Or are you offering an empty lakeside cottage with only cold running water? An accurate description will reduce misunderstandings with renters. Explain the type of place you have including the kitchen, kitchen utensils, living spaces, bedroom(s), bathroom(s), other rooms and any outdoor gear that is available. Provide an inventory of everything that could be removed and then walk through the cottage with them. Have them sign the sheet or give them the inventory sheet and have them contact you upon their arrival if something is missing. Explain the cleaning issues, how your renters will get inside and how to turn on appliances, water and heat. Putting everything down on paper before you rent will save you a lot of time and hassles in the future.

Services to Included

What type of services do you have and are they included in the rental fee, such as indoor running water (hot and cold), electricity, sewer (indoor or outdoor), heat, grass mowing, plowing, phone and cable? Describe what you provide in detail and clearly explain renter responsibility. This may vary greatly depending on the length of stay and how frequently you plan on renting it. If someone is renting for the summer, maybe they can take care of the lawn and pay for the services. Short term renters expect everything to be included.

Leaving a Boat and Related Items

A canoe, kayak, or even a small sail boat are pretty tame, but when you get into the area of speed boats, pontoon boats and sail boats, consider a separate lease and get a boating resume. Be sure home owner and liability insurance covers rental situations. Keep the life jackets, paddles, water skis and other miscellaneous beach toys in good shape to decrease liability concerns.

Allowing Pets

Choosing to allow pets depends on your tolerance for pets, your neighbor's attitude and the community's rules and regulations. You know your pet, but a renter's pet brings additional issues. Most pets are mannerly, tame and enjoyable—but not all. Requiring a deposit or extra fee for pets is appropriate. If you do allow pets, include the rules for pets, especially if you are part of an association that has additional pet rules.

Describing your Place

Whether you choose to list your property in a newspaper classified, create your own web site, list on a web rental site, or tack up a notice at the local general store, you must provide potential renters with a detailed description of your place.

Our property is:

Lakefront, oceanfront, near lake, near ocean, lake view, ocean view, in the woods, riverfront, ski slope, mountainside or other.

Type of vacation property:

Cottage, cabin, home, lodge, camp, other.

Property is available:

Summer, fall, winter, spring, all season, specific.

Will rent by the:

Year, month, week, weekend, night.

What are the amenities?

Water, hot water, electricity, other power types, heat (oil, gas, electrical, wood, coal), woodstove, fireplace, TV, VCR, telephone, kitchen, kitchen supplies, stove, refrigerator, oven, sink, bedroom(s), bedding supplies, bathroom (indoor, outdoor), bathroom supplies, towels (bathroom/beach) shower, bathtub, living room area, outdoor equipment, gas grill, outdoor furniture, others.

Remember:

Be careful about the number of people you say your place can sleep. You would be fine with 6-8 people but 16 sleeping on the pullouts and floor may be more than you want. Consider the burden it may put on your water and sewer system.

A Sample Description
Lake Miss You, Wisconsin

Great views from this 3-bedroom, secluded, lakeside cottage with an exceptional sandy beach, 150 feet of water front, fabulous sunsets, a large living room with fireplace, screened in sunroom, full bath and a large deck. Canoe, life jackets, firewood, water and electricity included. Perfect for up to 6 people. No pets or smoking. This property is available for one or more weeks during the month of July. Please call 888-888-8888 or email sample@sample.com for rates and more details.

Where to List Your Rental

If you want locals only, then let your neighbors know your place is available and post your rental at the general store. This limits your reach, but if you live in a hot spot or are renting for only one or two weeks, it may be enough. If you want to generate more rental interest and income, then consider a site on the Internet and in a vacation rental publication (some companies offer both). You can create your own web site complete with pictures of your property, your application and refer people to it. Research the web and see what other people have done. Contact a rental web site if you prefer.

Web Sites and Publications

How will you know what site is best for you? Do a search. What would individuals search for it they were looking for your place? A good start would be to type in your location followed by the words "rental, cottage." Once you put those into a search, you will come up with some rental sites that will be geared to service you. There are hundreds of sites, such as cyberrentals.com, cabins.com and cottagerentals.com. Be sure to look at a few, the costs and services provided vary greatly. A

rental publication specializing in your area is a good choice. Many rental publications host their own web sites so you can get two things done at once.

Think about a Property Manager

If you don't want to deal at all with applications, rent collection, phone calls, post-rent inspection and cleaning, and web messages, then outsource the process. Numerous property management companies and many real estate agencies will rent your place for you. The level of involvement varies as well as the price. Many property management companies take care of everything for you, including the cleaning, collecting the money, and dealing with the renters, all for a percentage of the rent. Some real estate agencies and rental groups will find the renter for you at no charge (they get paid by the renter), but then it is up to you to handle the rest. Contact several of them and decide who will provide the services you want and determine fee arrangement. Ask questions like: Will you list our property? What is your screening process like? Do you have your own application and lease agreement? Will you show the property? Will you make sure everything is in running order? Will you ensure it gets cleaned before rented again? How do you handle the finances? Do you have references? How does your fee structure work? The amount of work that goes into renting a cottage can be a fair amount and you just may want to pass that on to someone else, so be sure to consider this option before you go at it on your own.

Rental Applications and Leases

The type of application and rental lease you will use will depend on you, the amount of time you rent your place for and how many people are involved. My friends, Dan and Holly, rent their place out for a week with a friendly handshake. For others, a simple cottage application borrowed from the neighbor will do. There are many factors to take into consideration when renting, and if you are planning on renting your place often or feel like you need a little more security than a firm handshake, then you may want to consider purchasing a renting book such as, *Landlording*, by Leigh Robinson, a do-it-yourself handbook, filled with sample applications, leases and other forms. We rent out a cottage behind our own lake house (we have a complete application, do credit checks and have a detailed lease) and are pleased that we took the time to find great renters. Good renters can come back year after year, saving time and energy of having to find new ones!

No matter what you decide to use for an application and lease, you should use a sheet called "Rental Information," which is basic information about your cottage, such as the type of heat, how to use appliances, safety equipment location, sports equipment available, linens, and other items we mentioned. This way, your renters can get a basic understanding of what your place is all about before they move in. It will save you numerous phone calls and other hassles.

We have put a sample application in the worksheet section of this book. It is very basic and again, your level of confidence in your renters (are they your neighbor's kids or total strangers) will determine on the type of application you will ask people to fill out. If you do ask for references, check them; it only takes a few minutes. The best names you can get are previous cottage rentals. Call those owners and get an idea of what type of renters they were.

Special Treat

Leave a basket of goodies (with a $10.00 pre-paid phone card) for your renters upon their arrival; they will appreciate your gesture. Your thoughtfulness in all your renting comforts almost guarantees your renters will make an extra effort to show your cottage the respect it deserves.

"*Louie goes everywhere with me. He is my best friend. Every time we go for a walk on the twenty acres behind our cabin he clutches a stuffed animal in his mouth. In the spring we find a whole herd of the misplaced stuffed animals, it's like Christmas.*"

—Jerry
Boise, Idaho

Pets, Pests and Other Critters

It is difficult to overstate the love and enjoyment pet owners experience from their animals. When the dog is playing with the kids in the water, it is sheer delight for all. Curling up with the cat in the sunroom is a grand moment for a nap. Whatever your animal, there is a place and time for them at a cottage. My sister has two dogs she always brings to my parent's lakefront cottage. As a pet owner and vet tech she is well aware of situations that can occur for pets and their owners. When choosing to bring your animal to your cottage, many factors come to mind.

Protecting Your Pets

Unless you are very comfortable with the area, your neighbors and the wildlife, you may want to consider a fenced in area or an invisible electric fence around your cottage. These are easy ways to prevent neighbor misunderstandings or misfortunes for your animal.

Lyme Disease and Ticks

Ticks are serious hazards and should be treated properly and expediently. Since 1994, Lyme disease, a bacterial disease carried by ticks, has been reported in 47 states. Over 10,000 human cases have been diagnosed, making Lyme disease the second

Pet's Safety Questions

- ☐ What are the local regulations for pets?
- ☐ Is there a leash law?
- ☐ Do the neighbors have animals and how will they react?
- ☐ What is the nearby wildlife and will it threaten your pet?
- ☐ Are there any ticks around?
- ☐ Is there an area that can be blocked off for your pet's enjoyment?
- ☐ Where is the local vet?
- ☐ What are the emergency numbers for the pets?
- ☐ Do you have a local number on your animal's tag in case they get lost?
- ☐ Can your animal swim?
- ☐ Where are the best areas to take your pets for a walk?
- ☐ Are all poisons, moth balls and other items left from the closing season cleaned up?

fastest growing infectious disease after A.I.D.S. When an infected tick bites, the bacterium is transferred to the blood of the host animal, which could include your pet or yourself. For more detailed information contact your local veterinarian office for a pamphlet on ticks and Lyme disease.

You should inspect your pet daily for ticks. Start at the head and go to the tail, rubbing under the fur. Make it a playful game with your pet. Rub every inch of your pet for abnormalities such as ticks, fleas or other injuries that you may not notice otherwise. If you do find a tick on your dog, use tweezers to find the head of the tick and pull it straight out. The pamphlets you get from your local vet will have more details and pictures. You should keep these pamphlets at the cottage in the first aid kit. If you are concerned about Lyme disease, place the tick in a jar with a lid with rubbing alcohol and bring to your local vet for review. A variety of new tick and flea repellents are available (collars, powders, ointments) call your local vet for more information and a recommendation. **Important:** Be sure to check your kids and yourself as well everyday!

Playing in the Water

Many animals can get swimmers ear just like humans. If you have an animal that is prone to ear problems, inspect the inside of their ears and confirm they are dry before your animal settles down for bed. Also be confident of your pet's swimming ability before you head out too far in the water. In fact, I have seen several cottage owners put life jackets on their pets.

Be Neighborly

Be considerate of your neighbor and clean up after your animals. Also, have good communication regarding your animals: ask if they are bothersome.

Traveling with Your Pet

When traveling, carry a gallon of water, a dish, a leash, and a scooper for pit stops. Search out a local dog sitter, they come in handy for a late night out or a few days away.

Feeding your Pets

One of the favorite snacks mice, raccoons, bears and other animals love is dog or cat food. Bring in your pet's food at night and clean out the dish when you leave for the weekend to avoid attracting unwanted critter visitors, big and small.

Other Critters

Many people, like me, get a little squeamish about a variety of large animals, rodents, and insects. Others have no problem and can handle them with ease.

These creatures do have a place and purpose in this world, we just hope they don't choose our cottage for their home. When we learn more about their habits, we can reduce the chance that our home will become theirs. Have a healthy respect for wild animals and use safe preventive measures to repel them.

In addition to not enjoying sharing our space with unwelcome creatures, there are serious reasons to remove wildlife immediately. They can carry diseases such as rabies, plague, Hantavirus, or fleas, mites and ticks, all of which can afflict humans. Contact your local wildlife representative, the Department of Fish and Game, a local pest control company or research in books and on web sites for advice about rodent and insect removal. We have listed a few in the Resource List section.

Bugs

Whether it's a bad mosquito year or black fly season, you know you're going to be bugged in the outdoors. Even though bugs will be around, there are ways to lessen their annoyance and bite. Bats, which we discuss later, are one way to get rid of many insects. They can eat up to 7,000 mosquitoes per day! How's that for nature's bug zapper?

Standing water, or other moist areas are perfect breeding grounds for mosquitoes. Eliminate pools of water in old tires, kid's buckets, or birdbaths. Create screened in areas. Be sure to get the smallest mesh netting possible or you will have wasted your time and money.

Dress properly. When outside wear long pants, high socks, and long sleeve shirts. Light colored clothing helps repel bugs. Bug clothing is also available from www.bugshirt.com and outdoor stores and outdoor catalogs such as L.L. Bean and Campmor.

Citronella candles, electric zappers and other products are effective and available at hardware stores. If all else fails, hang out with someone bugs love. My aunt is infamous for getting bit. I just sit next to her and bugs leave me alone. (Mean and selfish? Yes, but effective.)

Know your bug season and then be prepared with clothing, screening and repellent. Learn to live with harmless, innocuous natural predators of insects.

Wear shoes, even if they are just flip-flops to protect from fire ants, wasps, bees and hornets that hang out in the grass or live in the ground.

Use bug repellent as a last resort. Read the directions of the repellents to know which one works best for specific insects. The ingredient in many repellents is DEET, which may be harmful in high concentrations. Other products that individuals have found helpful include Avon's Skin So Soft, citronella-based lotions, eucalyptus-based lotions, and combination sunscreen and repellent. Some repellents even come in a towelette form. There are a variety of natural repellents available today. Check for them at your health food store or in catalogs such as Harmony; see Resource List.

When you are applying a repellent of any type to your face, or your child's face, be cautious of eyes, nose and mouth areas. If you are using a spray, spray directly into your hands and then carefully apply to the face.

Mice

First of all, let us tell you what mice love: an empty cabin, uncovered trash, improperly stored food, dog food, unclean plates, toilet paper, and anything else that they may think is edible or good nest material. (Mice loved our cabin in the woods. Sleeping was peaceful, until in the middle of the night, you heard the rustling in the dresser next to your head.) Not to scare you but…a mice invasion can get out of control if not dealt with swiftly. Since young mice can go through a hole that is only 1/4 of an inch wide, they can quickly invade the entire cabin.

Removal and Prevention of Mice

Hardware stores sell a variety of traps, poisons and repellents. You can use a catch and release trap or a snap trap, depending on your values and time. If you are not around and you use the catch and release, it would be cruel to let the mice starve to death. If you do use the catch and release, be sure to release them miles away, not at your neighbor's house. Use plenty of traps and replace them often. Peanut butter works as well as cheese for bait. Be cautious when using poisons, especially if you or the neighbors have pets or toddlers. Follow the directions on the label carefully and poisons should not be used at all if there is a chance child or pets could come into contact with it. One cottage owner claims fabric softener sheets spread out throughout the cottage keep mice away.

Cleaning up after Mice

Cleaning up after mice is no fun-but crucial. It is very important that you use gloves and a facemask, especially in a dusty area. Mice and their droppings can carry Hantavirus or other diseases. Dispose of dead mice immediately where no other animal can get at the trash. Wash all the contents of drawers that show any signs of mice.

Blocking their Entry

Check for entry points into your home near plumbing fixtures, crawl spaces, openings around doors, windows, foundations, vents and cabinets. Cram course grade steel wool in the cracks to temporarily keep mice out. Mice like moving into the stove, so be sure to

clean that out before you use it for the first time (mouse poop is not the best incense). One cottage owner unplugs the stove and wraps moth balls into plastic bags and wraps the plastic bags around the bottom of the stove. If you aren't a fan of moth balls, wrap the bottom edge of the stove in steel wool.

Bears

It's wonderful to tell your friends you saw a bear while on vacation, but preferably not one in your vacation dwelling. Bears can cause havoc in your cottage, especially in the spring, when they are hungry after a long winter. Heavy-duty shutters and doors on your cottage will deter bears and vandals. Bears are voyagers who follow their nose and remember where a previous meal was found. Outdoor garbage cans and improperly sealed garbage lures them in too close for comfort. Use metal garbage cans with securable lids and remove any indoor food that may attract them. Don't leave picnic scraps or even a compost pile unkempt.

Due to a dwindling habitat, bears have become more aggressive when looking for food, so you need to be more and more diligent about putting things away, disposing of garbage, dog food and sealing the doors and windows. If a bear comes in close, you should contact your local wildlife authority to discuss how to handle the problem. Unlike a mouse, you can't put out a trap. Let the experts handle bears!

Raccoons

In a cabin near my parent's cottage, a raccoon family moved in over the winter. To hear the tale of carnage that the owners came back too was so gruesome we could have used it in the campfire ghost story section. Cornered raccoons are ferocious. Live traps are available, but check with your local wildlife agency for their trapping requirements, because many locations require a permit to trap raccoons and other wildlife. Usually it is best to leave raccoons to the experts. Request that whoever removes the raccoons release them at least 15 miles away—they have a keen homing instinct.

Secure your home from further raccoon invasion by blocking their entry points at night, after they have gone out to feed. Capping chimneys and extending heavy-duty screening into the ground is a good way to block entry points.

Cockroaches and Ants

Like most pests, ants are attracted by food. Keep you food in secure containers and keep your floors, counters and other cluttered locations clean of debris. You can also prevent carpenter ants by repairing any wood

---

Checklist for Keeping Wildlife at Bay

- ☐ Install motion detector light
- ☐ Chimney covered with mesh wire
- ☐ All holes discovered and filled with steel wool or suitable product
- ☐ All food is stored properly
- ☐ All cardboard is removed
- ☐ Recycle bins are clean and stored properly
- ☐ Firewood or other debris removed from side of cottage
- ☐ Damp areas ventilated and screened
- ☐ Pet food is stored in containers with secure lids
- ☐ Trash is staked to ground to prevent tipping
- ☐ Trash has secure lids
- ☐ Keep pets indoor at night
- ☐ Cover hot tubs and pools
- ☐ Soap and other detergents are stored properly
- ☐ Traps are left out (if necessary)
- ☐ Clean up fallen fruit from trees and other debris
- ☐ Cover vents with fine mesh screens

---

damage to your house, ventilating damp areas, and storing wood away from the house on a raised platform. Similarly, cockroaches are attracted by food, dampness and darkness.

A variety of traps, powders and sprays are available. Again, be cautious of children and pets, and read the labels carefully. You may also try some natural remedies such as red pepper, talcum powder, coffee grounds, eggshells and bone meal. Cover open vents with a fine metal mesh screen, get rid of all dirty, greasy rags and other food and water accumulation.

Skunks

Did you know that skunks don't see very well? They don't need to, they have an incredible line of self-defense. You can avoid most confrontations if you move slowly near them and avoid startling them. Unfortunately, most of our pets get sprayed because they rush right at them, making for a sad dog and put-off owner. Also, skunks are not afraid of humans and have no problem with our home's noises and movements, they could stay quite comfy co-inhabiting in a small crawl space.

The spring is when cottage owners usually notice a skunk is underfoot (quite literally). Skunks are looking for love and the male skunk is marking his territory with his distinctive cologne. To remove a skunk call the local wildlife organization and they will talk you through the removal process. Our advice—let the professionals do it.

If you or your pet does get sprayed you can try an old trapper's recipe as a smell neutralizer: 1 quart hydrogen peroxide, 1/4 cup baking soda and 1 teaspoon dish detergent. Be careful when using this mixture to avoid ingesting or eye contact. Read the labels for other precautions.

Tidbit: One cottage owner informed us that skunks dislike moth balls, so she places them under the camp before they leave for the season.

Like most other animals, skunks have a benefit. They can keep your home free of rats, mice, beetles and grubs. But you would have to live with the consequences of having a whole family of skunks living under your home.

Bats

Most of us have seen too many Dracula movies to appreciate bats, but actually they are a key part of a healthy environment. I have two friends who are bat gurus and they have given me a whole new respect for these amazing little creatures. One of the books they suggest for every family is *America's Neighborhood Bats* by Merlin D. Tuttle. This easy to read book is perfect for understanding bats and learning how to live with them. Bats are essential for the balance of nature and they even have economic benefit. Without bats, the bug world could take over! The Bat Conservation International, has a wonderful palm sized pamphlet about bats. Call 512-327-9721 or go online to www.batcon.org.

Did you know a single little brown bat can catch up to 1,000 bugs an hour? For those

them, they will die inside and cause an unpleasant odor.

Second, find out where the bats are coming out of the building by going outside and watching them exit at dusk several nights in a row. Then put up a bat house near the exit location. If there is more than one exit put up the house closest to the most active exit.

Then in late July install plastic netting (1/6" bird mesh from a hardware store) fastened at the top and sides but not the bottom on all exit points. Any hole that is 3/8" or larger must have netting installed. This type of netting will allow the bats to get out but not come back in. Hopefully the bats will use your bat house immediately, but in some cases, it takes up to a year before bats feel comfortable entering.

The day after the netting has been put in place, watch for existing bats again at dusk. If the bats are still emerging check again the next evening and if they are still coming out, you may have missed another entry/exit. Repeat the process until you have found all the exits.

When you are sure all the bats have been excluded you can then permanently seal up all the holes. You can use caulking, foam insulation, flashing, screening, steel wool or other similar materials.

To purchase a bat box you can go online to www.chiropteracabins.com or call 802-951-2501, or go to your local garden or hardware store. The book, *Bat House Builder's Handbook*, by Merlin D. Tuttle and Donna L. Hensley, shows how to build one.

of us who live in area's filled with mosquitoes, that is quite appealing. Besides making us more comfortable, bats help control bugs that cause nearly a billion dollars of damage in our country's croplands. Bats are indicators of a healthy environment; when they are not around, you should begin to worry. But, that does not mean you want them living upstairs in the attic. (As with any mammal, they can carry diseases and/or rabies, so get them out of the camp and into a bat house.)

Getting Bats Out of a Building

Now that you love bats, how can you get them out of your attic and into a bat house? First, do not try to relocate bats until late July, after the pups can fly on their own. If their mother cannot get inside and feed

Repellents, ultrasonic and chemical repellents are usually ineffective in removing bats permanently from buildings and may even cause harm to humans in large doses. Learn more about these alternatives before you use them and follow their directions carefully if you do.

Please teach your children and neighbors more about bat's beneficial value to our society. More than half of the North American bat species are endangered or in a rapid decline.

General Prevention

Being at your place in itself is a deterrent for many wildlife creatures. If you cannot be there regularly then try the preventative measures we suggested. Most creatures like food, dampness, and darkness, so keep your place clean and free of debris that attracts their attention. Store things in the freezer, remove all cardboard boxes and plastic bags, and replace food into storage containers that are not easy to get into, such as glass containers with tight lids. Patch all holes after you are certain wildlife is not in the house and double check for new entry holes regularly.

We truly did not mean to give you the e-bee-gee-bees with this chapter. Our intent is that you learned more about wildlife and that you respect the beneficial role they play in nature. However, before you go to bed tonight in your cabin, be sure to pull back the covers and peek inside!

"Keeping our lakehouse in the family is very important to us. We believe it shows our love and dedication to our children long after we are gone. That is why we are planning ahead to be sure family members understand our intentions and know what is expected of them and how they should handle the upkeep, both structurally and financially. We want our lakehouse to be a joy to our children and their children, not a burden."

—Sean, Lake Tahoe, California

chapter thirteen

Keeping It in the Family

The concept of a family cottage has been around since prehistoric times. The cave family shared the cave then passed it on to the next generation, without any major documents, attorneys or accountants. But those days are over and to be sure that your family continues to have the same happy memories you are creating today, you need to plan ahead. Nobody likes to think about life moving on without them, but unfortunately it will and if you want your children to claim ownership of the cottage smoothly, you need to think about these few things.

Ask Yourself These Questions

Do you have a plan in place to keep the cottage in the family?

Have you thought about spouses and if they will play a role?

Have you planned for a bump in the road, such as a divorce, lawsuit, or medical condition in your children's future?

Can your children afford the maintenance, taxes and upkeep of the cottage?

Have you set money aside for the maintenance, taxes and upkeep?

Do you know if all your children want to be a part of the cottage?

What situations would put the cottage in probate court?

What are your state's regulations in regards to passing on property?

Have you considered if a child wants to sell their part or financially cannot afford the cottage?

Do you know all the options available to you in regards to passing on your cottage?

Planning

We like to think that our children will get along splendidly with regards to the cottage. Planning ahead for unexpected events will ensure they do get along (or at least improves the chances) regarding the ownership and management of the property. How do you do that? First, you will need to sit down with your children and have a comprehensive discussion to properly assess and plan for these contingencies. Even if you love your daughter-in-law or son-in-law, many families prefer to keep the cottage solely in their children's names.

My father and mother have spoken of their preference to pass their lakehouse on to their children and not to the spouses of their children. For them, as well as many other

parents, it is always difficult to discuss the "what-ifs" because they do not like to consider that their children will disagree or argue with one another over the true "intentions" of the parent once the time comes to pass along the beloved property. Sometimes problems arise entirely outside of the family, such as when a sibling who has an interest in the property is sued and his or her assets are attached (made part of the lawsuit). Such a situation could eventually affect the other sibling's interest in the property if a court were to force the sale of the property to pay for any judgment and/or claim of the suing party. There are legal ways of avoiding this type of situation. An example is if the cottage is placed in a properly formed Trust or made part of a Limited Liability Partnership or Corporation, then there may be the ability to protect the property from being attached or subject to the interest of outside parties. To avoid such situations, you need to put together a detailed plan for the future of your cottage. It is advisable to speak with a lawyer in the state where the property is located to discuss both the legal implications and practicality of transferring the property into these types of entities.

When the cabin is passed on to third and fourth generations, it can become convoluted and difficult to manage, not to mention, how to share time. Be sure to think far ahead when you are laying out the plans of sharing a cottage. Meet with your lawyer and determine the best way to have the cottage transferred to your children or other family members. Keeping it organized and running properly takes a little bit of up-front effort and a lot of cooperation. Every family situation is different. You may share with aunts, uncles, cousins, or it might be just two siblings, so know your options and choose wisely for your family's specific situation.

Some Common Means of Transferring Interest in Property

As I mentioned before, every family situation is different and will require careful planning. Some of the ways a family or individual transfers property are as follows:

Do nothing... This is always an option. Most likely your assets will be dealt with in a probate court, with or without a will. The likelihood your children will have to deal with probate, financial issues, estate taxes and transfer problems is almost guaranteed.

Joint Tenancy... Some families transfer the property to their intended beneficiaries ahead of time. This is often accomplished by setting up a "joint-tenancy" with your spouse, children or both. A joint-tenancy permits the surviving "joint-tenant" to automatically acquire the property without the need of going through probate, meaning if one of the joint tenant's passes away, the others receive their interest. However, as this type of ownership has its own bag of pros and cons, it is advisable to ask your lawyer if this works for you. One point to consider with a joint tenancy occurs if one or more of the joint tenants are minor children. If they are, and for whatever reason you choose to sell or refinance the property while the children are still minors, then you may be required to have a court appoint a guardian for the children to approve of the sale or refinance as the children will be deemed to not have the capacity to make that decision for themselves.

Limited Liability Partnership or Corporation (LLP or LLC)... A popular way of holding property that is quickly making its way across the country is the Limited Liability Partnership (or Corporation). One of the benefits of placing property into a properly formed LLP or LLC is that the owner or owners can be shielded from lawsuits brought against the property or lawsuits that may indirectly affect the individual's interest in the property. Some of the things to discuss with your lawyer if you were to choose this type of holding entity is the cost of forming and transferring the property to the LLP or LLC and any tax advantages or disadvantages.

Life Estate... There are times when an individual or individuals choose to pass the actual ownership of the property to the intended beneficiary or beneficiaries while still living, but retain the right to live in the property, presumably until they pass away. The Life Estate is not all that common and has its quirks that warrant a thorough discussion with your lawyer.

Revocable Trust (also known as the Living Trust)... This is one of the most popular means of holding property with respect to Estate Planning. As with all the other holding entities, it too has its pros and cons. Yet, many people lean toward setting up a Revocable Trust as it provides a means to transfer property to beneficiaries without having to go through probate. It also permits the individual who is the transferring the property to change beneficiaries at any time prior to death and to keep those beneficiaries private *(some states may vary with respect to privacy of beneficiaries)*. Also, a Revocable Trust allows the current owner to specifically set out his or her intentions as to how the property is to be managed after they pass away and provisions for future generations.

These are examples of a few of the

options available to camp, cottage and cabin owners. Every state has its own laws and each method should be carefully considered after a discussion with your lawyer and your accountant.

Cottage Rules and Work Duties

It may sound a little dictorial to have rules and work duties at a camp, but once you define them and everyone is aware of them, then it is all fun and games. Sharing a cottage usually means having specific rules, such as not flushing anything except one-ply toilet paper in the toilet. Rules are beneficial to everyone. Work duties can also be little difficult to accept because that's what you came to the cabin to escape. But if no one mops the

floor or fixes the steps, the cabin's condition will deteriorate and it will not be around long for enjoyment. Sharing these duties, in a fair and business-like fashion, will keep family bickering to a minimum (we hope).

We recommend that you have your cottage manuals, financial information and upkeep records in one place. Then once a year, you sit down with your board of directors (i.e. everyone who has an investing share in the cottage) and discuss the maintenance, taxes, mortgage payments, other fees, opening, closing, cleaning, renting, and time sharing. If there is a trust, much of this might already been spelled out. If there isn't already an appointed trustee, choose one person to be the secretary and one person to lead the

sit down with everyone involved and figure out who gets what time to be there. Some will only want the place for a week, while others would be there every weekend if it was permitted. If you are renting the cottage part time, that also adds another element of difficulty. Who will manage the time schedule and be sure the place is being cared for properly? Who will get the Fourth of July this year? Who will get Labor Day weekend? Can someone have it for two weeks in a row? All these questions will come up, which means you will need to plan with all the interested parties and figure out how to make it work for everyone. The number of families sharing the cottage, when they want to visit, and the number of weeks it is available, will all become factors in your time sharing planning.

Keeping Records and How-To Lists

Throughout this book, we have worked hard to make you think of everything that you should consider for your cottage. An excellent way to be sure everything is shipshape at your place is to keep good records, how-to lists and all the manuals that belong with products or appliances at the cottage.

We bought an old wooden boat (yes, a true fixer upper) and the saving grace was the impeccable record keeping of the past owner. Every manual, license, permit, labor and maintenance receipt, map and every tidbit about that boat was recorded. We know who to contact about past repairs, how to order new parts and when the last time the boat

group. If you're not sure who should do it, sometimes picking a name from a hat is the best solution.

Time Sharing the Cottage

Many families are so large that they all can't be at the cottage at the same time. If this is the case, then each family should pick weeks and weekends that they can enjoy the cottage alone. Rules and work duties are especially handy in multi-family situations.

Picking Days

If this is not already spelled out in the will, trust or corporation, then you will have to

was registered. (Of course, how to get it to float is something we have to figure out on our own. I will add that piece of information to the manual when it happens.) Purchase three ring binders with sheet protectors for your record keeping and how-to manuals. This will save you time and money in the long run.

Cottage How-to Manual

This manual is for your guests, renters or other family members who share the cottage. Copy this book's Worksheets and create categories in your notebook. This is an instruction manual for the use of your cottage.

Cottage Product Manual

Label a binder "Product Manual." It should contain all your owners' manuals, product guarantees and instruction booklets. You may want to divide the manual into sections such as kitchen appliances, stereo systems, furnaces, plumbing and other miscellaneous products.

Boat Manual

This manual should contain all your information regarding the boat: contact information for repair work, take out and put in person, wrapping and storing information and other manuals and receipts. Place a "how to operate the boat" list in the front. If you have more than one boat than section the book for each boat.

Area Resources

When you stay overnight at a hotel, there usually is a booklet that tells you where to eat, what to do, what is happening, where to shop and such. You should create your own area resource manual. You can section it by restaurants, sporting activities, shopping, kid activities, calendar of events and other sections relevant to your area. Put all your brochures, menus, phone numbers and contacts in this manual. This is a great way for guests to discover new and exciting things to do. Do you have too many brochures for the surrounding area to fit in a binder? Fine, do what my Mom does; have a basket filled with maps, brochures and local information, which guests can easily thumb through.

Cottage Financials

If you are sharing your cottage it is especially important that everyone knows what it costs to run the place. Maintenance, water bills, electricity, taxes and other information can be readily available. You will also want to keep an inventory list in this manual and the values of the items. You may want to make a copy of this binder every year for safe keeping at home.

You might want to keep your cottage financial binder in a private location, or only put information in that you are OK with others reading. At the end of the season, be sure to bring your manuals home with you for storage.

"Part of our storytelling includes the stories of our siblings cutting their lip on the water tube, water skiing and falling not quite right, the poison ivy next door. These stories are a part of the every day happenings at the camp."
—Chris
Lake Michigan

chapter fourteen
Safety In and Around Your Place

Cabins come with a variety of unique safety issues besides the regular everyday knee scrape. It might be a strong undercurrent in the ocean, a cliff on the property, a barbed wire fence, a swift river in the spring time, or a variety of water crafts cruising close by. Consider having a Safety Issues section in your binder. If your guests are forewarned, appropriate safety precautions can be taken.

Emergency Contacts, Numbers and Facilities

In the back of this book are worksheets to write down important information such as emergency contacts. Please take a moment to write down all the local emergency information and then make a copy and tape it next to the phone. Be sure to drive to your local hospital, emergency center, rescue center, veterinarians and fire department to scope out the fastest and safest route. It may sound a little overly cautious, but from personal experience, it is important to know where your medical personnel are and how to get to them. If you have a family member who has special needs and you live in a small community, you should introduce yourself to the local volunteer rescue team or fire department and let them know where you live and what your situation is.

Basic First Aid Kit

You can purchase a first aid kit at most pharmacies, hardware and home goods stores. For a better stocked and less expensive first aid kit, you can create your own. Tool kits with double flap openings make good kits. They

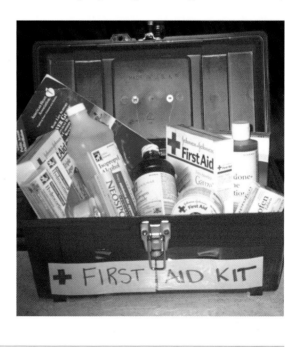

What Should be in your First Aid Kit?

☐ A first aid book, such as, *The American Red Cross First Aid and Safety Handbook*
☐ A copy of your emergency numbers and contacts

Dressings

☐ Adhesive bandage strips
☐ Butterfly bandages
☐ Elastic bandage
☐ Adhesive tape
☐ Roller bandages
☐ Cotton balls
☐ Eye patches
☐ Gauze pads
☐ Nonstick pads
☐ Triangular bandage

Instruments

☐ Blunt-tipped scissors
☐ Tweezers
☐ Bulb syringe

Equipment

☐ Cotton swabs
☐ Small plastic cup
☐ Instant-acting chemical cold packs
☐ Paper cups
☐ Space blanket
☐ Thermometer

Medication

☐ Activated charcoal
☐ Antiseptic wipes or solution
☐ Antiseptic/anesthetic ointment or spray
☐ Calamine/antihistamine location
☐ Syrup of ipecac

Other Items

☐ Candle and matches
☐ Flashlight and batteries
☐ Pen and paper
☐ Small bar of soap
☐ Disposable latex gloves
☐ Safety pins
☐ Tissues
☐ Change for phone

are easy to bring with you in the boat or car and you can have a child safety latch put on it. Do not lock your first aid kit! You, or someone else might need to get in it quickly and in a moment of anxiety and you might forget the combination or key. Every camp should have an extensive first aid kit and everyone should know where the kit is and how to use it.

Some Medicines to Have on Hand

Many of these medicines *should not* be used without professional medical advice:

activated charcoal, syrup of ipecac, antiseptic wipes or solution, antibiotic ointment, antiseptic/anesthetic spray, calamine/antihistamine lotion, antihistamines, hydrocortisone cream, bacitracin ointment, ibuprofen, children's antihistamine and children's ibuprofen.

Sunscreens and Insect Repellents

Why is sunscreen and insect repellent in the safety section? Because sun burns and insect bites can be serious if not treated properly. It is important that you protect yourself from the sun, both in summer and winter. Be sure to have plenty of hats at your cabin and a variety of sunscreens for adults, kids and babies. You should have a minimum of SPF 15 on at all times and a higher SPF on your children. You should purchase new sunscreen each season and don't leave them in extreme temperatures. Select types that will work best for your situation and if you have sensitive skin, check with the pharmacist or call your dermatologist to find out which product would be best for you.

A bad sunburn or sun poisoning is not fun and can be very painful, not to mention increasing your skin cancer risk. From experience, I know a bad sunburn can make you look like an alien from a old Star Trek sci-fi. Today's dark tan can become tomorrow's wrinkles and leathered skin. That is enough to make me wear sunscreen and a hat.

Bites and Stings

Check out the Pets, Pests and Other Critters chapter for preventative measures regarding bugs, bites and stings. If you do get bitten or stung, determine if it is a poisonous insect (check your Red Cross First Aid & Safety Book) and then react accordingly. If the bite is from something that could cause a serious reaction, immediately refer to the First Aid book. If it is from insects such as mosquitoes, house flies, gnats or fleas then wash the bite with soap and water and, if necessary, apply antiseptic or anesthetic ointment or a cold compress.

Lyme Disease and Ticks

We wrote about Lyme disease and Ticks in the Pets, Pests and Other Critters chapter, and the reason we mention it again is because it is a growing, serious problem. If you haven't read that section yet, please do so now. In the case of Lyme disease an ounce of prevention is worth a ton of cure.

If you are hiking in tall grass or areas with a lot of brush, it is best that you wear long pants and pull your socks up high to help prevent ticks from attaching themselves to you. Ticks may jump from your pet to you, so be sure you both are tick free before playing!

Removal of a Tick

According to the *Red Cross First Aid Handbook*, you should never forcefully pull off a tick that is attached to the skin because you may only get the body and not the head. Instead, they suggest you try to suffocate the tick by covering it with petroleum jelly, or another type of heavy oil, such as mineral oil. The tick may release immediately or take up to an hour. If the tick does not release through this method, then carefully pull it off with tweezers and try and get as close as possible to the mouth-part of the tick. Make sure it is completely removed. If you have concerns that you did not remove the tick completely or it has been there a long time, then you should call your doctor to see if you need a blood test.

Your Surroundings

Knowing where your spare keys, fuse box, circuit breakers, and emergency kits are located is important. But just as important, is knowing your surroundings and the danger areas near your cottage. Make sure everyone is aware of these areas and the dangers. An old well, a cliff, barbed wire, tides, rocks and sharp objects under the water, shallow water areas, poisonous plants, animal holes or caves, and other items should all be discussed and avoided.

Your Cottage's Safety Equipment

Things you *must* have on hand in your cottage are your first aid kit, smoke detectors, fire extinguishers, batteries, flashlights, candles, wool blankets, spare jackets, extra water and matches. (You may think of a few things that are unique to your location you should add to these lists.)

Courteous and Cautious

It is easy to add that extra touch during a guests visit to add comfort and give you peace of mind for their safety. Below are a few examples of what a variety of cottage owners do for their guests.

Rocky Beaches

A basket of water shoes by the door goes a long way in keeping your guests' tender feet safe from beach rocks and sharp shells. These inexpensive shoes are also great for wearing in the water when a mucky bottom might otherwise discourage your guests from entering. Have sizes that range from kids to adults so you are sure to accommodate all your guests. Write the camp's name on the shoes and rinse them with soap and water after every use.

Too Much Sun

No matter where you are, the strength of the sun can always catch you and your guests by surprise. Besides proper sunscreen and a hat, have a bag of men's long sleeve dress shirts close by (shirts that can no longer be worn to the office are perfect for the job). Large long-sleeve, white-cotton shirts are great cover-ups for any boating outing or for sitting on the beach. Keep a few in the boat at all times for you or your guests comfort. If you see your guest turning a shade of red that you considered painting your dining room in, by all means, hand them a shirt to put on. They will thank you!

Coming in from the Cold

Whether it is a fall hike or a winter snow-shoe excursion, it is likely that your guests' shoes and socks will be soaked. And many times they forget to bring extra shoes. So if you experience this situation at your cabin often, instead of having them be uncomfortable and chilled, have a basket of white cotton socks and slippers near by. Nothing spells cozy more than socks and slippers. White cotton socks are easy to wash and inexpensive to replace if your guest chooses to wear them home.

"My friend took a bunch of pictures of my cottage when I was not around and had color postcards made of the photos. She gave me fifty postcards and I mail them when we are at the cottage to say hello to folks back home. It was such as thoughtful gift!"

—Jackie, Nantucket Island

chapter fifteen
Bearing Gifts

Wondering what to get someone who owns a seasonal home? The ideas are endless. Whether it is a house-warming gift for a first time buyer, a visitor's thank you gift or a holiday present, shopping for a cottage owner can be fun. We talked to cabin owners and asked them what they would like to receive from their friends and relatives for their special place. We also added a few of our own ideas.

Camps, Cottages and Cabins
Of course this book is going to be our first gift idea! You can easily order another copy of this book by the order form in the back or by calling 1-800-860-5813 or going online to www.loveyourcottage.com. For only $21.95, *Camps, Cottages and Cabins* makes a great thank you gift for a weekend visit or as a holiday gift for your favorite cottage owner!

Magazines
We will be the first to admit there are other great books and magazines out their for the camp owner. There is the magazine called *Cabin Life*, which I believe every camp owner would enjoy. Just contact *Cabin Life* at 1-888-

287-3129 or cabinlifemag.com, for more information. *Cottage Life* is also a wonderful magazine published in Canada and well suited for any cottage. Everyone enjoys flipping through magazines like *Coastal Living, Country Living, Country Home, Better Homes and*

Gardens and *Martha Stewart Living*. What better way to enjoy a quiet moment than lounging in the Adirondack chair with a big glass of lemonade indulging in a wonderful magazine?

Books

As you can see in our Resource List, we think there are a lot of great books regarding camps. You can easily go online and look at almost all of these books on Amazon.com or another bookstore site. You can also go into your local bookstore and have them special order one or more for you. Many of these books are hardcover, coffee table type books, which make great gifts.

Adirondack Chairs

For years, the four of us kids have been pitching in together and purchasing two chairs for our parents every Christmas. They love it! (They are competing with the guy across the lake.) It is wonderful to drive up to our parents' lakehouse and see everyone sitting outside in the white Adirondack chairs.

Camp Sweatshirts, T-shirts and Hats

One cottage owner has sweatshirts made with their cottage name on them in a variety of sizes. When visitors come, they don't plan for the cool evenings so everybody gets to wear a cottage sweatshirt. You can go to most malls and have sweatshirts, t-shirts and hats embroidered with a cottage name. The cottage owner will be delighted at your thoughtfulness and will always have something for a visitor who forgot their hat, t-shirt or sweatshirt.

Unique Gift Baskets

We asked owners what kind of gift basket they would like to receive and some of them came up with some pretty interesting ideas. You will enjoy making up a unique basket.

Margaritas Basket

Maybe your friends throw a lot of parties. Consider a Margarita Basket. The basket could include an ice bucket, a blender, tequila, limes, orange liqueur, salt, plastic Margarita glasses and a bartender's mixed drinks book.

Breakfast Basket

For those who think breakfast is more important than a Margarita, a breakfast basket filled with maple syrups, gourmet pancake-mixes, jellies and jams will be the hit of the cabin. There are a variety of gift basket companies that can send one of these out for you, just get on the Internet a do a search for gift baskets.

Paperback Book Basket

Are you a person who goes to a friend's cottage, starts reading a book, and then asks to take it with you? That's o.k.— I do it all the time! Here is a great way to make it up to them; put a bunch of bestsellers, a mug filled with tea bags and a box of cookies into a unique gift basket. What's better than a rainy day at camp with a good book, tea and cookies?

First-Time Buyer Basket

When someone buys a cottage, the last thing they may think about are the essentials. Help them out by creating a unique basket filled with a flashlight, batteries, sunscreen, insect repellent, a disposable camera, a journal and a floating key chain. You can think of other items that are unique to that specific area, such as a hiking map, a tides chart or a gift certificate for a local restaurant.

Catalog Shopping

Specialty Catalogs such as *Waterfront Living, West Marine, Overton's, Campmor, L.L. Bean's Outdoor Living* and *L.L. Bean Hunting and Fishing* catalogs have hundreds of items that are perfect for camp owners. You can get personalized signs, rugs or bags. They carry standard items such as barbeque pits, beach towels and much more!

Camps and Cottage Stores

Want to go shopping? Stores such as *Camps and Cottages* in Berkeley, California, and *Maine Cottage Furniture* in Yarmouth, Maine carry a variety of furniture and unique items specific to cabins. See our Resource List chapter for more stores locations.

Homemade Gifts

In the Family Fun chapter we mentioned a few crafts that are fun to do with kids and make wonderful gifts. Look at those ideas again and think how you could package them. Think of something you could make that a cottage owner would love...soap, candles, or even postcards could be used on a daily basis at the cottage.

"My late husband was a plumber and there was never any doubt that the cabin would be properly shut down for the season. I still like knowing the cabin will winter well so I hire a professional to perform the duties that I don't understand and don't want to do."

—Bea, McCall, Idaho

chapter sixteen

Closing Time

When the leaves are falling off the trees at summer cottages, or the snow has finally melted around the winter cabin, preparing to leave can be bittersweet. Another wonderful season of memories will be ready to go home with you once you have properly prepared your place for departure.

A little work up front can save you a lot of work and headaches when you come back to open up your cottage next season. Before the car pulls away for the season, many things will need to be packed, cleaned, stored, tied down, brought in and boarded up.

A week before you begin to close, look in your kitchen cupboards and refrigerator and start making meals with what you have. You will come up with some interesting combinations in the process of cleaning out your kitchen. Many cottage communities bring all their food together and have a smorgasbord with their neighbors. It is a nice way to have a party and say goodbye to all your friends.

Why Close Down?

A variety of reasons justify spending the time to close your camp properly. Burst pipes, vandalism, rodents and structural damage are the main concerns of most cottage owners. Prepare for these possibilities and you will minimize the likelihood.

Freezing Temperatures

If your cottage will be battered with very cold temperatures during the closed season, you need to think of a few things besides your water pipes. If the temperature regularly drops below the freezing point, you will have to pack up anything that is water-based and bring it home. Paint cans may explode, as well as wine bottles, soda cans, laundry detergent and much more. Read the back of the container for specific storing information. Be cautious about what you store next to each other; you don't want to have a chemical party while you are gone.

Your Kitchen Duties

As you clean the kitchen, consider what is going to stay and what goes. Food that is packed in tin, glass canisters with screw-on lids or aluminum-lined storage containers provide adequate barriers against unwanted rodents and can stay. Any type of cereal or grain, no matter what it is in, should not be left behind. Even if bugs don't get into it, it will turn stale.

Clean out all the cupboards and wash them down with a mild soap and water. If you are going to leave a cabinet full of food, line the cabinet in tin or aluminum for extra protection, then you can wash down the outside of the cans and canisters and place them back into the cupboard.

Clean out the refrigerator (and freezer) completely and wash it thoroughly. Unplug it and leave the door open, otherwise you will find a lot of mildew upon your return.

Be sure to wash down the counters and floors before you go. Selfish as this may sound, you don't want to leave even one crumb for any bug to get excited over!

In the Bedrooms

Rodents have to sleep too and what better place than your blankets and sheets. If you are going to leave your bedding behind, bundle it up and store it in heavy duty plastic containers, suitcases, a metal box or blanket chest. Add a few pieces of cedar to the container and place it on the top bunk. (Mothballs are an effective but less fragrant option.)

If you leave clothes behind, do the same thing to them. If you wash anything before you pack it, be sure it is completely dry. Even a slightly damp shirt or blanket can cause mildew damage.

Blocking off the Flues and Stove Pipes

In a lake house I rented years ago, birds frequently came down the woodstove chimney.

Both the birds and I were frantic in trying to get them out of the stove and the house. To keep birds and rodents from coming down or creating a home in your stove pipes or flues while you are gone seal them off with a metal cap. Your dampers should also be closed tightly. If you don't have a damper, plug your pipe with paper, BUT BE SURE to leave yourself and others a note on the fireplace or woodstove that the paper and metal cap must be removed before using.

Covering the Windows

If you cover all the windows with cardboard (on the inside) you not only will save your furniture from fading over the winter season, but you will discourage vandals from checking out what you have in your place. You can also use curtains, but cardboard totally blocks the view and adds a little thermal protection by blocking wind.

Many cottage owners I know place plywood on the outside of the house over all the doors and windows. This is a serious deterrent for anyone, man or beast. If you do use plywood, number each one to correspond with a particular location and place handles on the outside of the plywood for a better grip and to reduce your sliver count. Don't forget to use galvanized or brass screws.

Keep all the Doors and Drawers Open (Sometimes)

To help air circulation, keep all your cabinet doors open, closet doors ajar and bureau drawers pulled out. If you leave the heat on low this will help in areas that have water pipes in them (under the sinks). If there are rooms or areas on the house you can close off without frozen pipe concerns, then close them off and cover the doorway with a towel or blanket to block heat from going into those areas. It is better to have a musty room than an expensive heating bill.

Remove all Fire Hazards

Eliminate all trash, stored papers, matches, chemicals, old rags, plugged in appliances, lights left on and other fire hazards.

Remove your Valuables

Besides taking home the bottle of wine that might burst in the cold, be sure to bring home your valuables such as paintings, jewelry, antiques, your financial records, old books

and photo albums. It is nice to know those things are safe and sound with you at home.

Wrapping the Shrubs

If you are concerned about your shrubs freezing or deer enjoying their taste, then wrap them in burlap. It is an easy and inexpensive insurance policy.

Stacking the Lawn Furniture

Many cottage owners stack their lawn furniture and store them in a shed or chain them to the side of the house or tree. Adirondack chairs and other nice lawn furniture can easily be picked up and taken away during the winter months when no one is around.

Bringing in the Dock

Most people store their dock on the lawn or the edge of the water. (My uncle's advice is to keep a pair of waders at the cabin, because it's cold when you put it in and cold when you take it out.) Allow plenty of room for a spring flood, and if you can, lock it down. Be sure to mark the pieces with duck tape and black marker before you remove them or just after, so you won't have to spend time in the spring putting together what seems to be a dock puzzle (it is a chilling experience for those who are in the water without waders).

Cleaning Every Corner

Yes, once again I am asking you to clean every corner of the cabin. Of course, it is easier for me to say, and type, than to do, but trust me, it is important. You want to keep any pest problems to a minimum, and I am talking about rodents and human. If you have left your cottage clean and free of debris, and you come back to find newspapers or other items strewn

about, you know you have had a squatter. A few squatters are kind and will leave the house in decent order (maybe a beer or two short, if you left any). Even so, it is important you report it, if you suspect someone has been in your cottage.

Another way to deter unwanted visitors is to make the cottage look uninviting. Stack all your furniture in one room, take all the cushions off the couch and place everything in a pile that looks haphazard. If someone wants to stay, they have to set everything back up to make the cottage even somewhat inviting.

Keeping the Heat and Water On

My parents keep the heat and electricity on at their lakefront cottage because it is winterized, and we like to spend time there snow-shoeing and skiing. What my father does in addition to making a list of how we should open and close after we leave, is have a trigger switch on the heating system. If the temperature in the cottage goes below a certain point, it triggers a response at the electricity company and they call Dad. There are other ways to help you sleep at night knowing the heat is still on and the pipes are not broken and spewing water. My husband connected a thermostat to the phone at our cabin. He would call the cabin and if he got a busy signal, he knew the heat was too low. Similar devices will tell you if the water is running when no one is there.

Develop a plan for emergency situations. Leave a key with a year-round neighbor, the electric company, or hire a service that periodically checks, or go there yourself. Watch

Boat Closing Checklist

- [ ] Clean the boat, inside and out
- [ ] Remove all life jackets or other items that will mildew
- [ ] Take all boat paperwork home and be sure to bring it back in the spring
- [ ] Make sure the boat is stored above the high water mark
- [ ] Open drain hole and face drain hole down hill
- [ ] Be sure no debris can block the drain hole
- [ ] Turn canoes and kayaks upside down and lift them off the ground
- [ ] Block the wheels of boats on trailers
- [ ] Shrink wrap or tarp larger boats

the weather so you can catch the potential problem before the cottage gets too cold and the pipes freeze. There are a variety of programs and devices that you can use to ensure your cottage is at the right temperature. Contact your local electric or heating company or go online and search for companies such as www.freezealarm.com or www.intwoplaces.com.

Shutting off the Utilities

Electricity can be shut off either at the service entry or for individuals appliances, or sections of the house, at the breaker panel. If you have to keep some appliances running, then unplug all the other non-working appliances, including lamps, clocks, stoves, etc. This prevents animals from chewing on the wires and causing an electrical short. Gas appliances must be shut down to only pilot light operation. Follow all your appliance instruction manuals carefully. Most new appliances have safety shutoffs, but if they are old, they do not and should be shut off entirely. If propane gas escapes it will collect at floor level and could be ignited by turning on the pilot light of another appliance. It is very important that the propane gas is shut off completely, including the tanks.

Storing the Boat

Canoes and Kayaks

For canoes and kayaks this is pretty easy, store them in a locked facility or bring them home with you. If they are going to stay outside, set them upside down so they do not collect water. Bring all life jackets and paddles inside and make sure they are dry before stored.

Small Boats

Small boats, if left upright, should be covered, drain plug removed, and the drain hole aimed down hill and not blocked. Remove outboard motors, lubricate the lower unit (waterproof grease) and remove the spark plug and spray lubricating oil on the piston. Pull the starter a few times to allow the piston and shaft to receive the lubricating oil. If you have freezing weather, make sure all water is drained out of the motor.

Large Boats

For larger boats, many people are excited about the new shrink wrap process. Instead of

wrapping your boat in tarps that may cave in during heavy snowstorms or blow away in strong winds, you can shrink wrap your boat in a couple of hours (alright, maybe a little longer if it is your first time). If you don't want to do it yourself, you can have a professional boat service do it. Some will even come to your home if your boat is not going to be stored at a marina. It can cost as little as $8 a foot, which might be worth the money. Watch how they do it. You might feel confident enough after that to do it yourself. Instructional videos and internet instructions for shrink wrapping your boat are available.

If you decide to use tarps instead of shrink wrapping, make sure the tarps are heavily weighted down. (I have seen concrete blocks, jugs filled with water, and the like hanging from ropes tied to the tarps). This will help keep the animals out and the wind from blowing the tarps away. Create a wooden frame inside the boat, underneath the tarps, so they are not lying directly on the boat. This further protects your boat from damage. Make sure that the trailer is in a secure location and block the wheels.

Draining the Water

Closing down your water systems is one of the most important things you will need to do before locking the door for the season. This will also be one of the last things you do because you will need the water to clean the cottage. Most cabin closing procedures can be done by the owner, but if you feel that this is not your strong point, then it would be

Make sure your service contacts (a plow person, plumber, and a heating company) know how to contact you when you are not at the cabin.

Phone System

If a lot of people will be staying at your cabin, especially unknown renters, we recommend a phone with local service only. As an inexpensive courtesy, leave a prepaid 100-minute calling card near the phone. This way you don't have to worry about your phone service if you want to leave it on.

If you want to leave the phone service on, but still don't want anyone to make calls, even local ones, take the phone home with you. Then if someone does borrow your cottage, uninvited, there is no phone to use, even if the jack is still working. Just remember to bring it back when you visit. It is also easy to shut the phone down for a few months or at least take off the long distance service; just contact your phone company or your long distance service.

Security

If winter crime is a problem in your cabin community, consider organizing a neighborhood watch. Whether it is hiring a year round resident to make rounds, or periodic visits from each cabin owner over the season, together you can reduce the numbers break-ins over the season. Other measures to take include having good deadbolt locks, removing all tools, boat motors, liquor and pricey items. If you do leave the electricity on,

worth it to call in a professional. Consider hiring a plumber the first time and ask him or her to show you how to do it. This way you will feel comfortable enough to do it yourself next year. If other co-owners or guests will be shutting down the cabin, write step-by-step instructions for closing all systems, especially shutting down the water and utilities. The Water, Sewer and Heating chapter gives you points for closing.

Mail Forwarding

If you had your mail forwarded to you, fill out the forms to forward it back to your house.

consider a motion sensor light to deter away unwanted visitor, including the wildlife.

Saying Goodbye

Before you pull out of the driveway with your loaded down car take a moment to think about the wonderful season it has been. Think about all the new things that happened and the special moments that will be imbedded in your mind forever. Say goodbye to your cabin and let it know that you are already looking forward to next year. Closing up properly will make coming back much more pleasant.

"One of the best things about our cottage is the outdoor shower! Not only do we get to enjoy the views while scrubbing up, we also give the septic system a break from too much water!"
—Paul, Yarmouth, Maine

chapter seventeen

Water, Sewer and Heating

I know…when you think about your cottage, the last thing you want to talk about is can you drink the water? Should you flush the toilet? Or, is this the furnace's last hurrah?

That is why we didn't even bother putting this chapter in color—we figured you had a pretty good imagination without the "graphic" details. Thanks to my husband, Stephen, and a few camp owners, this chapter outlines the most common systems seen in camps and cottages. Changing or adding systems to your cottage is one of the most important choices you make. Understand your choices and choose the one that works best for your place and area.

Your Water Systems

Cabin water systems vary significantly in complexity from having a nearby stream to splash in, to having modern indoor toilets, sinks, and showers all served by pressurized and thermostatically controlled water systems. It is up to you to decide how rustic a system you want to live with (or can live with).

Water systems consist of a source for the water, a means to get it to the cabin and a distribution system within the structure. The source for the water varies greatly from location to location. Some examples include: lakes and streams (surface water), shallow wells and springs, deep wells, rain water systems, and municipal systems. We have compiled a list of the most common ones and some basic information to help you at your

Water Usages and Saver Chart

Shower: Average 5 minutes: 25-37 gallons
Wet down, soap up: 2 minutes: 10-15 gallons
Tub: Full: 20-35 gallons
Limited level: 7-10 gallons
Wash Hands: Running water: 2-3 gallons
Fill basin, rinse: 1 gallon
Brush Teeth: Running water: 10 gallons
Wet and rinse: 1gallon
Shave: Running water: 20 gallons
Fill basin: 1 gallon
Toilet Flush: 5-7 gallons
Washer: Full load: 60 gallons
Outdoor Watering: 10 gallons
Washing Car: 10 minutes: 100 gallons

camp. With all of the types of systems, installation of water saving fixtures will help reduce flows, which, in turn can reduce the cost and size requirements for pumps, piping, and septic systems.

Want to conserve water for the health of your system and to be a good citizen? No matter what system you have, water conservation is a good idea. For many cottages it is a necessity; whatever your reason, we found these water saving numbers interesting. Let your family know how they can help save water by posting the water usage and saver chart of approximate estimates of water usage.

Pumps

Unless you are fortunate enough to have a good source of water substantially higher than your cabin, or a municipal system, you will need to have a pump. Generally the pump will be located below or up to slightly above the surface level of the water, and pump uphill to the cabin. Pumps can be either submersible, or mounted above the water. Submersible pumps have the advantage that they do not require priming, and are naturally freeze-protected. Above surface pumps are often used to pump from springs, shallow wells, and surface water and usually are the less costly option. Once primed, surface pumps can draw up water by vacuum (usually limited to about 20' vertically, less at higher elevations), and then pressurize the water to push it to the elevation and pressure required for service.

Piping System

Water is transferred from the pump to the cabin in pipes or tubing. Historically the pipe was made of almost anything including wood, ceramics, iron, steel, galvanized steel, copper, and brass. These days pipes are usually soft copper or plastic. The least expensive and most reliable option that most people use is coils of polyethylene tubing. The tubing is very flexible and can be run almost anywhere, can be either shortened by cutting with a saw, or extended, divided, valved, or terminated with the use of inexpensive fittings and hose clamps. Copper is almost as easy to run, but requires special tubing cutters to divide, and soldering or expensive mechanical fittings to connect. To protect the pipe from physical damage and/or freezing it is usually buried below the frost depth.

Controlling Water Pressure

Once at the cabin, the water pressure is controlled to maintain a relatively uniform pressure to the plumbing fixtures. A gravity system controls pressure using gravity by placing the water system above the plumbing fixtures. One pound per square inch (psi) is equal to 2.4 feet of elevation. The minimum desirable pressure at a plumbing fixture is typically 8 psi which requires 8 x 2.4 ft/psi = about 20 feet of elevation of the water surface above the fixture outlet. Unfortunately, the flow is restricted by friction. For example, a 3/4" tube, running at 3 gallons/minute has a frictional pressure drop of about 1 psi for each

100 feet of pipe. Therefore gravity systems work best with steep sites, and/or oversized (low friction) pipes.

With pumped systems the pressure is controlled by a combination of a pressure tank and pressure switch. The pressure switch monitors the pressure in the system, and starts and stops the pump to maintain the pressure set-point. The pressure tank acts as a reservoir for the system so that the pump doesn't have to run every time water is used in the cabin. The pressure tank is as its name sounds: a tank, that is partially filled with water when the pump is running. The remainder of the tank is filled with a cushion of air, often with a rubber bladder separating the two. When the pump is running, the water pushes on the air and compresses it. When the air is compressed to the high pressure set-point on the pressure, switch the pump shuts off. A check valve is installed between the pump and the tank to prevent water from leaking back through the pump when the pump isn't running. When a faucet is opened in the cabin, the water is pushed out of the tank by the compressed air cushion and out the plumbing fixture. When the air decompresses to the pressure switch low set-point the pump is started and the process begins again.

Water Heating

If hot water is required it can be heated in pots on a fire or stove, or more commonly with the use of pressurized water heaters mounted inline in the water system. The water heaters can be heated with electricity, LP or natural gas, or #2-fuel oil. Typically natural gas or fuel oil fired water heaters are the least expensive to operate from an energy purchasing perspective. LP gas and natural gas fired heaters have the advantage that they can be configured to operate without electricity. However, electric water heaters may be the least expensive and simplest to operate if the heat in the cabin is to be used a limited

Checklist for Basic Maintenance

☐ Clean, replace, or service filters

☐ Oil pump if required

☐ Verify correct operation of pressure switch (a pressure gage installed by pressure tank aids in this check)

☐ Listen for correct pump operation

☐ High pitched whine and continued operation may indicate loss in prime or air in system

☐ Frequent cycling of pump could indicate dirty filter, air in system, or incorrect pressure switch adjustment

☐ Check for adequate draft of fuel fired water heaters (could indicate bird's nest, etc., are plugging chimney)

☐ Periodically test water quality and treat water as required to maintain a healthy source of good, clean water

number of hours/year. If a check valve exists between the cold water fill and the water heater, an expansion tank or compensator should be installed to prevent the system from over pressurizing when the water heats and expands.

Cleaning the Water Supply

With any type of water system it is important to know how clean the water is, and if it is to be consumed, whether it is potable. Nothing dampens the wilderness experience more then intestinal problems. It is always a good idea to test the water quality routinely by getting a test kit from your local Department of Health, or Environmental Water Quality testing agency. It is important to test for both biological and chemical contaminants. If there are biological problems they can be treated by cleaning the source; for example, by adding Chlorine bleach to a well, cistern, or spring, or adding sand filters. Chemical problems can be treated by adding sand or other types of filters or water softeners in-line in the water delivery system.

Opening for the Season

Each water system will have different requirements for annual opening and closing. The following is a list of typical items that may be in your system. If different people will be performing these functions from year to year or from visit to visit, it is a good idea to write down the individual system requirements and their locations.

The first step, if a system has been drained, is to close all the drain valves. Clean or install the intake to the pump. Clean or replace any filters. Prime the pump (often requires filling the discharge side of the pump with water). Turn on the power to the pump. At this point the pump should start, and the system will begin to fill. The system will be full of air which must be bled from the system by opening faucets and allowing the pump to run until the air stops sputtering out the outlets. Close the outlets, and observe the operation of the pressure system to determine if the pressure is being adequately maintained, and that the pump is starting and stopping correctly. Once the system is filled and operating correctly, turn on the power, (or light the pilot) to the water heater and observe if the system is heating correctly. Open the faucets and run the system for a while to clean out the pump and piping. Finally, take a hot shower; you'll probably need it at this point.

Closing for the Season

Closing for the season generally requires shutting the systems off and draining the components. The first step is usually to turn off the electricity or fuel to the water heater, and the power to the pump. If the water intake is from a surface source of water, often the intake system is removed from the water source. Next, the water must be drained from all the system components. If the system has low points that aren't drained it may be beneficial to install low point drains. If the drains are not practical, non-toxic anti-freeze is available to pour into these pockets. Also make sure you drain the water heater, the pump, and filters.

Your Sewer Systems

Sewer and septic systems serving cottages often vary significantly in quality and effectiveness from what is normally encountered in cities and residential neighborhoods throughout the country. Rustic sites often operate satisfactorily with simple outhouses. Many folks require indoor plumbing as a basic necessity in any living situation. For all systems it is essential that the system doesn't adversely effect the environment. This non-

exhaustive discussion will address the most common systems encountered and the basic elements of each. Check with local authorities to determine the types of systems allowed at your site, and the disposal requirements.

From the broadest perspective there are two types of systems. The first type includes systems in which all waste from sinks, washing machines, toilets, etc. is collected together and disposed in one system. These systems include: septic tanks and leach fields, cesspools, and holding tank systems. The other type of system requires the separating of wastes, typically liquid wastes from solid waste, and the individual disposal of each component. These systems include: outhouses, composting toilets, incinerating toilets, and chemical toilets for the disposal of human wastes. Liquid or grey water systems include dry wells, cesspools and surface disposal fields that are used to dispose of liquids not easily handled by the toilets.

Outhouses

Outhouses are the lowest tech, simplest, least costly, and one of the more environmentally friendly of your waste disposal options. They consist of small shacks (usually 5' x 5' x 7' tall) built on top of a hole dug in the ground (usually 3' x 4' x 4' deep). In the shack is a bench with one (or more) holes through which one places their excretions (poop, pee, etc.). The number of holes used depends on the expected traffic and the familiarity of the operators. The holes are often equipped with toilet seats which can

be lifted to aid in sanitation, and lids to contain smells when not in operation. More sophisticated installations include separate funnels to be used as urinals. It is usually a good idea to vent the waste pit with a 3-4" pipe up through the roof of the structure to carry sewer gases up and away from the building. The cabin of the structure is usually ventilated with a crescent moon shaped hole in the door (above eye level), screened to reduce bugs. It is often a good idea to hang fly strips to reduce the number of bugs that will still manage to get in.

The outhouse should be located 100' from and when possible down hill of your water source and down wind of your cabin, and as far from your neighbors as possible. When the pit becomes full, a new pit is dug and the outhouse moved to the new location. Fill in the old pit with soil. If the odors from the active pit become excessive, soil or chlorinated lime can be shoveled on top. If mice are present it is a good idea to place the toilet paper in covered containers, unless you're willing to use confetti to complete the paper work for the job.

Sub Surface Disposal Systems

The most common and often most convenient systems for waste disposal are the sub-surface systems. These include: septic tank and leach field, and cesspool systems. Septic systems consist of a tank and a leach or disposal field. The tank is made of concrete, fiberglass, plastic, or steel although concrete seems to be the most common material. Within the tank are two sets of baffles to limit mixing and to separate the solids being decomposed from the liquid effluent. Sewage enters the tank at one end and drops below the first baffle.

Solids float to the surface in the middle area to be digested by anaerobic bacteria. The digestion process produces water, gases, and dead bacteria. The dead bacteria sink to the bottom with other heavy materials forming sludge on the bottom of the tank, the gasses leak out the top of the tank and the plumbing vents, the water/liquid flow over past the second baffle and are distributed into the soils through the leaching field. In the leaching field the final stage of digestion takes place as aerobic bacteria complete the process. In a properly working system all solids remain in the septic tank and all liquids eventually overflow out to the disposal system. After several years solids will build up in the tank, requiring the tank to be pumped out by a professional septic disposal company. Signs indicating the need for a pump-out include gurgling of drains, the slowing of toilet flushes, and smells outside the house.

The leaching field or disposal area can have a number of configurations including seepage pits, and seepage beds. The seepage pit is typically a covered well (or a series of wells) surrounded by gravel. The effluent overflows into this area from the septic tank, aerobic bacteria complete digestion, and the liquids leach into the soils. This system is not always permitted, but can often work well in areas with very sandy soils. The seepage bed is a series of perforated pipes lying horizontally and parallel to one another in gravel trenches or beds. Usually the pipes are located about 24-30" below grade, and any of the lengths of piping are limited to about

100'. Similar to the seepage pits, the liquids are distributed into the gravel where digestion and leaching into the soil takes place. The lengths of pipe and area of gravel in the system is determined by design and is a function of the permeability of the soil. Sandy soils require fewer pipes and less gravel; heavy or clay soils require more pipe and gravel. Over time disposal fields can clog-up and become saturated. When this occurs an alternate field must be developed for replacement. Usually the location for the alternate field is determined at the time the first field is laid out.

Cesspools are an older style of system that is not allowed in many areas. They consist of a single sub-surface tank usually constructed on site of stacks of stone or un-cemented concrete blocks. Sewage from the house is piped into the tank, digestion of the waste

Maintenance Checklist

- [ ] See individual systems
- [ ] Pump out septic tank. At first pump out every three years. Ask the service person if there is evidence that it should be pumped out more or less frequently
- [ ] Install layers of soil in outhouse pit
- [ ] Clean and empty composting and incinerating toilets
- [ ] Refresh anti-freeze in traps if used in the winter in freezing conditions

manhole shaped structure with sewage pumps that pump the effluent up to the required elevation. Aerobic systems are similar to septic tank systems but include aeration fans or pumps to raise oxygen levels in the effluent and speed digestion. These systems can solve some of the problems associated with insufficient tank volume or disposal area, but can add significantly to the price.

Grey water systems are similar to cesspool or seepage pit systems in construction and operation, but are designed for the disposal of non-human, liquid wastes only. They dispose of waste from washing machines and sinks in order to reduce the load on the septic systems, and they dispose of these liquids when alternative toilet systems are employed.

When using sub-surface disposal fields it is a good idea to avoid putting egg shells and coffee grinds into the system. These materials don't break down in the septic tank and form a type of concrete at the bottom. Also avoid disposing chemicals, paints, and certain types of detergents and cleaners into the system. These materials can kill the bacteria in the tank and cause the system to fail. It is best to determine if the cleaners you use are "safe for septic systems."

happens in the "pool," and liquids leaching through the sides are disposed of through the soils. Because all digestion and disposal happens in a single area, these systems are much more prone to failure, and should be pumped out more frequently.

Variations on subsurface disposal systems include: raised beds, pumped systems, and aerobic systems. Raised beds are used when soils are of poor quality (clay), or ground water is high. They are similar to leach fields but consist of soils imported from off-site piled above existing grade. Pumped systems are used when the outlet of the house or septic system is below an area suitable for disposal. The pump station usually consists of a

Holding Tank Systems

Holding tank systems are simple systems often employed when cottages are very close to the waters edge, or when there are not sufficient soils for disposal. They are simply tanks above or below ground that accumulates waste until the waste can be pumped out by a septic disposal service. These systems often have monitors which indicate when the tank is full and in need of a pump-out.

Alternative Systems

Composting Toilets

Composting toilets function much like a sophisticated outhouse with provisions for the aeration, decomposition, and drying of the waste stream. They can be and should be located indoors, especially in colder climates. Proper operation requires temperatures above 40 degrees F year around. Therefore continuous heating may be required if winter operation is anticipated. Models often require fans and electric heaters to promote decomposition and drying. To aid in decomposition, soil or vegetable matter must be added on a regular basis, and the waste must be turned with hand cranked or electric aerators.

Periodic maintenance requires removing the waste chamber when full (real fun) and properly disposing of the waste. Disposal regulations vary from place to place. Some authorities having jurisdiction allow the use of the composted product as a fertilizer, others require disposal in a septic system or a sewage treatment facility. Problems with this type of system include energy consumption, smell, or noise from exhaust fans to reduce the smell.

Incinerating Toilets

Incinerating toilets are electric, propane, or natural gas fired systems that heat waste to about 1,200 degrees F, evaporate the liquids, and convert the solids to ash. Chimneys are required to vent the products of combustion up above the roof. The ash pan for these systems must be emptied regularly (up to several times per week). Incineration in electric units happens after each use, and can be interrupted as the need arises. Gas fired units can be a good option at cottages without electricity. These units typically store wastes for a day at a time and must be locked down for incineration for a 4-5 hour period each day. If occupant levels are high, often more then one unit is required with one ready for use, and the other incinerating. Requirements for the disposal of the ash vary with locality. Operating costs can be significant for electric models, and smell and heat given off by the units can sometimes cause difficulties.

Chemical Toilets

Chemical toilets are essentially basins filled with chemicals into which people dispose of their wastes. The chemical bath is full of bacteria killing agents, perfumes, and dyes. Once the basin is full it must be pumped out by professionals and recharged. Frequent addition of poisonous chemicals is required. Usually the smell and disposal problems discourage most people from using these systems, but in locations where no other alternative is available they are an option.

Opening for the Season

Generally there are no special requirements associated with the use of these systems other than cleaning for use, turning on the power, and/or gas to the toilets.

Closing for the Season

Closing for the season varies with type of system. With an outhouse, clean the overall structure, and add fresh soil to the top of the pile. Subsurface systems typically require no maintenance other then periodic pumping out. Composting and incinerating toilets should be cleaned and emptied, and power or gas shut-off. Holding tanks should be pumped out to avoid freezing.

Throughout the cottage, traps for sinks, washing machines, and toilets should be filled with non-toxic anti-freeze. Pockets of water in washing machine pumps must also be drained out to reduce failure caused by freezing.

Heating Systems
Heat

Heating systems for camps and cottages vary greatly. Rustic cabins can have very crude systems that are inexpensive to operate, and very effective. More sophisticated second homeowners can spend tens of thousands of dollars installing complex heating plants and control systems. In trying to decide what system is right for your spot, several questions must to be answered. Will you use the cabin year round, or just in the summer? Do you want to maintain uniform temperature in all spaces, a few key spaces, or just take the chill off the main living space? What fuels are available to you, wood, natural gas, fuel oil,

LP gas, kerosene, coal, electricity, etc? Is the cost of heating important to you, or just the convenience?

If a cabin will be used just in the summer to take the chill off on cold nights and mornings, very simple systems may be perfect. If you plan to use the cabin year round and need to protect plumbing from freezing, a more complex system may be required. Many simple systems will work well to heat a single space, but won't work well if different zones of heating are required. Many heating systems require electricity, some do not; if the system is seasonal only, and requires electricity for pumps, fans, or controls it might be practical to provide this power by generator. If you hope to heat the whole cabin electrically, a utility power connection and a large breaker panel will be necessary. If you plan to heat year round, is the cabin accessible for deliveries of LP gas, fuel oil, kerosene, coal, etc? Many fuel delivery companies won't risk their livelihoods by making deliveries to remote cabins in the winter.

Wood Heat

Wood heats you three times: when you cut it, when you stack it, and when you burn it...

Heating with wood for many is an essential part of cabin life. It reflects back to centuries past when families gathered around campfires to cook, talk, keep away wild animals, and stay warm. Heating with wood covers the gamut from being very simple and inexpensive to being complex and expensive. In some locations trees fall down or can be cut down adjacent to the cabin, they are cut, dried, and then are burned. In other areas trees are part of the landscaping, or are not available, it will be necessary to purchase the wood and have it trucked in. Many believe that heating with wood is the least expensive fuel source. However, if you calculate in chain saw purchase, repair and maintenance, wood truck purchase and maintenance, doctors bills relating to dismemberment and crushed or lacerated body parts, chiropractic bills relating to resultant back issues, and your own time to cut, stack, haul, and stoke, wood heat can be an expensive fuel source.

Typically hardwoods (oak, maple, hickory) are a better choice then soft woods (pine, spruce, aspen) as fuel sources. Hard woods produce more heat, burn more slowly, and are cleaner. Soft woods burn quickly and the soot generated forms creosote on the insides of chimneys that can lead to chimney fires.

Generally wood is burned in open campfires, fireplaces, wood stoves, and wood furnaces. Campfires and fireplaces heat occupants sitting adjacent to them radiantly. If you see the fire, you feel its warmth. Unfortunately, open type fires typically are very inefficient because the airflow around and to the fire can't be controlled. Often more heat is drawn up the chimney then actually enters the cabin. Wood stoves are much more efficient because the draft can be controlled, and they can be esthetically pleasing if units are selected with stone or enameled walls, and with glass doors which permit occupants to view the fire. Wood stoves heat a space both conductively (air moving over them), and radiantly (similar to the sun). Wood furnaces and boilers are effectively wood stoves with heat exchangers to warm air or water, respectively. These devices typically require electricity to run the fans, pumps, and controls and have the advantage that the furnace or boiler can be located remotely and heated air or water can be blown or pumped to the area it serves.

Other solid fuels such as wood pellets, and coal can be burned in the same manner as wood, and often require only small modifications for the addition of racks (to hold the

cool, pellets) in stoves, boilers, and furnaces.

Typically solid fueled appliances must be vented in masonry or double walled, insulated, stainless steel chimneys. When using single walled vents, make sure that clearances to combustibles are maintained to prevent house fires.

Gas Heat

Gas for heating is generally available in two forms: bottled, or piped from a utility. Bottled gas, often referred to as LP (liquefied petroleum) is typically either butane or propane depending on your location. LP gas is stored

Opening Checklist

- ☐ Remove ashes from wood or coal stoves, fireplaces, and furnaces.
- ☐ Clean chimneys to remove ash, creosote build-up, birds nests etc.
- ☐ Open chimney dampers before lighting a fire or starting an appliance.
- ☐ Open gas valves and oil valves (where applicable) at the tank and/or at the appliance and inspect for leaks. Questionable fittings can be sprayed with a soap and water solution to uncover leaks (bubbling will occur at the leak).
- ☐ Check oil lines for leaks, (can be performed visually and detected as oily substance on surface of pipes or on ground under piping).
- ☐ Turn on breakers serving appliances.
- ☐ Fill LP gas or oil tanks.
- ☐ Light pilot in gas fired appliances (when so equipped).
- ☐ Perform annual burner service on oil-fired appliances.
- ☐ Replace air filters in furnaces, and oil filters at oil tanks.
- ☐ Check that all appliances are properly vented with adequate clearance to combustibles. If building materials adjacent to a vent are warm to the touch, shut the appliance off and correct the problem.
- ☐ Provide smoke detectors in rooms with space heaters, and verify batteries are fresh.
- ☐ Last but not least, check that all combustible materials are clear of space heaters including curtains, blankets, and rugs.

under pressure in cylinders which vary in size from very small (used in gas grills) to 500-1000 gallon tanks (used for large heating systems). The tanks are stored outside the building either above or below the ground depending on ground type, required portability of the tank(s), esthetics, and required vaporization rates. Gas inside the tank is a high-pressure liquid that vaporizes at the top of the tank. The vaporized gas passes through a regulator that drops the pressure to a point that is safe to use inside a dwelling. The vaporizing process cools the gas, so in cold climates it is often necessary to oversize the tank (to reduce the vaporization rate) or bury it (to keep the tank warmer) to prevent the tank from reaching a temperature where the gas will freeze. A local delivery service is contracted to come to the site and refill the tanks periodically (larger tanks) or the tanks are brought to a refilling depot (smaller tanks). The price of LP gas varies significantly, up to 200%, depending on the quantity you purchase and your use of the gas. Generally, if you use small amounts for cooking or clothes drying, the price is much higher than if used for year round heating.

Gas piped from a utility is typically referred to as natural gas. The gas is in a high-pressure vapor form in the pipes leading to the dwelling. At the building wall the gas is passed through a gas meter/regulator that reduces the pressure to a safe pressure to use inside a home. Natural gas is a simple and inexpensive fuel source if you have it available at your location.

Natural or LP gas can be used in a variety of heating units ranging from non-electric wall or floor heaters to very complex boiler and furnace arrangements. The simple heaters are available in vented and non-vented varieties, but the author prefers to use the vented systems to reduce the risk of carbon monoxide poisoning. Non-electric heaters are very beneficial at locations without electricity or in locations where the electricity is un-reliable. These systems are available with non-electric thermostats that can be remotely mounted.

Whichever gas system is selected it is important to properly vent the units using type-B gas vent for gravity vented systems, or manufacturer approved venting for forced draft units. The vents should be installed maintaining proper clearance to combustibles to prevent the risk of setting building components on fire. Please remember that if you smell gas in the home to extinguish all open flames, leave the building, and contact a qualified gas service technician or the fire department.

Oil or Kerosene Heat

Fuel oil is available in a number of grades from #1 to #6. #1 fuel oil is thin and light colored and is typically referred to as kerosene. #2 fuel oil is dyed reddish, is slightly heavier then #1, and has a higher freezing or gel point then #1. Apart from some additives, #2 fuel oil is identical to the diesel used in cars and trucks. The higher grade numbers refer to less and less refined grades of oil. #6 is thick and black and one could stand a stick in it at room temperature. In colder climates the thicker grades of oil must be heated in order to keep them liquid enough to pump and pipe. For home heating applications typically kerosene or #2 fuel oil is used. The oils can be stored in tanks inside or outside the cabin and above or below the ground depending on local regulations. Typically up to 660 gallons can be stored inside a home but 275-330 gallon tanks are the norm. If the tanks are stored outside above ground, fuel oil is typically mixed with kerosene or anti-gel compounds to prevent the tank from forming into a giant tube of Chapstick.

Kerosene is used in a variety of heaters from simple non-vented, non-electric, fill from a jerry can, stand-alone, room heaters to more complex space heaters which require power for venting, burners, and controls, and piped fuel from a central oil tank. The small portable kerosene heaters could cost under $200, and are very effective for heating small spaces, but should only be used in reasonably leaky (air wise) cabins to prevent the contamination of the room air. The larger space heaters have the benefit of automatic operation and good control, but the disadvantage is that they typically require electricity to operate and can be expensive to install ($1,500-$2,000).

Home heating oil is typically used these days only in central furnaces and boiler plants. At one time it was possible to find non-electric kitchen stoves and space heaters that burned #2 fuel oil, but these have gone the way of the Dodo. Now heating oil appliances have 1/3 to 1/2 horsepower electric burners and controls, and electric pumps and fans to distribute heated water or air from boilers or furnaces to heating terminal points. These heating systems tend to be complex and beyond the budgetary price range for many small camp and cottage owners. The flue gases of an oil system are typically much hotter then natural gas systems, and sometimes under pressure, therefore it is important that the chimney and venting material be rated for the application. If you have questions check with the appliance manufacturer to verify recommendations.

Electric Heat

In general, electric heat is not recommended. The fuel cost is typically three to four times the cost of the fuel sources discussed above, and when you need it most (in a winter blizzard) is when the power usually fails. Also, in many parts of the country it is against code to install electric heat in a dwelling due to the negative impact on local power generation. Heating is not considered one of the best and brightest uses for electricity.

Closing Checklist

☐ Close dampers on solid fuel fired appliances.

☐ Clean ashes from stoves, fireplaces, and furnaces.

☐ Shut gas and oil valves at the tanks.

☐ Turn off oil burner switch.

☐ Shut off breakers to electrical appliances.

With that said, electric heat can be very inexpensive to install, and very convenient to use for short periods of time in small spaces. Simple systems consist of plug-in quartz and electric resistance portable heaters. More complex systems consist of hardwired baseboard systems. The most complex systems consist of electrically heated furnaces and boilers that heat air or water and blow or pump the heated medium to terminal distribution systems.

Often in cottages that have plumbing freeze-up problems, plumbing pipes are wrapped with electrically heated wire to prevent the freezing and cracking of pipes.

Taking the time to understand and properly care for you systems will allow you to spend less time dealing with them and more time playing and relaxing at your cottage.

"As first-time cottage owners we are blessed with the abundance of information we have gathered from friends, family and other resources to help us enjoy our new place on the water."

—Kim, North Hero, Vermont

chapter eighteen
Resource Lists

Here is a list of books, magazines and web sites that we used for our book research or cottage owners have suggested you might enjoy yourself. Some of the resources have brief descriptions (sometimes the book's own) that we added for your convenience. If you have a suggestion for a good resource, please send it our way! (See survey in back.)

BOOKS

CAMPFIRE FUN

The Campfire Collection
By Eric Martin, Chronicle Books, San Francisco, California. ISBN 0-8118-2454-3. As the sun goes down and the darkness settles and brings its creepy creatures and noises, be ready to share the scariest campfire stories ever told with *The Campfire Collection*. These collections of true stories, told from the people that have lived to tell their tale, will surely make your camping experience memorable and chilling.

Campfire Songs
By Irene Maddox and Rosalyn Blandenship, The Globe Pequot Press, Old Saybrook, Connecticut. ISBN 1-56440-372-6. More than 100 of your favorite campfire songs, including the musical notes.

Campfire Tales: Ghoulies, Ghosties and Long-leggy Beasties
By William Forgey, M.D., ICS Books, Inc., Merrillville, Indiana. ISBN 0-934802-50-5. Campfire Tales is the perfect book filled with stories of adventure, ghosts and other scary encounters that will surely make the night memorable. Enter different worlds and discover the mysteries of the dark while sitting close by firelight with *Campfire Tales*.

If you and your family enjoyed *Campfire Tales*… check out William Forgey's first book, *Campfire Stories… Things That Go Bump in the Night*.

Campstoves, Fireplaces and Chimney
By A.D. Taylor, United States Government Printing Office. ISBN 0-8466-6055-5. *Campstoves, Fireplaces and Chimney* is a complete guide in constructing your own campstove or fireplace for best all-around usage and safety.

Cooking On a Stick: Recipes for Kids

By Linda White, Gibbs Smith Publisher, Layton, Utah. ISBN 0-87905-727-0. Campfire cooking is fun and easy with recipes from *Cooking on a Stick!* Following these easy instructions on preparing delicious campfire food is enjoyment for the entire family!

The Kids Campfire Book

By Jane Drake, Kids Can Press Ltd., Tonawanda, New York. ISBN 1-55074-539-5. This book illustrates how much fun you and your family can have around a campfire with fun songs, scary ghost stories and entertaining activities! There never will be a dull moment for your family again with this book. Also, there are many handy tips for safeguarding your camping area and fire.

A Little Book of Campfire Songs

By Brian Denington, Chronicle Books, New York. ISBN: 0-8118-0821-1. This book is a perfect pocket size filled with traditional campfire songs. Each song includes music and chord notations.

COOKING

Cabin Cooking- Good Food for the Great Outdoors/ William Sonoma Outdoors Collection

By Time Life Books and Tori Richie. ISBN 0-78354-620-3. This is the perfect little book to take with you and your family for some quick and helpful hints in preparing a wonderful meal in your vacation home. *Cabin Cooking,* is filled with easy and delicious recipes that you and your family will love.

Cottage Life's More Summer Weekends

By Jane Rodmell, Firefly Books. ISBN 0969692234. This wonderful book, created by Cottage Life Magazine, is simply filled with great quick and easy recipes, suggestions on what to serve for any summer occasion and hundreds of beautiful photos that are completely irresistible.

The Great Grilling Cookbook

By Annette Yates, Macmillan of Canada. ISBN 0771576331. This book is packed with over 200 exciting ideas for everyone's taste. Also this book is a great source for important and beneficial grilling methods and serving tips.

Smoke & Spice

By Cheryl Alters Jamison, Harvard Common Press. ISBN 155832061X. The art of grilling and barbequing are described in detail in this book filled with helpful tips for making the mot delicious meal in your own backyard.

GARDENING RESOURCES

101 Essential Tips: Basic Gardening

By Pippa Greenwood and Deni Bown, DK Publishing Merchandise. ISBN 078942777X. A small, useful handbook is filled with easy to remember tips and ideas for any gardener.

Fun with Gardening, 50 Great Projects Kids Can Plant Themselves

By Clare Bradley, Southwater, United Kingdom, ISBN: 1-84215-138-X. These projects teach all the basic gardening skills.

The Garden Primer

By Barbara Damrosch, Workman Publishing, New York, ISBN: 0-89480-316-6. Detailed guide to every type of plant, tree, shrub, and vegetable you want to grow. This book includes a common-sense approach to gardening.

GENERAL COTTAGE BOOKS

Sparkle Island

Ellen Rosewall, Raven Tree Press, Green Bay, Wisconsin. ISBN 0-9701107-0-7. *Sparkle Island* is filled with true tales of camping memories that are all heartwarming and inspiring. Enjoy, and let the stories of a special family who loves the outdoors and Lake Wobegon into your camping experience.

The Night the Bear Ate Goombaw, Rubber Legs and White Tail-Hairs, The Grasshopper Trap, Never Sniff a Gift Fish, They Shoot Canoes, Don't They? A Fine and Pleasant Misery, and The McManus Treasury

All these books are by Patrick F. McManus, one of America's leading outdoor humorist. Every cottage should have his collection of short stories ranging from every mishap you can imagine or have lived through at your camp, cottage or cabin.

The Cottage Book: A Collection of Practical Advice

By Frank B. Edwards, Hedgehog Productions Inc., Newburgh, Ontario. ISBN 1-895261-04-x. This book has over 60 full-length articles. Full of environmental-friendly advice for your cottage experience, including birdfeeders, animals, sun block protection and more.

INTERIOR DECORATING AND ARCHITECTURE

Cabin Fever: Rustic Style Comes Home

By Rachel Carley, Simon and Schuster Editions, New York City, New York. ISBN 0-684-84422-2. This book gives you a charming insight into our countries most rustic, cozy and comfortable cabins with hundreds of colorful photographs perfect for your enjoyment.

Cabin Fever: Sheds and Shelters, Huts and Hideaways

By Marie-France Boyer, Thomas and Hudson Publishing, New York City, New York. ISBN 0-500015-759. Come into a world of magical hideaways that will leave you simply breathless. *Cabin Fever* is filled with colorful photographs that exemplify the true solitude of cabin living.

The Cabin: Inspiration for the Classic American Getaway

By Dale Mulfinger and Susan Davis, Taunton Press, Newtown, Connecticut. ISBN 1-5615839-28. *The Cabin* is filled with a broad spectrum of cabins that are filled with both style and design. This book exemplifies the need for simplicity in giving your cottage that warm and cozy feeling, with an array of colorful photographs that will give you numerous ideas on how to create that sort of atmosphere with ease.

Camps and Cottages: A Stylish Blend of Old and New

By Molly Hyde English, Gibbs Smith Publisher, Salt Lake City, Utah. ISBN 1-58685-056-3. One of the latest cottage style decorating books which is filled with great decorating ideas, blending both old and new rustic living with a stylish kick!

The Cottage Book

By Richard Sexton, Chronicle Books, San Francisco, California. ISBN 0-87701-636-4. *The Cottage Book* is a showcase of colorful and exquisite cottages. The photographs give a descriptive look of both the interior and exterior of some of the most gorgeous Bay area cottages.

Cottage Comfort

By Lynette Jensen, Laudauer Corporation. ISBN 1-89062-119-6. Lynette Jensen shares with you her secrets and suggestions for combining your favorite collectibles, decorations and antiques and creating a new form of cottage comfort. This book gives you helpful hints through descriptive pictures and text, on changing your older looking cottage into something modern.

Cottage Living

By Better Homes and Gardens, Better Homes and Gardens Books, Meredith Publishing Group, Des Moines, Iowa. ISBN 1-567-99979-94. This Better Homes and Gardens book, *Cottage Living*, captures the most expensive and rustic-looking cottage homes ever imagined. This book gives you many ideas for remodeling your vacation getaway, with Scandinavian flair!

Cottage Retreats

By Lisa Jill Schlang, ISBN: 1-58663-306-6. This colorful book is filled with photograph and text that helps incorporates decorating ideas for every mood.

Cottage Style

By Better Homes and Gardens, Better Homes and Gardens Books, Meredith Publishing Group, Des Moines, Iowa. ISBN 0-696-20777-X. Decorating ideas for any cottage or camp near the beach or the lake! Created from the well known and acclaimed *Better Homes and Gardens Magazine,* this guide book will help you give your special place a warm, friendly and welcoming touch.

Country Weekend Homes

By Cristina Montes, ISBN: 0-8230-0969-6.

Creating Country Style: Inspirational and Practical Decorating Projects for the Home

By Stewart and Sally Walton, Lorenz Books. ISBN 1-85967-614-6. Do you enjoy small decorating projects around your home? Well this book is the perfect tool to help you give your own special getaway home your own personal creative kick! *Creating Country Style* has many great ideas that will get you working and your home looking fantastic.

Getaways

By Chris Casson Madden, Crown Publishing Group, New York, New York. ISBN 0-609-60320-5. A getaway home can be found in various locations and for every season. In addition to viewing the breathtaking landscapes of the United States, enjoy your own personal viewing of some of our countries most notable and famous celebrities' private getaways.

Great Escapes

By Judith Miller, Ryland Peters and Small, Inc., New York, New York. ISBN 1-84172-106-9. Throughout history, people have been escaping the realities of real life and flocking to their own private getaways. *Great Escapes* is filled with unforgettable pictures and narrative that will inspire you in creating your own perfect getaway.

House and Garden Book of Vacation Homes and Hideaways

By Leonie Highton, Vendome Press. ISBN 0-86562198. This book features key elements of design for vacation homes throughout the world.

The Illustrated Cottage: A Decorative Fairy Tale

By Nina Williams, Hearst Books. ISBN 0-68816-541-9. Are you interested in making your home into an imaginative fairyland? This book shows the creative steps in making your house into your own home with a sort of French flair! Nina Williams fills her book with the most beautiful and imaginative pictures that will just take your breath away.

A Little House of My Own

By Lester Walker, Black Dog & Leventhal Publishers, New York. ISBN 1-57912-151-9. This book is filled with hundreds of ideas, illustrations and photographs for tiny shelters, cottages and hideaways.

Little Retreat

By Jane Tidbury, Clarkson Potter Publishers, New York City, New York. ISBN 0-609-60902-5. The thirty-one little retreats featured in this book describe the very nature that a small retreat would bring, such as comfort, privacy and a rest from everyday life.

Log Cabin Living

By Daniel Mack, Gibbs Smith Publishing, Layton, Utah. ISBN 0-879059-206. If your perfect idea of a vacation home is of a homey, small and warm little log cabin, this book is right for you! Log Cabin Living is filled with colorful photos of some of the warmest log cabin homes ever dreamed about! Get great ideas for giving your log cabin that warm, rustic feeling.

Mary Emmerling's American Country Cottages

By Mary Emmerling, Clarkson Potter Publishers, New York, New York. ISBN 0-517-58365-8. *American Country Cottages* is filled with suggestions for the average American cottage that's in need for the perfect country look with minimal maintenance. Its charming full-color photographs present you with images of country living that can be easily created in your own American cottage.

The New Cottage Home

By Jim Tolpin, Taunton Press, Newtown, Connecticut. ISBN: 1-56158-229-8. Jim Tolpin shows you a world of new cottages, evoking storybook dreams. Through beautiful photography and detailed description of each well crafted cottages by the lakes, in the woods and in the fields.

The Not So Big House

By Sarah Susanka with Kira Obolensky, The Taunton Press, Inc., Newtown, Connecticut. ISBN 1-56158-130-5. This book is targeted to the cottagers that are in favor of smaller and more personal spaces. The *Not So Big House* gives great suggestions to those who desire new and creative ideas in making their homes more comfortable and cozy.

Perfect Country Cottage

By Bill Laws, Abbeville Press, New York City, New York. ISBN 1-55859-784-0. *Perfect Country Cottage* gives you a full comprehensive and historic view of some of the world's most famous cottage homes and why they were built the way they were. Bill Laws manages to cover and give a descriptive look at all the aspects, from large to small, of each of the historic and notable cottages mentioned in this exceptional book.

Second Home

By Better Homes and Gardens, Better Homes and Gardens Books, Meredith Publishing Group, Des Moines, Iowa. ISBN 0-696-21152-1. If you enjoyed the previous Better Homes and Gardens books mentioned above you are going to fall in love with, *Second Home*. This book is perfect for planning the second home of your dreams! Filled with colorful and fun photos, *Second Home* is a handy book filled with tips, facts and websites to get you started on your own dream vacation home!

Snow Country, Mountain Homes and Rustic Retreats

By Elizabeth Clair Flood, Chronicle Books

Waterside Homes

By Marcie Stuchin and Susan Abramson, PBC International. ISBN 0866366318.

Waterside Living

Inspirational homes by lakes, rivers, and the ocean. By Leslie Geddes-Brown. ISBN 1-84172-213-8.

Weekend Houses

By Penelope Rowlands and Mark Darley, Chronicle Books. ISBN 0811825434. More than 200 color photographs and editorial based on twenty-seven exceptional retreats.

Waterfront Homes

By Joaquin Russell, Franciso Asenio Carver and Watson Guptill ISBN 0823066185.

KID'S STUFF

Buck Wilder's Small Twig Hiking & Camping Guide

By Tim Smith & Mark Herrick, Buck Wilder Books, Williamsburg, Michigan. ISBN: 0-9643793-3-3. This is an adorable book for kids who want to learn more about hiking and camping. Great illustrations and editorial that keep kids interested and teaches them and their parents a thing or two about camping, the National Parks, tracking and safety.

Buck Wilder's Small Fry Fishing Guide

By Tim Smith & Mark Herrick, Buck Wilder Books, Williamsburg, and Michigan.

Outdoor Adventures Series
By David Armentrout, The Rourke Press, Vero Beach, Florida. Kids books about the outdoors, about 20-25 pages each. The series includes books about boating, camping climbing, fishing, hiking and hunting. You can get these books at your local library, kid's section.

Parents Play and Learn
By Parents Magazine, Roundtable Press, Inc., New York, New York. ISBN 1-58238-005-8. *Play and Learn* is a combination of creative ideas to entertain your child on both rainy and sunny days from the notable editors of Parents Magazine. Keep your child busy with all these activities that will help your child develop and build learning skills while having fun!

Summertime Treats
By Sava Perry and Jonelle Weaver, Chronicle Books, San Francisco, California. ISBN 0-811823237. *Summertime Treats* is filled with fun recipes for the entire family, ranging from drinks to beach food! *Summertime Treats* also has many fun ideas and crafts that don't require expert skills, just happy faces!

Water Sports, An Outdoor Adventure Handbook
By Hugh McManners, DK Publishing, New York. ISBN: 0-7894-1479-1. A 48-page handbook, filled with pictures and descriptions for kids of all ages regarding basic water safety. It discusses water confidence, using a kayak, how to sail, water rules and much more.

Children's Magazine's Book of Children's Parties
By Angela Wilke, DK Publishing, New York. ISBN 1-56458-853-X. Thinking of many creative ideas for planning a children's party can be difficult, so let the *Book of Children's Parties* help you out! It's completely filled with fun, new and exciting games that will keep everyone happy and having a great time.

The Little Hands Art Book and The Little Hands Craft Book
By Judy Press, Williamson Publishing, Charlotte, Vermont. ISBN: 0-913589-86-1. These books are filled with wonderful indoor and outdoor ideas to do with kids, who are 2-6 years old.

MAINTENANCE

All Thumbs Guide to Home Plumbing
By Robert W. Wood, Tab Books, Summit, Pennsylvania. ISBN: 0-8306-2545-3.

This 125-page book has detailed instructions with step-by-step illustrations that lead you through 10 of the most common plumbing problems.

Cabins and Cottages: Home Repair and Improvement
Time Life Editors, Time Life Books, Alexandra, Virginia. ISBN 0-8094-2412-6. Fix all your problems in your cottage or cabin with this easy-to-follow home repair manual. This improvement guide is filled with descriptive diagrams and illustrations that are essential for any cabin or cottage to have, in case of any repair emergencies or quick fixer-uppers.

Campstoves, Fireplaces and Chimney
By A.D. Taylor, United States Government Printing Office. ISBN 0-8466-6055-5. *Campstoves, Fireplaces and Chimney* is a complete guide in constructing your own campstove or fireplace for best all-around usage and safety.

Cottage Projects
By Charles Long, Warwick Publishing, Los Angeles, California. ISBN 1-895629-75-6. From canoe racks, chimney cleaning, wood steps, hammock hanging to tire swings, *Cottage Projects* is filled with easy and affordable projects to do around your cottage. There is always a project to do to make your cottage more appealing, let the *Cottage Project* guide help you.

Cottage Water Systems
By Max Burns, Cottage Life Books, Toronto, Canada. ISBN 0-9696922-0-X. This manual gives you helpful tips with an easy-to-understand style, about how each component of your own water system works. *Cottage Water Systems* is filled with diagrams and illustrations that will help you point out the problem in your water system. Also, tips on how you can safeguard your system so that you will be able to eliminate future problems and or detect them from the start.

Country Plumbing
By Gerry Hartigan, This 80-page book is full of information regarding your plumbing problems, systems and disasters. A must have for every country cottage, camp or cabin.

The Dock Manual
By Max Burns, Storey Books Publishing, Pownel, Vermont. ISBN 1-58017-098-6. If you want to build your own customized dock, this manual is ideal for you! *The Dock Manual* is an easy-to-use guide that is devoted exclusively to your residential dock, with helpful tips and upgrades.

Heating with Wood
By Larry Gay, Garden Way Publishing, Charlotte, Vermont. ISBN 0-88266-036-5. Learn the real facts of wood, and how it is our economical and ecological energy alternative. This is a great book to learn all about burning wood, stoves and fireplaces.

How to Build Your Home in the Woods
By Bradford Angier, Hart Publishing Company, Inc., New York City, New York. ISBN 0-911378-103. This is an illustrated how-to guidebook showing how to build log cabins, camping shelters, cabins without logs and rustic furniture. This book provides many drawings and plans to give you step-by-step information.

Home Basics: The Complete Guide to Running Today's Home
By Gill Chilton, Barnes and Nobles, Inc., New York, New York. ISBN 0-7607-2719-8. Get expert advice with step-by-step guidelines for those everyday tasks around the house. Run your home efficiently with ease with the *Home Basics* guidebook.

The Homeowner's Handbook of Plumbing Repair

By K.W. Sessions, John Wiley and Sons, New York City, New York. ISBN 0-471-02550-X. Now you can successfully tackle your own plumbing repairs with this helpful handbook. This book gives you information on how to handle the largest to the smallest problems with your plumbing.

Shelters, Shacks and Shanties

By D.C. Beard, Charles Scriber's Sons, New York City, New York. ISBN 0-684-12805-5. This is one of the best guidebooks on construction of outdoor shelters that only requires your own maintenance and materials. The author gives clear instructions on numerous projects to help you create your personal home.

Outdoor Adventures

The 2 oz. Backpacker: A problem Solving Manual for Use in the Wilds

By Robert S. Wood, Ten Speed Press, California, ISBN 0-89815-070-1. This is a perfect back pocket guide to day and overnight hiking, walking and outings for the whole family.

Outdoor Recreation Areas

By the editors of Time-Life Books, New York, New York. ISBN:0-8094-7354-2. Full of information on how to build grass fields and surfaces courts, children's gyms and playhouse, badminton courts, tire swings, a Jacuzzi and more.

PETS AND PESTS

American's Neighborhood Bats

By Merline D. Tuttle, University of Texas Press, ISBN: 0-292-78148-2. 92 page book on how to understand and learn to live in harmony with bats. Filled with helpful information on how to remove them from buildings and relocate them and much more.

Bat House Builder's Handbook

By Merlin D. Tuttle and Donna L. Hensley.

RENTAL AND OWNING INFORMATION

Landlording

By Leigh Robinson, Express, El Cerrito, California. 0-932956-11-4. A handy manual for home owners who want to rent their own place, filled with detailed information, worksheets and record keeping information. A must have for any property owner thinking of renting.

The Estate Planning Sourcebook

By Dawn Bradley Berry, J.D., Lowell House, Los Angeles, California. 0-7373-0076-0. This book discusses wills, living trusts, family limited partnerships, joint tenancy, life insurance policies, probate and tax-reducing trusts.

SAFETY

The American Red Cross First Aid & Safety Handbook

By the American Red Cross and Kathleen A. Handal, M.D. ISBN: 0-316-73646-5. This book shows you how to handle every type of first aid emergency...a must have for every cottage.

First Aid for Children Fast

By Johns Hopkins Children's Center. ISBN 1-56458-702-9. An instruction color photo first aid book geared specifically to children.

Handbook for First Aid and Emergency Care

By The American Medical Association. ISBN: 0-679-72959-3. A Comprehensive, Step-by-Step Guide to Dealing with Injuries, Illnesses and Medical Emergencies.

PERIODICALS AND MAIL-ORDER CATALOGS

Cabin Life Magazine: Cabin Life Editorial Team, Fladmark Publishing Company, Duluth, Minnesota. This magazine gives you updated stories, tips, recipes, decorating and suggestions with in improving your cabin or camping life. This magazine that is essential for any cabin owner or renter. Online: www.cabinlifemag.com or Phone: (888) 287-3129.

Campmor: This mail order, retail store and web site, feature a variety of camp, cottage and cabin accessories. Online: www.campmor.com or Phone: 800-525-4785 to request a catalog.

Coastal Living Magazine: For people who love the coast, recent colorful photographs and interesting articles of breathtaking landscapes throughout various coastlines of the U.S. Online: www.coastallivingmag.com or Phone: 888-252-3529.

Cottage Life Magazine: A wonderful magazine for those who own or rent a cottage. Articles on every subject including opening up your cottage, docks, boating, wildlife information and much more. Based out of Canada, this magazine is also very popular in the United States. Online: www.cottagelife.com or Phone: 800-465-6183.

Cyberrentals: Your rental guide to find your perfect vacation rental spot all over the world with over 3,250 rental properties listed. Call for a rental guide or go online and see what they have available. Online: www.cyberrentals.com or Phone: (800) 628-0558.

Harmony: A catalog that sells a variety of items including organic cotton sheets, natural insect repellants, outdoor furniture, garden tools and natural cleaners. Online: www.gaiam.com or Phone: 1-800-869-3446.

L.L.Bean Outdoors: This catalog has a variety of equipment, clothing and other items needed for outdoor living. Online: www.llbean.com/outdoor or Phone: 800-226-7552.

Overton's World's Largest Watersport Dealer Mail-Order Catalog: Items ranging from waterski equipment, wet suits, bathing suits, boat covers, safety equipment, watercraft accessories and more. Online: www.overtons.com or Phone: (800) 334-6541.

Soundings, The Nation's Boating Newspaper: This magazine lists over 9,000 boats for sale, plus hundreds of waterfront properties. Plus, each month this magazine features a different waterfront town or city. Online: www.soundingsonline.com or Phone: 800-244-8845.

Waterfront Living Mail-Order Catalog: Put the finishing touches to your camp or cottage with the decorative items listed. Items ranging from deck chairs, welcome signs, decorative throw rugs and more. Phone: (800) 341-5280.

West Marine Master Mail-Order Catalog: Various items great for your boating experience! Items ranging from fenders to boat shoes, everything you need to equip your boat. Online: westmarine.com or Phone: (800) BOATING or 262-8464.

WEB SITES

Boating/Fishing/Water

www.uscgboating.org

www.bugshirt.com

www.the-fishing-network.com

www.fishingline.net

www.westmarine.com

www.overtons.com

www.waterworkswonders.org

Crafts/Gardening/Cooking

www.artisticflair.com

www.Childparenting.about.com

www.home.att.net/~Dleddy/kids.html

www.fulcum-gardening.com/html/easy_ga

www.kidscook.com

www.propane.ca/safety/understanding.html

www.bbq.about.com/library

Gifts/Products/Furniture

www.adirondackcountrystore.com

www.beachcottagelinens.com

www.camps-and-cottages.com

www.llbean.com/outdoor

www.greenmountaingiftbasket.com

www.marthabymail.com

www.shabbychic.com

www.vermontoutdoorfurniture.com

www.wickerwarehouse.com

www.potterybarn.com

Home Repair/Plumbing/ Maintenance

www.achilles.net/~cco

www.freezealarm.com

www.intwoplaces.com

www.homedepot.com

www.usinspect.com

Pets/Pests/Other Critters

www.doyourownpestcontrol.com

www.animalrepellents.com

www.ChiropteraCabins.com

www.batcon.org

Renting

www.agetaway.com

www.cyberrental.com

www.cabinrental.com

www.cottagerentals.com

Traveling with Pets

www.tips4trips.com/Tips/pettips.htm

www.traveldirt.com/FamilyTravel/pets.htm

STORE LOCATIONS

Adirondack Store
109 Saranac Ave.
Lake Placid, NY 12946
518-523-2646

Adirondack Country Store
252 N. Main Street
Northville, NY 12134
518-863-6056

Beach Cottage Linen's
225 Redfern Village
St. Simmons Island, GA 31522
877-451-6994

Bungalow
1850 South Coast Highway
Laguna Beach, CA 92651
949-494-0191

Camps and Cottages
1231 North Coast Highway
Laguna Beach, CA 92651
949-376-8474

Camps and Cottages
2109 Virginia Street
Berkeley, CA 94709-1613
510-548-2267

Coming to America
276 Lafayette Street
New York, NY 10012
212-343-2968

Maine Cottage Furniture
PO Box 935
Yarmouth, ME 04096
207-846-1430

Quimby's Arts and Antiques
8535 S.E. 13th
Portland, Oregon 97202
503-235-7460

Tippycanoe
475 North Lake Blvd.
Tahoe City, CA 96145
530-581-1669

Village Antiques
419 Main Street
Colchester, Vermont 05446
802-288-8089

STATE RESOURCES

STATE	OFFICE TITLE	PHONE
Alabama	State Park and Recreation Office	(800) 252-7275
Alabama	State Park and Recreation Office	(877) 226-7652
Alaska	Alaska Travel Industry Association	(907) 929-2200
Alaska	Fish and Game Department-Anchorage	(907) 344-0541
Arizona	Tourism Office	(888) 520-3434
Arkansas	State Parks	(501) 682-1191
California	Tourism of California	(800) 862-2543
California	State Parks Office	(800) 777-0369
Colorado	State Parks	(303) 866-3437
Connecticut	State Parks Division	(860) 424-3200
Delaware	State Parks Office	(302) 739-4401
Florida	State Parks Information Line	(850) 488-9872
Georgia	State Parks	(800) 843-6420
Hawaii	Department of Parks and Recreation	(808) 961-8311
Idaho	State Parks Office	(208) 334-4199
Illinois	Dept. of Commerce-Bureau of Tourism	(217) 785-6276
Indiana	State Park Office	(317) 232-4125
Iowa	State Tourism Office	(800) 472-6035
Kansas	Department of Wildlife and Parks	(620) 672-5911
Kentucky	Visitor Services	(502) 582-3732
Louisiana	Tourism Department	(225) 342-8119
Maine	Bureau of Parks and Lands	(207) 287-3821
Maryland	Forest and Park Services	(800) 830-3974
Massachusetts	Division of Forest and Parks	(617) 626-1250
Michigan	State Parks	(800) 447-2757
Minnesota	Office of Tourism	(800) 657-3700
Mississippi	Department of Wildlife, Fisheries and Parks	(601) 432-2400
Missouri	Natural Resources Information Services	(800) 334-6946
Montana	Travel Montana	(406) 444-2654
Nebraska	Game and Parks Commission	(402) 471-0641
Nevada	Division of State Parks	(775) 687-4384
New Hampshire	White Mountain National Forest	(603) 528-8721

STATE RESOURCES

STATE	OFFICE TITLE	PHONE
New Jersey	Department of Parks and Forestry	(800) 843-6420
New Mexico	State Parks Office	(888) 667-2757
New York	State Parks	(518) 474-0456
North Carolina	State Parks	(919) 733-4181
North Dakota	Dept. of Commerce-Tourism Division	(701) 328-2525
Ohio	Travel and Tourism	(614) 466-8844
Oklahoma	Oklahoma Tourism Office	(800) 652-6552
Oregon	State Parks and Recreation Department	(503) 378-6305
Oregon	Fish Division	(503) 872-5252
Pennsylvania	State Parks Reservation and Info	(888) 727-2757
Rhode Island	Department of Parks and Recreation	(401) 222-2632
South Carolina	Parks and Recreation Tourism	(803) 734-0122
South Dakota	Department of Fish, Game and Recreation	(605) 773-3391
Tennessee	Convention and Visitor Bureau	(615) 259-4700
Texas	Parks and Wildlife Office	(800) 792-1112
Utah	State Parks and Recreation	(801) 538-7220
Vermont	Forest and Parks	(802) 241-3670
Virginia	Conservation and Recreation	(804) 786-1712
Washington	State Parks	(360) 902-8500
West Virginia	Tourism	(800) 225-5982
West Virginia	Division of Parks and Recreation	(304) 558-2764
Wisconsin	State Parks Department	(608) 266-2181
Wyoming	State Parks Office	(307) 777-6323
Wyoming	Fish and Game Office	(307) 777-4600

ADD YOUR OWN RESOURCE LIST

Books

Magazines

Web Sites

Stores

ADD YOUR OWN RESOURCE LIST

State Contacts

Local Contacts

Other Resources

"We keep a log on all the different things that need to be done; how to drain the water systems, how to protect the shrubs from the deer eating them, where to store screens, draining oil in the boat, etc. It has taken us several years to get "the manual" completes— now we finally have a working manual."

—Jana, Lake George, New York

chapter nineteen
Worksheets

Emergency Information

Our Camp Name _____

Address _____

_____

EMS _____ Fire _____

Poison Control Center _____

Ambulance _____ Other _____

Police _____ Non-emergency Police _____

Family Physician: Name _____ Phone _____

Nearest Hospital: Name _____ Phone _____

Address _____

Driving Instructions: _____

Other Emergency Numbers

In case of Emergency Contact:

Name_____ Phone_____ Cell Phone_____ Relationship_____

Name_____ Phone_____ Cell Phone_____ Relationship_____

Other_____

Neighbor's Numbers

Neighbor's Names _____

Address _____

Home Telephone Number _____

Camp Telephone Number _____

Neighbor's Names _____

Address _____

Home Telephone Number _____

Camp Telephone Number _____

Neighbor's Names _____

Address _____

Home Telephone Number _____

Camp Telephone Number _____

Neighbor's Names _____

Address _____

Home Telephone Number _____

Camp Telephone Number _____

Neighbor's Names _____

Address _____

Home Telephone Number _____

Camp Telephone Number _____

Contact Information about Cottage and Emergency Contacts

Owner _____

Contact Name _____

Address _____

Home Telephone Number _____ Work Telephone Number _____

Cell Phone Number _____ Fax _____

Email _____

Relationship _____

Additional Owner(s)

Contact Name _____

Address _____

Home Telephone Number _____ Work Telephone Number _____

Cell Phone Number _____ Fax _____

Email _____

Relationship _____

Insurance Company

Name _____

Address _____

Home Telephone Number _____ Work Telephone Number _____

Cell Phone Number _____ Fax _____

Email _____

Relationship _____

Utilities and Maintenance Information

Electricity

Electric Company Name _____

Telephone Number (workday) _____

Emergency Telephone Number _____

Location of the service entry _____

Location of the main switch or circuit breaker, if different _____

_____

Where new fuses are kept _____

Gas

Name of Gas Company _____

Telephone Number (workday) _____

Emergency Telephone Number _____

Location of the meter _____

Location of the main shut off valve _____

Location of inside shut off valves _____

Location of the tools necessary to turn off valve _____

_____

Coal, Fuel Oil, Propane Delivery

Name of service _____

Telephone Number (workday) _____

Emergency Telephone Number _____

Time delivered _____

Location of chute or tank _____

Special instructions _____

Water

Name of the Water Company _____

Location of the meter _____

Telephone Number (workday) _____

Emergency Telephone Number _____

Location of the street valve or pump _____

Location of the main valve for the camp or cottage _____

Location of the inside shut offs _____

_____

Location of the valve for draining the system _____

_____

Location of any necessary tools to shut off the valves _____

_____

Sewer or Septic Tank

Name of the Company or Plumber _____

Telephone Number (workday) _____

Emergency Telephone Number _____

Location of the clean-out _____

Location of the septic tank _____

Garbage and Trash

Name of the Company _____

Telephone Number (workday) _____

Emergency Telephone Number _____

Location of the garbage can _____

Day garbage is picked up on _____

Location where picked up _____

Items to be recycled and pick up day _____

Telephones

Name of Telephone Company _____

Telephone Number (workday) _____

Emergency Telephone Number _____

Location of telephones _____

Location of Answering Machine _____

How to start and stop answering machine _____

_____

How to access call answering _____

What types of telephone calls are to be returned _____

_____

What callers are to be told about where you are and when you will return _____

_____

General Maintenance and Contracting Services

Name of Service _____

Contact Person _____

Telephone Number (workday) _____

Emergency Telephone Number _____

Special instructions _____

Lawn and Landscaping Services

Name of Service _____

Contact Person _____

Telephone Number (workday) _____

Emergency Telephone Number _____

Special instructions _____

Snowplowing and Shoveling Services

Name of Service _____

Contact Person _____

Telephone Number (workday) _____

Emergency Telephone Number _____

Special instructions _____

Appliances Information

All appliance manuals are stored in _____

_____

_____

Information and limitations and special instructions on use of dishwasher, washer, dryer, toaster, oven, microwave, television, VCR/DVD, stereo, etc. _____

_____

_____

_____

_____

Special information, such as inability to use certain appliances at the same time due to electrical or other issues. _____

_____

_____

_____

_____

_____

_____

_____

_____

Local Companies Used

Grocery Store/Location _____

_____

Drugstore/Location _____

_____

Video Rental/Location _____

_____

Department Store/Location _____

_____

_____

Dry Cleaners/Laundry Mat/Location _____

_____

Post Office/Location _____

_____

Mechanic/Auto Body Shop/Location _____

_____

Boat Shop/ Repairs Location _____

_____

Canoe/Kayak Rental Company _____

_____

Other Services _____

_____

_____

_____

_____

Consent and Contact Form

This form is to be signed and filled out by the parents/legal guardian of child.

Name(s) of child (children) _____

In the event the child (children) named above is (are) injured or ill, _____ will attempt to contact us at the numbers below. In the event that we cannot be reached, we give permission to _____ to provide first aid for the child (children) or to seek medical attention or other appropriate measures for the child's (children's) well being and safety.

Parent's (legal guardian) name _____

Telephone Numbers _____Days/Hours _____

Telephone Numbers _____Days/Hours _____

Cell Phone Numbers _____   _____

Other Emergency Contacts:

Emergency Contact _____

Relationship to child _____

Phone Number _____   _____

Cell Phone Number _____

Emergency Contact 2 _____

Relationship to child _____

Phone Number _____

Cell Phone Number _____

Allergies/Medications _____

Other Medical Conditions _____

Phone Number of our Pediatrician _____

Medical Insurance Plan _____ Number _____

Signature _____ Date _____

Local Hunting Information

State Fish and Game Contact _____

State Fish and Game Telephone Number _____

Season _____   Dates _____

Season _____   Dates _____

Season _____   Dates _____

Season _____   Dates _____

Where to go in the area: _____

_____

Where to obtain a hunting license: _____

_____

Other Important Information _____

_____

_____

_____

_____

_____

_____

_____

_____

Local Fishing Information

State Fish and Game Contact _____

State Fish and Game Telephone Number _____

Where to go in the area _____

_____

_____

_____

_____

Where to obtain a fishing license _____

_____

Cost of fishing license _____

Types of fish in our area _____

_____

_____

_____

Types of fish you are not allowed to catch _____   _____

_____

_____

_____

Types of fish you can catch and release _____

_____

_____

_____

Where fishing equipment is stored _____

_____

_____

Basic Checklist for Your Boat

- [ ] Ring Buoy
- [ ] VHF Radio
- [ ] Heaving Line
- [ ] Fenders
- [ ] First Aid Kit
- [ ] Flashlight
- [ ] Mirror
- [ ] Search Light
- [ ] Tool Kit
- [ ] Chart and Compass
- [ ] Boat Hook
- [ ] Spare Propeller
- [ ] Mooring Line
- [ ] Food and Water
- [ ] Binoculars

- [ ] Spare Batteries
- [ ] Sunscreen
- [ ] Extra Clothing
- [ ] AM/FM Radio
- [ ] Anchor and Tackle
- [ ] Overall Boat Condition
- [ ] Electrical Systems
- [ ] Fuel Systems
- [ ] Weather Forecast
- [ ] _____
- [ ] _____
- [ ] _____
- [ ] _____
- [ ] _____
- [ ] _____

Opening Your Cottage for the Season Checklist

- [ ] Turn on water/septic system
- [ ] Turn on electricity
- [ ] Turn on phone
- [ ] Check for rodents/mice holes
- [ ] Air out entire camp/cottage
- [ ] Dust
- [ ] Wash countertops
- [ ] Wash windows-inside and out
- [ ] Scrub sink/bathtub/toilet
- [ ] Throw away any leftover spoiled food
- [ ] Scrub oven/microwave/refrigerator
- [ ] Wash linens/curtains
- [ ] Air out blankets
- [ ] Clean slip covers on furniture
- [ ] Wash all dishes
- [ ] Wash down walls

- [ ] Mop/vacuum floors and rugs
- [ ] Place linens on beds and curtains on windows
- [ ] Wipe down outdoor/porch furniture
- [ ] Hose down house/porch
- [ ] Sweep shed/garage
- [ ] Wipe down boat and inspect for any rotting
- [ ] Replenish first aid kit
- [ ] Check for repair necessities
- [ ] _____
- [ ] _____
- [ ] _____
- [ ] _____
- [ ] _____
- [ ] _____
- [ ] _____

Valuables Inventory

- ☐ Television(s)
- ☐ VCR/DVD player
- ☐ Stereo
- ☐ Microwave
- ☐ Computer
- ☐ Printer
- ☐ Deck Equipment
- ☐ Water Skis
- ☐ Tubes
- ☐ Jet Ski
- ☐ Snowmobiles
- ☐ Trampoline
- ☐ Boat
- ☐ Beach Chairs

- ☐ Bikes
- ☐ Artwork
- ☐ Antiques
- ☐ Dock
- ☐ Canoe/Kayaks
- ☐ _____
- ☐ _____
- ☐ _____
- ☐ _____
- ☐ _____
- ☐ _____
- ☐ _____
- ☐ _____
- ☐ _____

*Keep a copy at your home office and be sure to give the make, model and replacement cost to your insurance company.

Basic Closing Checklist

- [ ] Clean out refrigerator and freezer
- [ ] Throw away/use all perishable food
- [ ] Pack all paint cans, wine bottles, soda cans, etc that could explode in winter
- [ ] Do not leave cereal or grain
- [ ] Clean out cupboards and wash with mild soap and water
- [ ] Wash counters and floor
- [ ] Store all bedding and clothes in heavy-duty plastic bin & add a few pieces of cedar
- [ ] Block off flues and stove pipes—leave a note to remind you it is there!
- [ ] Close dampers tightly or block off pipes
- [ ] Cover windows
- [ ] Remove all fire hazards
- [ ] Take home all valuables
- [ ] Wrap the shrubs
- [ ] Stack lawn furniture

- [ ] Take in all other outdoor equipment
- [ ] Bring in the dock
- [ ] Stack inside furniture
- [ ] Turn off water/heating system
- [ ] Shut off electricity/gas
- [ ] Forward mail
- [ ] Turn off phone
- [ ] Say goodbye to neighbors!
- [ ] _____
- [ ] _____
- [ ] _____
- [ ] _____
- [ ] _____
- [ ] _____
- [ ] _____
- [ ] _____

Sample Rental Application

Knotty Pine Camp, 233 Turn Key Road, Big Little Island, Our Beautiful State

Thank you for your interest in renting Knotty Pine Camp. This application will be your tentative reservation until we confirm the dates are available and check your references. Your deposit will be refunded if Knotty Pine Camp is not available for rent.

Rental Terms

1. Knotty Pine, the 3-bedroom cabin, 6-person maximum, is available from July-September for $1200.00 a week, starting Saturday at 4:00 p.m. and ending Saturday at 11:00 a.m.
2. A $300.00 security deposit must be mailed with this application.
3. Knotty Pine is fully furnished with 3 double beds, bed linens, towels, hot and cold water, fireplace, a small stack of wood, a charcoal grill, kitchen stove, refrigerator, sink and basic kitchen utensils, plus a canoe, paddles and two adult life jackets.
4. Utilities and garbage removal (two barrels) is included in the rent.
5. Knotty Pine must be left clean and all linens put in a laundry bag by the door.
6. No pets or smoking allowed.
7. Long distance calls must be made by a calling card. Local calls are free.

Name _____

Home Phone _____ Work Phone _____

Current Address _____

_____

Name and Relationship of all Renters _____

_____

Want to Rent the Camp: _____ Deposit Due: $300.00

Past Property Rented _____

Contact for that Property _____ Phone _____

Reference _____ Phone _____

Reference _____ Phone _____

Emergency Contact _____ Phone _____

(You may want to ask for Social Security Number and Driver's License Number and if you rent often, you may want to consider credit checks.)

Let us know what suggestions, tips or ideas you may have by filling out the survey on the next page. You will have a chance to win a beautiful picnic set. Enjoy the book, we had fun putting it together—now, we're off to the beach.

Win a Picnic Set! Just Fill Out Our Survey

We want to thank you for filling out our survey, it is greatly appreciated. Drawing for the picnic basket sets will be on January 15th and June 15th.

Name _____

Address _____

City _____State _____ Zip _____

Phone _____

Location of Camp, Cottage or Cabin _____

Type: (circle) Summer Only   Winter Only   All Season   Other _____

How Much Time Do You Spend There? _____

Do You Rent Your Place Out? Yes or No

How did you hear about *Camps Cottages and Cabins?*_____

Where did you purchase this book?

___ Bookstore ___Specialty Store ___ Our Web Site ___ Our 1-800 Number

___Received as a Gift ____ Other _____

Is there any additional information that would be useful in our next edition of *Camps, Cottages and Cabins?* (Please feel free to send a separate sheet of information)

How has Camps, Cottages and Cabins helped you?

Would you recommend the book to a friend? Yes or No

What other books about *Camps, Cottages and Cabins* would you be interested in?

____ Easy Cooking ____ Simple Decorating _____ Product Resource Book

____ Picture Book of Camps, Cottages and Cabins ____Other _____

I give Happy Hollow Promotions and the *Camps, Cottages and Cabins* series permission to quote me from this survey.

Signature _____ Date _____

Please mail to: Happy Hollow Promotions, P.O. Box 5152, Burlington, VT 05402

Easy Order Form

Telephone Orders: Call Toll Free: 1 (800) 860-5813 (9-5 Eastern Standard Time)
Online Orders: loveyourcottage.com
Fax Orders: Fax this form to: 802-985-9399
Postal Orders: Happy Hollow Promotions, P.O. Box 5152, Burlington, VT 05402
(Make Check Payable to: Happy Hollow Promotions)

Mailing Address:

Name: _____

Address: _____

City _____ State _____ Zip _____

Telephone: _____

If a Gift: Note to Say: _____

_____

_____

_____

Book Price: $21.95 each $ _____

Sales Tax: Please add 5% for book(s) shipped to Vermont address. $ _____

Shipping: $4.00 for the first book, $3.00 for each additional book. $ _____

                                              Total $ _____

For a pop singer or group, being photographed is a vital part of the pop process. The result can be a visual manifesto: this is what we are, what we want to be, where we're from and where we're going; these are our influences; this is what we want to say.

At the beginning, in the Fifties, it was maybe more innocent. You were either sexy and rebellious or the boy/girl next door (or somehow both). Then, The Beatles came along and suddenly art was on the agenda. John Lennon had been to art school and the influence of the art schools on British pop from the Sixties onwards was immense: if you were producing pop, it was gonna be presented as pop art. After Robert Freeman's cover for *With the Beatles* (1963), pop photography ceased to be simply reportage or 'publicity' but became an intentional collaboration between the photographer and the photographed with the aim of making a statement about the music, the philosophy behind it, the fame. The thrill of emergence, the quasi-royal ubiquitousness of established fame, the imperial phase of world domination, the disciplined strategies of survival, are each encapsulated in new images: a statement is issued.

In the Seventies and early Eighties, the statement was often about gender. The most resolutely heterosexual musician might happily collude in creating a feminised image of himself. In the late Eighties and the Nineties, the apparently iconic visual statement could probably be read as ironic.

The past is always with us. Every generation finds it own way of dealing with Billy Fury's (or Elvis's) gold lamé suit or Keith Richards' black mascara or punk's cut-up fashion and slogans.

All of this does not apply to all varieties of pop star - many, even the majority, of pop musicians shun the personality cult of the pop star - but it tends to be true of those who want their music to mean more.

This century-end survey of the contribution made by British acts and British photographers to the iconography of pop music spans forty-one years. It is illustrated by fifty photographs taken by top photographers, and serves also as a short history of British pop photography. The selection leans heavily towards chart success and image-led acts who have had an enduring visual impact based on their portraiture and singles chart success. Whenever possible the choice of an iconic or definitive image is taken from an early moment in the career of the artist featured.

Pop, for us, begins in November 1958 when Cliff Richard's first record 'Move It' reached number two in the charts. With its distinctive guitar riff and Cliff's American influenced vocal phasing, 'Come on pretty baby/ let's a move it and a groove it...' provided Britain with its first home-grown teen pop icon. Although a writer for the *New Musical Express* complained of his 'violent hip-swinging' and 'crude exhibitionism', this only helped to confirm his rock and roll credentials with a legion of screaming teenage fans exulting in the eighteen-year-old's uninhibited sexuality . *NME* readers nominated him in force as 'Favourite New Singer' of the year so he could appear at a poll-winners' event. The Lionel Bart-written 'Livin' Doll' was his first number one. Derek Allen's studio portrait was one of eight poses taken, two others appearing on the front and back cover of his 1959 *Oh Boy! it's Cliff Richard* tour programme. In 1997 Lorenzo Agius would achieve his digital Spice Girl portraits for the *Spiceworld* poster with the same few frames .

Forty years later, Cliff, the rock and roller of 1958-9 would, with fellow pop people Paul McCartney and Elton John, become a 'Sir', and the twenty-three-year old veteran ex-Take That member Robbie Williams, with his three 1999 Brit Awards, would inherit Cliff's mantle as the new King of Pop; the deep-voiced Helen Shapiro and Cerys Matthews are the equivalent Pop Queens. Closing this survey is Hamish Brown's photograph of Robbie Williams with dyed blond hair and, like Cliff, wearing a small cross on a chain around his neck. After a wild period Robbie's three major hits in a year encompass their own pop history: an Elton John-like 'Angels', a Neil Hannon and Neil Tennant-backed Pet Shop Boyish 'No Regrets' and the James Bond/John Barry inspired 'Millennium' (Barry did much to help launch Adam Faith's breakthrough in 1959): 'We've got stars directing our fate/ And we're praying its not too late.../Millennium'. Though the stars referred are in the celestial plane the alternative pop icon meaning is equally valid for the influence that pop stars exert.

Iconic status in pop is achieved by the combination of many elements: image, presence, personality and musical talent. As in the theatre and cinema a name change is often crucial. Harry Webb found fame by adopting two first names, one borrowed from a friend at the Two I's coffee bar, to become Cliff Richard; Reg Dwight and Georgios Panayiotou similarly became Elton John and George Michael. Terence Nelhams chose two first names from a book of boys'names and a book of girls' names to become Adam Faith. David Jones had to change his name in 1966 to avoid the confusion with the lead singer of the American-manufactured group The Monkees, and became David Bowie.

Hairstyles and make-up have played equally important roles in the definition of images. Cliff and Billy Fury had Elvis-inspired styles and Adam Faith's early image was based on James Dean. Sixties groups rebelled with the long-haired Beatles, and the unkempt Rolling Stones. Pop girls Helen Shapiro and Dusty Springfield had piled-high hairstyles as unique selling points. 1980s gender-bending produced Annie Lennox and her mannish crop which complemented Boy George's decorative plaits. George Michael took sharp suits and patented designer stubble as his template for image changes. In the Nineties, Prodigy have reinvented and updated the Sex Pistols' style.

Modern pop iconography was first celebrated in a gallery context by Sue Davies, founder-director of the Photographers' Gallery in May 1981. 'Pop People' surveyed thirty years of pop history and was drawn from the archives of two key photographers Harry Hammond (covering 1951-1963) and Gered Mankowitz (covering 1963-1981). The exhibition broke attendance records, with 62,000 visitors in three weeks; this,together with a book published in 1984 (reprinted in 1990), confirmed the continued interest in these historic moments of pop culture.

Hammond, the 'father of pop photography', learnt his craft in a fashionable London portrait studio before the Second World War but his pop photographs, in contrast to those of Mankowitz ,were shot entirely on location, at concerts, in dressing rooms and on the sets of the first television programmes to feature pop music. These shows started and encouraged the whole pop phenomenon. Jack Good's *6.5 Special* ran for two years from 1956-8 before being succeeded by his next show, *Oh Boy!*, which helped launched Cliff Richard's career; elsewhere regular exposure on *Drumbeat* helped give Adam Faith his first number one in 1959 with 'What Do You Want (If You Don't Want Money?)'. ABC's *Thank Your Lucky Stars* went nationwide in September 1961, and on New Year's Day, 1964, *Top of the Pops* was first broadcast. Harry Goodwin remained resident photographer for the show for nine years. David Redfern, who took the portrait of Sandie Shaw used on her first album, did so on the set of *Ready,Steady,Go!*, where other photographers such as David Wedgbury, Val Wilmer and Dezo Hoffman would also find their subjects.

One of Billy Fury's many iconic images is the cover of his *Halfway to Paradise* LP. It was taken by Fayer of Bond Street (late of Vienna), one of a number of studio professionals who shaped the image of early pop performers. Other important photographers worked occasionally in pop. In the Sixties Cecil Beaton photographed The Walker Brothers and The Rolling Stones, as did Terence Donovan, who later produced style statements for Bros and Robert Palmer. Dusty Springfield's early publicity photographs were taken by 'Vivienne', before she turned to the legendary Czech-born show-business photographer Dezo Hoffman for a series of key images that defined her look in the 1960s.

Hoffman had begun his career as a clapper-boy in Prague on Hedy Lamarr's 1933 film *Ecstasy* and on arrival in England in 1940, worked as a war photographer. In the Fifties he photographed celebrities such as Dietrich, Monroe and Chaplin and joined *Record Mirror* as star photographer in 1955, becoming The Beatles' official photographer from 1962. It was Hoffman who created the images that adorned souvenirs from tin trays to wallpaper, produced to satisfy the demands of burgeoning Beatlemania. Hoffman also documented the early Rolling Stones, and only fell out with The Beatles in their drug phase. Hoffman's career finds its mirror in Brian Aris, who covered wars and global catastrophes before turning to celebrity and pop portraiture in the mid 1970s. Aris would later create a series of images for George Michael from *Wham!* to the *Ladies and Gentlemen...* compilation. Michael's acute style consciousness harks back to the importance paid to image as seen in album covers by top Sixties groups.

Realising this early on, The Beatles and their management selected their photographers carefully. Eschewing the first choice of a Hoffman shot taken outside their recording studio, they used instead a carefully-posed portrait by Angus McBean for the important first album *Please Please Me*. Shot on the staircase at EMI's offices in Manchester Square, the pose was reprised many years later by McBean for the 'Blue' singles compilation album, with now bearded Beatles hanging over the same stairwell.

Robert Freeman, one of the emergent younger talents created the most iconic of early Beatle photographs, for their second album *With The Beatles*. It was taken against a maroon curtain in a Bournemouth hotel dining-room during one of their tours. Shot in black and white, it emulated Freeman's jazz photographs, but was an unusual image for a pop album cover. John, George and Paul appear on the top row almost silhouetted, the trademark haircuts and black turtleneck sweaters emphasising this artfully contrived image. Ringo, who joined the group last, is placed below them on the right to balance the title and text on the top left of the sleeve: the result was a compelling graphic composition. Freeman also shot *Rubber Soul*, *Hard Days' Night* and *Help!* covers. From early on, The Beatles themselves were aware of the importance, not only of photography, but of the photographer: in 1963, Paul McCartney told Michael Braun, 'We work much harder with someone like Robert Freeman or (Norman) Parkinson than with the nationals who only want a cheesy grin....' As Neil Tennant says in his foreword, these photographers' images set a standard that inspired and raised the art of record sleeve portraiture, photography and design.

As the Beatles' chief chart rival, The Rolling Stones first album cover shows them dimly-lit against a black background. Photographed by Nicholas Wright, it established their darker image. Their second album, shot by David Bailey continued the menacing agenda through their scowling poses. For their third album, *Out of Our Heads* (1965), Andrew Loog Oldham commissioned Gered Mankowitz who had come to his attention through his 1964 photographs of another of his artists, Marianne Faithfull.

In the 1980s Mankowitz shared a studio space with Red Saunders, where they traded as the Rembrandt Brothers. Here Eric Watson, straight from art college, first assisted, before becoming chief photographer for the wildly successful 1979-launched *Smash Hits* magazine, a return to glamour after the grit of punk which the black and white *NME* successfully fed into. *Smash Hits*' photographers of the1980s are a who's who of pop style photography, elsewhere luxuriant in the new 1980s style guides *The Face*, *Blitz* and *i D* which provided a gallery for new portraiture. The later Eighties saw the launch of more serious in-depth monthlies such as *Q*, *Mojo*, *Select* and the shorter-lived *Vox* (drawing in part on the pioneering American *Rolling Stone* of the late Sixties). They provided another platform for a maturing pop appreciation, not only of the music, but of its images, too.

From all these sources, the images on the following pages have been chosen by myself and my colleagues. We hope they will find some resonance in the collective pop memory. Enjoy.

Lorenzo Agius b.1962

Agius studied Art and Art History at the University of East Anglia, moved to London in 1983 and started to assist in photography. In 1989 he became a freelance photographer specialising in fashion and portraits. His work has been published in *Vanity Fair, Vogue, Elle* and *i-D*. His film poster commissions are instantly recognisable and include *Trainspotting, Jude, Spiceworld, Trees Lounge* and *Sliding Doors*. Agius' portraits of Ralph Fiennes and Kate Winslet are on display in the National Portrait Gallery's Twentieth Century Galleries.

Derek Allen b.1925

Allen was born in Reigate, Surrey and was introduced to photography through a fortuitous game of golf between his school Maths master and local photographer Frank Woods. On the strength of this experience he moved to Carlton Studios in London where he worked for three years, doing still lives for trade magazines before joining the RAF. In the early 1950s Allen found premises for a studio in St.James's, London next door to the impresario Sandor Gorlinsky. Here he was encouraged to start taking pictures of conductors including Sir Malcolm Sargent. Building up an archive of music-related people, he was approached by EMI and asked to work for them directly which he continued to do for the remainder of his long career.

Brian Aris b.1946

Born in Kilburn, London, at fifteen Aris had his first newspaper front page with a picture of a fire that he had taken with a camera given to him for a birthday present. In the early 1960s he photographed many of the major Sixties groups who appeared at The Ballroom, Gaumont State Cinema in Kilburn for the *Kilburn Times*. His big break came in 1969, freelancing for the *Daily Mirror* when he covered the arrival of the British Army in Ulster. Commissions for global news events followed including the Middle East War. He worked in Vietnam, leaving two days before the fall in April 1975. He later changed direction moving into celebrity portraiture, concentrating on the rock and pop scene. He was in Africa when he met Bob Geldof, and became the official photographer of Live Aid in 1984. More recently he has taken golden wedding photographs of Queen Elizabeth and Prince Phillip.

Alan Ballard b.1943

Ballard's grandfather was the sports editor at the *Evening Standard*, so when Ballard was sixteen he left school and worked on the picture desk for a year. In 1960 he went to assist the famous fashion photographer John Cowan in his studio in Chelsea. He travelled with Cowan for three years and began to take more photographs which were published in the *Sunday Times*. In 1963 he began to work for the paper from his studio in Primrose Hill. He was represented by Hatton (now Scope) which was considered to work with the most respected photographers and credited names in the international press. In 1966 he became involved with film and worked on the publicity shots for Ken Russell's films *The Devils, Women in Love* and *Tommy*. In 1974 he became the official photographer to the Bay City Rollers. He has worked with musicians including Bryan Ferry, Elton John, Slade and Status Quo.

Edgar Brind

Brind was a celebrity photographer working in the late 1950s and 1960s. His portraits of pop stars such as Russ Conway and Herman's Hermits appeared in the press, on record sleeves and annuals of the time. Connected with Murray's nightclub he is also known for his glamour photographs of Mandy Rice-Davies.

Harry Borden b.1965

Borden was born in New York but grew up on a pig farm in Devon. He is the son of an advertising art director and a celebrity chef. He attended Plymouth School of Art from 1985-1987 where he studied photography. Borden moved to London shortly afterwards, where he worked as an assistant for Lester Bookbinder, Barney Edwards, David Montgomery and John Swannell on a variety of projects including advertising work. Attracted by the work of Anton Corbijn and Steve Pyke he approached the *NME* who used his portrait of Tom Petty. He is now gaining a more global presence but still works regularly for *Select, Q*, the *Independent on Sunday* and is one of the main photographers for *Observer* 'Life'.

Hamish Brown b.1968

Brown bought his first camera in 1996 with the money he won from a radio competition. He attended the London School of Fashion in London for six weeks before deciding to work for himself. Gaining valuable experience by assisting Steve Gullick (official photographer for Prodigy) and using the considerable contacts he had in the music industry, (being a musician himself) he built up a portfolio of images of music people. In 1997 he started to work for the *NME* covering live gigs. His cover work for the magazine has included portraits of Massive Attack, Primal Scream and The Beastie Boys. After being approached by Robbie Williams' record company to go on tour, he built a relationship with the star and many of his portraits can be seen in the official Robbie Williams book - *Let Me Entertain You* (1998).

Brian Cooke b.1947

Cooke attended Hull College of Art where he gained formal photographic training. His first job was as a photographic technician and lecturer at Teeside College of Art. Always passionate about music, he photographed many local groups and in 1971 moved to London to pursue his career. It was in the same year that he set up Visualeyes - a company that offered photographic and design services to record companies. During the early days of this company Cooke took pictures of a variety of musicians including Jethro Tull, Robert Palmer and Bryan Ferry. He took the first ever press pictures for Roxy Music and went on to do album covers for them including the experimental design for *Inside Out*. Cooke also set up the company Cooke Key Associates which became the design agency to Virgin Records. Cooke Key were credited with over 150 album covers. In 1981 he decided to focus more on stills photography which took place during the shooting of videos.

Kevin Cummins b.1953

Born in Manchester, Cummins attended Salford College in the mid 1970s where he gained a degree in Industrial Art and Design, concentrating on photography. Whilst teaching at the college a year after graduating Cummins used the college equipment to take pictures of the musicians involved in the vibrant Manchester music scene and bands who played at the Electric Circus - such as Buzzcocks. It was the heyday of punk and the *NME* first used his images in a double page spread about Manchester bands. They continued to publish him as their Northern contact until 1987 when he moved south to London. For the next ten years Cummins continued to work for them on a full-time basis. He now works for a variety of publications including *Esquire, Newsweek* and *Observer* 'Life'.

Andy Earl b.1955

Born and brought up in Sussex, at sixteen Earl went to work for James Hunt as a mechanic. He attended Worthing College of Art to do a foundation course and from 1974 to 1977 and studied art at Trent Polytechnic where he was encouraged to use photography as a tool for artistic expression. During his second year Earl won a photography scholarship to study in Baltimore, where he was strongly influenced by American colour photography. In 1978 Earl was offered a show at the Photographer's Gallery, London and the following year represented Britain in the Venice Bienniale. On the strength of his Photographer's Gallery show Malcolm McLaren offered him a commission for the controversial *Bow Wow Wow* album cover. A hugely successful career within the international music business followed, including over twenty videos for musicians such as The Rolling Stones. His work is characteristic but diverse, often incorporating dramatic natural backdrops and architectural elements to create a surrealistic effect.

Chris Floyd b.1968

Floyd started photography when he was fourteen, using his father's camera and setting up a darkroom in his garage. In 1988 he attended North East Surrey College of Technology for six months to do a BTec photography course. During the holidays he got a job in a studio in Chelsea and stayed on working as an assistant. Three years after he left the studio he phoned The Orb's manager and convinced him to let him take their picture. He took the work to *Select*, where work followed including portraits of Reeves and Mortimer. He then went on to work for *Loaded* in 1994 continuing until 1996. One of his first jobs for them was a week in America with The Verve; he continued to work with the band until 1998. His work is now published in *GQ*, American *Esquire, Flaunt, The Face*, the *Guardian Weekend* and the *Sunday Times Magazine*.

Jill Furmanovsky b.1953

Furmanovsky was born in Rhodesia and in 1965 moved to London with her family. Her first picture of a pop icon was of her two school friends with Paul McCartney outside his house in 1967. Always acutely aware of the music industry, she recognised the links between musicians and art school. Pointed toward textile design whilst at Harrow School of Art, Furmanovsky then attended Central School of Art and Design (1972-1974). Using their equipment and blagging her way into gigs she started to work as the Rainbow Theatre's official photographer until 1979. She became a regular contributor to the music press in publications such as *Smash Hits* and *The Face* during the 1980s and early 1990s. Her book on The Human League was published in 1982. She has regularly photographed icons such as Sting, Chrissie Hynde and Oasis. Her images of Oasis formed a book titled *Was there Then* published in 1997 and was accompanied by a major travelling exhibition. Her autobiographical *The Moment* was published in 1997.

Harry Goodwin b.1924
Born in Manchester. In 1943, when he was nineteen, Goodwin was called up to join the RAF. For seven years he travelled and started taking photographs. His first images to be published once back in England were glamour shots of a beauty pageant which were used on the front page of the *Daily Mirror*. In 1964 he worked as a scene shifter at the BBC and from here he started taking pictures of presenters and musicians such as Val Doonican, Ken Dodd and Harry Worth which were used in the *Radio Times*. In 1964 the new music show *Top of the Pops* commissioned him to take stills for the show which were used to illustrate the chart count-down. Goodwin worked on the show for nine years in both the Manchester and London studios. From 1973 onwards Goodwin concentrated on photographing footballers.

Steve Gullick b.1967
Gullick never considered that he would be anything other than a music photographer. He first started using his pictures for fanzines for friends' bands whilst studying photography in the Midlands. Shortly afterwards he dropped out of college and in 1990 started to work for *Sounds*. A year later the magazine folded and Gullick moved to *Melody Maker*. It was around this time that the grunge scene happened and Gullick was involved with a number of the bands. He regularly photographed Nirvana until Kurt Cobain's death in 1994.

After five years at *Melody Maker* he began to work for the *NME*. His work is also published in *Uncut* and *Kerrang!* featuring American bands such as Smog, Palace and Mercury Rev. His first book *Pop Book 1* was published in 1995. Gullick is the official photographer for Prodigy and his pictures of Nirvana will be exhibited at the Proud Gallery in November 1999.

Harry Hammond b.1920
Universally hailed as the 'Father of Pop Photography', Hammond was born in the East End of London and was apprenticed to Fleet Street in 1934. From here he gained experience with one of the leading London portraitists, Bassano Studios in Dover Street. In the late 1940s after service as a war photographer, Hammond went freelance away from the studio. Starting with general news features he quickly progressed to photographing musical personalities, concentrating on location shots. For more than thirty years Hammond photographed leading personalities on both sides of the Atlantic. His book *Pop People* was published in 1984. Hammond's work is in numerous collections including the V&A (who hold his original negatives) and The National Portrait Gallery.

Bay Hippisley b.1950
Son of Pamela Booth, the society portrait photographer, who was an ex-pupil of Rudolf Koppitz the legendary 1930s art photographer. From 1968-1971 Hippisley attended Regent Street Polytechnic, originally to study film, then taking an option in stills photography. His photo-journalism was published in the *Telegraph*. From 1978 he spent five years working in his Sackville Street studio, on advertising work, and collaborated with the designer Pete Barrett, photographing the sixteen year old Lisa Stansfield for her first record. He also took The Pretenders *2000 Miles* cover, using models. The success of the record led to doing campaigns for John Player Special cigarettes. In 1983 he photographed Bananarama at Pineapple Dance Studios for the cover of their album *Deep Sea Skiving*. From 1980 to 1997 he was the official Sindy photographer and later Action Man. He is currently concentrating on advertising and commercial work.

Dezo Hoffman 1910 -1986
Hoffman's career started as a newsreelman when he covered the Spanish Civil War. During the Second World War he worked for the Ministry of Information covering the war from Burma to El Alamein and was a member of the Czech army. After the war he did film work which eventually led him to doing work for the *Record Mirror* and *Melody Maker*, as well as working as house photographer at the London Palladium. In 1962 Hoffman went up to Liverpool to take pictures of The Beatles and was captivated. He had so much material on them so that when eight months later they broke, Hoffman was able to supply the press with the images. From his studio in Gerard Street he worked with them until 1965 and did the famous 'jump shot' for the *Twist and Shout* EP. He helped shape their clean cut early image and his intimate style can be seen in his book *With the Beatles*.

Klanger and Boink
Wolfgang Klanger (Paul Jeff) b.1957
Betsy Boink (Elizabeth McDonough) b.1965
After meeting at University of Derby (1984-1987) whilst studying Fine Art Photographic Studies, Klanger and Boink became a partnership in 1988. Their approach was strongly influenced by pop bands of the time such as Kraftwerk and Devo. They first started to photograph pop personalities for *Time Out* - commissions included Shonen Knife, the Japanese pop outfit. Whilst working on the art direction for a video for Fuzzbox (1990) they became involved with musicians working under the Warner label. Through this they photographed Marc Almond for the cover of his hit single 'Jacky' and the album *Tenement Symphony* (both in 1991). Based in Cardiff, they regularly photographed pop personalities and designed the set for the *Mal Pope Show* shown on BBC Wales. Klanger and Boink officially broke up in 1995 to pursue solo careers, but like so many of the bands which first influenced their whole concept they are currently enjoying a revival.

Angus McBean 1904-1990
McBean is renowned for his theatrical and inventive photography of the 1930s and 1940s. Copied and imitated all his life, his influence, especially in advertising, is still prominent today. In 1934 he was assistant to the Bond Street portraitist Hugh Cecil. In 1935 he opened his own studio; and his imaginative and bold style made him stand out and his work was soon being published in

a variety of glossy magazines. The infamous 1936 Surrealist exhibition had a dramatic effect on McBean and he started to use many of the styles and effects, seen in his portraits of theatrical stars. After World War Two he opened a bigger studio in Covent Garden, and during the 1940s and 1950s was inundated with commissions from major theatre companies. In the early 1960s he photographed the Beatles for their first LP. In the 1980s his importance in the place of British photography was realised and he enjoyed numerous exhibitions, TV documentaries and a renewed demand for his work.

Gered Mankowitz b.1946
Born in London, the son of playwright and screen writer Wolf Mankowitz - the author of Cliff Richard's first film *Expresso Bongo*, Mankowitz's first professional photographs were taken in 1962 in Barbados for British West Indian Airways. By 1963 he had opened his first studio in the West End of London. Through various contacts he was able to build up a large client base of musicians, and his work included early shots of Marianne Faithfull and the Rolling Stones. The cover *Out of Our Heads* (1965) was a turning point in his career and he toured with the Stones to America taking many of the iconic images so often associated with the band; he was their 'official' photographer until 1967. Mankowitz continues to photograph musicians for publications such as *Mojo*.

Barry Marsden b.1954
Barry Marsden was born in South Yorkshire. He attended Loughborough College of Art from 1972 to 1976, where he gained a first-class honours degree in Painting, with commendations in History of Art and Electronic Music. He had no experience with photography until 1981 when he was thirty years old, and decided that it was the right visual medium for him. His big break came with *Time Out* when they used his photographs of football managers that he had been pursuing as a personal project. He has since been commissioned for a variety of magazines and papers including the *Sunday Telegraph* and the *Mail On Sunday's* 'Night and Day'. Pop icons were taken for *Vox* magazine. He was recently commissioned by the NPG to photograph thirty leading chefs and food-related people to be shown in the new café.

Keith Morris b.1938

After reading Maths at the University of London and travelling in Asia, Morris felt that he needed to do something that satisfied the technical and creative side of his character. He saw photography as the tool for this and from 1965 to 1967 attended Guildford Art School to study it, leaving a term early in order to assist David Bailey for a few months before John Swannell took over as his main assistant. In 1968 Morris became involved with *Oz* the underground magazine. A shot of the 1960s group The Incredible String Band was noticed by Island Records and an association followed which lasted until the 1980s. Perhaps his most iconic image of this time was of Nick Drake. In 1972 Morris was the official photographer for T.Rex, touring and with them, shooting their record sleeves and promotional posters. Morris has covered a wide range of pop stars from Led Zeppelin to Barry Manilow.

Terry O'Neill b.1938

O'Neill left school at fourteen with dreams of becoming a drummer in America. However, when he was eighteen he had to do his National Service. Afterwards he started to work for BOAC in their technical photographic unit: this involved going to art school once a week, and O'Neill's interest in photojournalism grew. In 1959 O'Neill took a picture of a man sleeping at the airport: the following day the picture was on the front page of the *Sunday Dispatch* as the sleeping man turned out to be 'Rab' Butler, the Home Secretary. From 1960 to 1963 O'Neill worked for the *Daily Sketch*, and having established a name for himself went freelance, for *Vogue*, *Paris Match* and *Rolling Stone*. During the 1960s and 1970s he became one of the world's most published photographers. O'Neill often spotted talents and stuck with his subjects such as Elton John and David Bowie.

Steve Pyke b.1957

Pyke moved to London from his home town Leicester in 1977. Having toured for a year with his band the RTRs, he felt it was time to move to London and became involved with the punk scene. He was singer in a variety of bands and became involved with the setting up of an independent record label, as well as a variety of 'fanzines'. In 1979 he became a photographer, and from 1981 to 1984 worked continuously for a diverse mixture of publications including *The Face* and the *NME*. His first assignment for *The Face* was to photograph John Lydon for its cover. Pyke's work has been shown internationally and is in collections world wide. He is currently photographing the astronauts who walked on the moon and the people that got them there: the project coincides with the thirtieth anniversary of the first moonwalk and will be published in a number of forms including a TV documentary.

Mick Rock b.1948

Mick Rock graduated from Cambridge University with a degree in Modern Languages. Soon afterwards he attended London Film School where his interest in photography grew. In the late Sixties he became fascinated with faces, and through contacts started to do publicity shots for local bands such as The Pretty Things. In 1972 he met David Bowie during his Ziggy Stardust mutation and became Bowie's 'official' photographer - mainly due to the fact he was one of the few photographers interested in following his rise to fame. Prominence and cache in the world of rock photography continued to strengthen and he produced some of the most iconic images of the 1970s including artists such as Lou Reed (*Transformer* album cover), Queen, Blondie, Thin Lizzy and Mott the Hoople. Between 1977 and 1983 he divided his time between New York and London. He now lives and works in New York and is currently working on books on David Bowie, Queen and Glam to accompany his already published book *Mick Rock - A Photographic Record 1969-1980*.

Sheila Rock

American born but based in London, Rock's photographic career was launched through the commissions given to her by Nick Logan, editor of *The Face*. Starting in the late 1970s Rock's pictures of The Clash and Generation X were published and she continued to work for the magazine on a regular basis until the late 1980s. Concentrating on punk and enjoying the artistic freedom of working with such bands she also complemented her documentary style with more classically posed portraits in black and white. She is currently working on a personal project of portraits of Tibetan monks as well as doing advertising work and posters for the National Opera.

Pennie Smith

Born in London, Smith went to Twickenham Art School in the late 1960s where she studied graphics and fine art. She first worked on *Friendz* magazine with Barney Bubbles and Nick Kent, and her first major commission was to cover Led Zeppelin touring in the early 1970s. Smith worked on the *NME* as staff photographer until the early 1980s, having numerous covers and becoming an icon herself, influencing a younger generation photographers. She left the publication when the direction and format changed to colour. In 1980 she published a best-selling book on *The Clash, Before and After*. She still lives and works in the railway station she bought and converted when she was a student, and freelances in black and white reportage.

John Stoddart b.1957

Born in Liverpool, Stoddart became a trained sniper in the army (1972-1975). It was during this time he became interested in photography, inspired by extensive travelling. On his return to Liverpool he started taking pictures of local musicians such as Echo and The Bunnymen and Wah! which were subsequently published in the *Liverpool Echo*. The *NME* started to use him as their Liverpool contact, he began to build up contacts with record companies, especially EMI for whom he did record covers for a variety of bands. Stoddart started photographing Frankie Goes to Hollywood in the early 1980s and followed them throughout their career. In 1982 he moved to London and set up a studio and during the mid 1980s worked primarily for the music press and for record companies. This lead onto movie stills and posters, including *Letter To Breshznev*. Stoddart now works for a variety of journals internationally including *Vanity Fair, Loaded, Esquire* and *Harpers & Queen*. His book *Its Nothing Personal* was published in 1997 and he is currently working on an exhibition titled *Peep World - Women Only*.

Peter Vernon b.1946

During his last year at school Vernon became interested in photography and art and in 1963 went to Croydon College of art to study Fine Art. It was here that he decided to become a photographer and after he left he went on to assist Lindsay Willby for a year at the fashion studios 'Tunbridge', then situated off Regent Street. After a series of other photographic-related jobs he returned to Croydon Art College in 1968 to teach and stayed there until 1971. That year he joined EMI as their resident photographer. During this time he photographed all aspects of the industry, including gold and platinum disc presentations, recording sessions, contract signings and band line ups, as well as numerous album covers including Marvin Gaye, Diana Ross and Cliff Richard. In 1978 he went freelance, concentrating on pictures within the music industry.

Eric Watson b.1955

Born in Newcastle, Watson attended Hornsey School of Art from 1977-1980 where he gained a B.A (Hons) in Fine Art and Art History: fellow students included Stuart Goddard (Adam Ant) and Mike Barson from Madness. Unusually for the time he was encouraged to use photography, even though he was on a painting course. Straight after college he assisted The Rembrand Brothers (Gered Mankowitz and Red Saunders). In the year before he joined *Smash Hits* in 1981, he worked for Stiff Records doing covers for Madness, and OMD and the inside cover of *Sid Sings* soon after the death of Sid Vicious. Up until 1986 Watson was the *Smash Hits* main photographer. He subsequently concentrated on videos, directing musicians such as Rod Stewart, Chris Rea, Holly Johnson, Pet Shop Boys and Dusty Springfield. He is currently concentrating on writing and pursuing fine art photography.

David Wedgbury 1937-1998

Wedgbury is best known as the head photographer for Decca records, based in Black Prince Road in Lambeth, supervising a staff of twelve and working throughout the 1960s. His 1993 book *As Years Go By* documents his career from the early 1960s Liverpool scene to his iconic portraits of Marianne Faithfull, The Rolling Stones and particularly The Who and The Small Faces. His portraits appeared uncredited on their record sleeves and defined their images. In the 1970s he turned to painting working for Victor Lowndes and the Playboy Club. A memorial exhibition of his work was held in October 1998 at the Chris Evans Well Hung gallery in Notting Hill.

Cliff Richard

1958

Derek Allen

The British pop scene was already well established by the late 1950s, born out of the skiffle craze and American rock and roll; the first TV pop show, *6.5 Special* had been running since 1956. But it was only with Cliff Richard that the country produced its own truly modern, young pop star as a teenage role model.

'From John O'Groats to Lands End the Cliff Richard name is a household word. Think of Pop songs. Think of Cliff Richard. Cliff, The Boyfriend of the year', announced the 1961 *Boyfriend* annual. Few could have guessed, from the Teddy boy, hip-swinging, proto-rebel image which raised Cliff Richard to stardom, that he would still be a marketable force forty years later. It is ironic - given its transient nature - that pop's Peter Pan was only ever fashionable once: here, with his pomade and smouldering good looks, the very essence of 1950s rock'n'roll. Cliff would remain outside the cycle of fashion; indeed, that is the reason for his longevity. Even now, he is the innocent face of pop, a memory of its infancy. As Michael Bracewell writes in *England Is Mine* (1997), Richards' 'represents youth as an Edenic state of being'. Like Elvis Presley, his image was adeptly if ubiquitously promoted in the medium of film, from the rebellious sneer of *Serious Charge* (1959) and 'wannabee rock star' in *Expresso Bongo* (1960), to *Summer Holiday* (1962), which hermetically sealed his virginal innocence for ever in the public imagination.

For photographer Derek Allen, his 1958 session with Cliff was the 'nicest one I can remember, very friendly, helpful - he was the perfect sitter, a pleasant young man doing a job in front of the camera.' In marked contrast to modern photographic marathons, the session in Allen's studio lasted just one hour, and he shot a mere ten exposures on a quarter-plate Soho reflex. 'He was just another of the EMI acts', recalls Allen. 'He got the same treatment as Ruby Murray whom I'd photographed the previous week - except she got more attention because I thought she had more potential.'

Adam Faith

Edgar Brind

1962

Coming out of the coffee bar scene of the late Fifties, Adam Faith (Terry Nelhams) had an unprecendented run of seven successive singles in the top five of the charts. A teen idol with a 'little-boy-lost' image, his blond hair, handsome face and yearning voice struck passion into teenage hearts, and powered a remarkable career on a trajectory from singing to acting to finance.

'I'm inclined to think that acting will be my real medium of acceptance' he announced in 1960, having already played a 'beatnik strummer' in *'Beat' Girl* (1960), a 'dynamic drama of youth mad about living for kicks!', in which Faith uttered the pivotal line, 'I ain't fightin no Teds, fightin's for squares...' In the Seventies he became a TV personality in *Budgie* - in platforms, check wool jacket and fake fur collar - and a smooth romantic lead in *Love Hurts*, meanwhile managing his own pop prodigy, Leo Sayer, and conducting business meetings over breakfast at Fortnum and Mason.

Faith wrote about his search for an image in his autobiography, *Act of Faith*: 'I wore out the mirror trying to figure out which bit of me would produce a change to impress Jack Good [the producer]. I needed something that didn't frighten the girls off but could look different enough to get me noticed. Then it struck me, my hair. I'd change my hair.' Hitherto heavily Brylcreem'd, Faith went to a barber in Chiswick called Eddie Jones 'who was getting a reputation for doing to men's hair what women took for granted: styling'. Jones washed out the Brylcreem. 'And out I slithered from Eddie's chair a new man. Without knowing it Eddie had created the Adam Faith trademark. That funny little crop, tight to the head, with a short fringe probably became my most recognizable feature'.

Faith was photographed by Edgar Brind in 1962 looking more like a movie star than a pop idol: the immaculate grooming might come straight out of a hairdressing ad, were it not for Brind's exquisite lighting and dynamic composition. The portrait was used for the album cover of *From Adam With Love*, 1962.

'Birkenhead's answer to Elvis Presley' made his name at Soho's 'Two Is' coffee bar, birthplace of British rock'n'roll. Having begun life in Liverpool 8 under the more prosaic name of Ronald Wycherly, he was seen at a concert in Liverpool by impresario Larry Parnes, who rechristened him Billy Fury because it made him sound wild. In fact, Fury was an essentially shy character, almost bemused by his success, a quality somehow reflected in his hunched-shoulder stance. Incipient heart disease gave him a faintly helpless, if not fatalistic air. 'He needed looking after', said one girlfriend. 'That was part of his attraction to women'.

Publicly Fury was the gyrating, microphone-grabbing idol of millions with songs such as 'Colette' and 'That's Love' (1960); privately, he retreated from fame. His iconic status was confirmed by the ten-inch album, *The Sound of Fury* (1960) followed by nine top ten singles in three years. Having become assimilated into the cultural mainstream with hits such as 'Halfway to Paradise' and 'Jealousy' (1961), Fury lost his cutting edge to Merseyside compatriots The Beatles (although he was, ironically, younger than all of them). Fury became a recluse in Wales for eight years, caring for wild birds, but remained a pivotal star, a bridge from the Fifties to the Sixties and beyond. Not only were his singing voice (and skinny frame) prescient of future stars such as David Bowie's, but his stage lamé became a symbol of what Michael Bracewell calls 'pop's alchemical promise to turn nobodys into big stars', passed from glam to punk to Eighties pop: from Elton John to ABC and Morrissey.

In 1973, Fury emerged from semi-retirement to appear in the rock'n'roll movie *That'll Be the Day* as Rocky Tempest, a virtual version of his former self. Strangely preserved, half-young, half-ancient reminder of pop's birth, his traces were remembered in such pop-born christenings as Iggy Pop, Johnny Thunders and Billy Idol. He died of heart disease in 1983, at the age of 41.

Harry Hammond's photograph shows Billy Fury and the Tornados at the *NME* Poll Winners' concert in April 1962. The Tornados - featuring the peroxide-blond Heinz - would later that year become the first British group to reach number one in the USA with 'Telstar'. The *NME* reported that Fury 'was welcomed with a fantastic ovation that reflected in no uncertain manner his current popularity. In his silver-grey lame suit he twisted through "Sticks and Stones". After "Halfway to Paradise", we were treated to the inimitable Fury gymnastics. Billy, too, had to rush off for an evening show, so he was given his award... and a spontaneous gift of a giant teddy bear from his fan club secretaries'.

With her back-combed bouffant adding height and her belting voice belying her slight frame, Shapiro's success heralded a new generation of female singing stars, but her pop career was all too short-lived, ending with her last Top Forty - 'Fever '64' - in 1964. However, Shapiro went on to become a respected jazz singer.

This picture was taken in 1962 (the session provided the cover for Shapiro's *'Tops' With Me* album) by Angus McBean, famous since the Thirties for his surrealist compositions, and for his portraits of theatre personalities. McBean photographed The Beatles for their first album cover (*Please Please Me*, 1963). Here he has put Shapiro literally on a pedestal - a modern Sixties glass-topped table - and arranged a spiky abstract halo behind, demonstrating his ability to move with the times, although his glamorous vision of his sitters did not concur with the encroaching realism of the decade.

In a medium as evanescent as pop, the name of Helen Shapiro is now almost forgotten, but the diminuitive singer with a formidable voice (and equally formidable hairdo) was the teen pop sensation of her day. Her incredibly youthful start predates present-day teen sensations (Billie, for instance), and indicates the strength of her appeal - she headlined a tour in 1963 for which her support band were The Beatles. Born in Bethnal Green, she was called 'foghorn' at school because of the masculine timbre of her voice. At fourteen, she made her first single for EMI - 'Please Don't Treat Me Like A Child' - which went straight into the Top Ten in 1961. By the end of the year, number ones with 'You Don't Know' and her signature tune, 'Walking Back To Happiness' had followed.

A contemporary billing for a New Zealand tour date (reproduced in *Helen Shapiro's New Book For Girls*, 1963) sums up her iconic status at the dawn of Britain's first fully pop-conscious decade, and trumpets her attraction as a role model and aspirational figure for a generation of girls just discovering the liberating joys of being a teenager in the 1960s: 'Britain's wonder girl!! Helen Shapiro. Top of the bill at the London Palladium! Star of motion picture "It's Trad, Dad" and "Play It Cool". Sensation of the vast Paris "Olympia!". Star of ITV's "Saturday Night At the Palladium" & her own radio & TV show."'

Brian Aris

With The Beatles, the British pop image switched from the pervasive influence of America (under which the likes of Cliff Richard and Billy Fury had evolved) and the notion of a youth-oriented extension of show business to a discrete, home-grown phenomenon. It was a crucial part of their appeal. 'You usually think of film stars, pop singers and so forth as living in glamorous places, Hollywood and so on', one contemporary fourteen-year-old girl told the *Observer,* 'But the Beatles aren't like that. It's Liverpool - where *Z-Cars* comes from.'

This was Merseybeat, and its success was specifically linked to a new spirit in 1960s Britain. As Beatlemania broke - adeptly stage-managed by ex-furniture salesman Brian Epstein - even national press editorials commented on their image. The *Daily Mirror's* prose sounds like an advert from the new commercial ITV station, and flies the flag for the first incarnation of cool Britannia: 'They're young, new. They're high-spirited, cheerful. What a change from the self-pitying moaners crooning their love-lorn tunes from the tortured shadows of lukewarm hearts. The Beatles are whacky. They wear their hair like a mop - but it's WASHED, it's super clean. So is their fresh young act. They don't have to rely on off-colour jokes about homos for their fun. Youngsters like the Beatles are doing a good turn for show business - and the rest of us - with their new sounds, new looks. GOOD LUCK, BEATLES!'

As John Lennon laconically observed to another journalist, 'Ours is a today image'. It was an image which would be used as a marketing tool in itself - quite outside their own control - resulting in a plethora of clothes, books, posters, bubblegum cards, Beatle wigs, boots, suits, china, toys - practically every artefact their likenesses could endorse. The Beatles, as the commercial product of a new youth-centric culture, had been truly commodified.

Brian Aris's portrait was taken backstage at The Ballroom, Gaumont State Cinema, Kilburn on April 9th 1963. For Aris, it was a remarkable introduction to 'rock and roll mayhem';the band themselves remained calm at the centre of the storm of hysteria around them. 'I was impressed at how well-groomed they were, and how professionally they responded to the camera', says Aris. 'Of course, by that stage, they were already well used to it.' Aris's portrait shows the group together, yet somehow looking apart, as if prescient of things to come: within their very uniformity - and the dynamic of the picture's composition - is a sense of the centrifugal force of fame which would eventually pull the group asunder. The coherent image of the foursome would not outlast the decade, but their influence would dominate pop for the rest of the century.

The Rolling Stones

1965

clockwise from top left

Charlie Watts
Keith Richards
Bill Wyman
Mick Jagger
Brian Jones

It is a measure of The Rolling Stones' iconic status that Gered Mankowitz's photograph looks so contemporary. From the Sixties to the Nineties, their style has been much emulated, not least by recent bands - Primal Scream, Stone Roses, Oasis, The Verve. The originals were as carefully positioned to represent youthful rebellion. The Stones were promoted by their manager, Andrew Loog Oldham as the 'anti-Beatles', rockers to the Merseysiders's mod-ish suits, ruffled where fellow bands seemed smooth, raw where their rivals appeared manufactured. An arch manipulator who had worked as publicist for Brian Epstein and Mary Quant, Oldham circulated the slogan 'Would you let your daughter go out with a Rolling Stone?'.

Photographers like Mankowitz benefited from a new spirit of artistic experimentation in the Sixties. They were encouraged both by young managers who saw the importance of their charges' image and its propagation, and by new art directors and designers at magazines who gave them the freedom to explore different ways of presenting pop groups. Moving away from the staged portraits of previous generations, they brought their subjects out of the studio and onto the streets as if to physically connect them with their audiences; to show that they were not artificial products of Brylcreem and tungsten lighting, but real people whom their fans could emulate.

Mankwitz shot this, the cover image for the *Out of Our Heads* album, opposite his studio in Piccadilly. The session also produced an image of the band caught in a builder's wire cage, thereby emphasising their feral appeal. 'It was all part of the first shoot I did with them', recalls the photographer. 'There was a huge office building going up next to Ormond Yard and I asked the foreman if it would be OK to bring a band along. They're posing in a gap created by two huge pieces of shuttering used to protect the building at night - I thought it would make an interesting shape. It's particularly interesting because they all have equal space, but Mick is almost on the edge, and Brian Jones is in the forefront. Brian was very charismatic and good-looking, but I don't recall any argy-bargy about who was the leader of the band. There wasn't much problem about who took the lead in photos. Andrew wanted to keep the five as equal figures.'

Mankowitz was 'completely knocked out when it was selected as a cover - it was an amazing coup, and confirmed my position with the band.' Then aged eighteen, Mankowitz was asked by Oldham to accompany the band on their second 1965 tour of the USA; he became the Stones' official photographer for the next three years.

Marianne Faithfull

1964

Gered Mankowitz

Few performers emerged from the 1960s with such a credible, iconic image as Marianne Faithfull's. From virginal scion of Mittel European aristocracy to protegé of the Rolling Stones' manager and ringmaster of Sixties rock decadence, Andrew Loog Oldham, Faithfull became the knowing, worldy alternative to her more commercial counterparts, part angel, part harlot, part heavenly-voiced chanteuse, summed up in her anthem to lost innocence, the Jagger-Richards penned 'As Tears Go By'. Her later descent (literally) into the gutters of Soho, and subsequently rehabilitation as a charismatic cabaret performer merely underlines her status as pop icon. 'I've gone through life standing there saying, "Look at me, aren't I pretty? Please buy me." Which is what I did as a pop singer, and I've done it with every man since, and I don't like to be like that anymore.'

Gered Mankowitz's portrait was taken at the Salisbury pub in St Martin's Lane as part of a session to promote her first album, provocatively entitled *Come My Way*. Mankowitz was impressed with the nascent Sixties icon. 'I was completely goo-goo for her', he recalls. 'Marianne was just so beautiful, and generated an extraordinary, innocent sexuality that seemed to capture the times really well. Those knee socks!' Unaware of the famous Bill Brandt session with Dylan Thomas done in the same location, to Mankowitz the picture seemed redolent of Brassai's work in Paris in the Twenties and

The Kinks

1966

Dezo Hoffman

L to R

Dave Davies
John Dalton
Mick Avory
Ray Davies

In 1963 Ray Davies left Hornsey Art College to join his brother Dave's band, The Ravens. In his book, *X-Rated*, Davies describes how the band arrived at their new name. 'One evening, we were having a drink in a pub with Larry Page [their manager] and somebody commented on the fake-leather capes Dave and Pete [Quaife] were wearing. Someone else said that we were wearing kinky boots, similar to those worn by Honor Blackman in *The Avengers*. Larry overheard someone calls us "kinks" and concluded that, because of the kinky clothes we wore, and the fact that the new drummer [Mick Avory] looked a little like a police identikit version of a pervert, we might as well call ourselves the Kinks. We looked at one another in an unimpressed sort of way, said no more, finished our drinks and left.' Later, they were taken to the theatrical costumiers Berman and Nathan. 'We tried on what we thought were clothes from the Victorian era, but Monty Berman explained that they were in fact hunting jackets. He matched the red hunting jackets with white frilly shirts from another period in history, put us in black riding trousers and Chelsea boots, and lo and behold, we looked like us.'

The band played their first official concert in Oxford, February 1964, and became the dandy face of British pop in the Sixties. The nervy sexual neuroticism of 'You Really Got Me' and 'All Day and All of the Night' (both 1964), the ironic stab at Carnaby Street in 'Dedicated Follower of Fashion', and the lyricism of 'Sunny Afternoon' (both 1966) and 'Waterloo Sunset' (1967) were the idiosyncrasies of songwriter Ray Davies, a true English talent. Davies's self-destructive bent contributed to a mystique reflected in the revival of Kinks numbers such as The Pretenders' 'Stop Your Sobbing' (whose lead singer Chrissie Hynde would marry Davies). Highly stylised in their music and their image, their mod-ish wire-rimmed sunglasses, velvet jackets and Regency looks pre-empted many of the visual themes later explored by Paul Weller, and the BritPop bands.

Harry Goodwin

A sixteen-year-old plucked from obscurity when Adam Faith discovered her backstage, Sandie Shaw exemplified the new body image of the Sixties. She was photographed for a fashion spread for the *Daily Express* by Michael Williams in 1963: 'I was just sixteen. I had recently been to Vidal Sassoon to have my hair bobbed and wore hardly any make-up. Lit like a dream, I was totally unaware of my visual impact. The lanky body, endlessly long legs and boney, square-jawed face that had made me feel so clumsy and ugly compared with the curvaceous *Photoplay* and *Reveille* pin-ups were suddenly transformed into streamlined assets under the loving stare of the camera lens'. By 1964, her second single, '(There's) Always Something There To Remind Me' had gone to number one.

'Just a few incident-packed months ago, Sandra Goodrich was just a teenager from Essex, avidly following the trends of teenage fashion - gulping in huge rations of pop music in between working as a punch-card operator at Ford's massive factory at Dagenham. Now, as Sandie Shaw, she SETS the trends. As a Barefoot Princess of Pop, with Adam Faith as her personal Prince Charming, the angularly beautiful girl, with her intuitive "feel" for a good song, has become one of the most exciting vocal discoveries in years'. So ran the sleeves notes for *Sandie*, Shaw's debut album, released in 1965, when the singer was just eighteen. The shoeless look was a crucial gimmick that gave her a sense of vulnerability: she sang barefoot because she felt 'more relaxed, more able to get the mood of a song'. Thirty years later, she was to admit, 'Its symbolic potency is immense'.

Since her Sixties heyday Sandie Shaw has passed - via a career lacuna - into icon status. After winning the Eurovision Song Contest with 'Puppet On a String' (1967) she went into semi-retirement, to be reinvented in the Eighties, initially by Heaven 17 (singing 'Anyone Who Had A Heart'), and then by The Smiths, with whom she recorded a version of 'Hand In Glove' (1984). Harry Goodwin's photograph shows her at the height of her Sixties fame: bright, fresh and girl-next-doorish, with a hint of modern sexuality. It was taken, like many of his shots for *Top of the Pops*, in the studio dressing room. He remembers Sandie Shaw as a true star, but rather 'moody - she had terrible eyesight...'

Like many Sixties groups, The Who's visual impact was determined by an outsider with a vision of what their image could be, and how it could sell their music: in this case, their publicist (and, briefly, manager), Pete Meaden, who was determined to find the perfect band to express his purist mod obsession. Meaden - who had previously worked as a publicist for The Rolling Stones with Andrew Loog Oldham - defined mod as 'a euphemism for clean living under difficult circumstances', and in 1964 renamed the band The High Numbers, dressing them in the cutting-edge mod fashion.

That year mod had erupted into the public consciousness via the infamous south coast 'riots' - Clacton in March, Brighton, Margate and Bournemouth in May - the first specifically British youth cult since the Teddy boys of the Fifties. Whilst The Small Faces might lay claim to the title of true mod band, Meaden made 'his' group the new 'faces' of the movement, taking them into the mod subculture of Soho clubs and amphetamine rushes - the same rush which would fuel their chaotic onstage behaviour. Pete Townsend in particular took up the look with Ivy League jackets and button-down shirts (although for Townsend, there was a personal motivation: 'When I was a kid I had this enormous great hooter and I was always being baited about it. So I used to think, "I'll bloody show them. I'll push my huge hooter out at them from every newspaper in England - then they won't laugh at me." It was the reason I did everything.') But it was Keith Moon, already a sharp dresser, whose Fred Perry shirts and brushed-down fringe proved the most perfect mod image, a certain look born of poor post-war nutrition and a working-class pride in clothes.

The songs written by Meaden - 'I'm The Face' and 'Zoot Suit' (1964) - encapsulated the intense narcissism and fashion-fetishism of mod. But it was only when the band were discovered by manager Kit Lambert, and reverted from The High Numbers to The Who, with their graphic male symbol logo and 'Maximum R'n'B' slogan, that they achieved fame. A January 1965 *Melody Maker* review of a Marquee gig declared that The Who 'must surely be one of the most trend-setting groups of 1965'. Few singles could have been as anthemic as 'My Generation' (1965), with its time-tempting cry of 'I hope I die before I get old', and a sleeve which featured this photograph - an image reprised in the bands' own mod musical, *Quadrophenia* (1973).

Decca's inhouse photographer David Wedgbury appeared to draw on The Who's pop art style for this overhead street-credible shot (taken from a crane), prescient of the street cred of punk. Emblematic of a specific moment in British pop culture, the band wore Pete Townshend's art school credentials literally on their sleeves: the Union Jack (which, like Fury's lamé, would be reprised in pop history, from The Jam to The Spice Girls and the Eurythmic's 1999 Brits' appearance) was worn here by John Entwistle 'as a highly ambiguous statement about national and personal politics, laden with nihilism and irony', notes Michael Bracewell. The nihilism was evident in the band's social-realist lyrics, feedback frenzies and auto-destructive performances which owed much to Townsend's time at Ealing College of Art, where he witnessed the artist Gustav Metzger destroying a bass guitar in illustration of his art theories.

The Who's concerts became set-pieces of performance art where violence met creativity, a mix of art credentials and laddishness which would later surface both in punk, and in the BritPop bands of the Nineties. For Brian Eno, The Who were an example of the way 'it was possible to occupy an area between fine art sensibility and popular art, and have the ambiguity work'. Their live performances remained their greatest artistic achievement; and by 1970, The Who had become the biggest - and loudest - band in the world, the progenitors of stadium-rock.

clockwise from top left

Pete Townshend
Keith Moon
Roger Daltrey
John Entwistle

Harry Goodwin

Ex-builder's labourer and vacuum cleaner salesman Tom Jones, all sideboards and swivelling hips, strode into Sixties pop from the Welsh Valleys to the bright lights of London. The songs that got him there drew on country and western and soul (US DJs thought he was both American and black). His 1964 hit, 'It's Not Unusual', originally written for Sandie Shaw, reached number one, and was followed by 'What's New Pussycat?' (1965), the theme from *Thunderball* (1965), 'Green Green Grass of Home' (1967), and 'Delilah' (1968), heart-tugging stuff which had middle-aged women in tears.

His TV series, which ran from 1969 to 1974, earned him a transatlantic contract worth £9 million. Apparently destined for the Las Vegas/cabaret circuit, 'The Voice' was repositioned in the íronic Eighties/Nineties, covering Prince's 'Kiss' with the Art of Noise, and duetting with Robbie Williams, and Cerys Matthews from Catatonia.

Harry Goodwin, the offical photographer at *Top of the Pops* for nine years, took this shot in the dressing room - 'the only place with a white wall'. BBC cups adorn the dressing-table, while clearly visible dangling from Jones's belt is his lucky rabbit's foot which always accompanied his performances. 'He never gave me a bad time' says Goodwin of the professional Mr Jones, but he regrets one thing about the singer's modern incarnation - 'I prefer him with a nose like that'.

Instantly recognisable by her panda-black eyes, pale pink lips and candy-floss backcombed hair (in fact a wig, her natural hair being red), Dusty Springfield was the best pop singer of her generation. Born of Irish stock in Hampstead (her real name being Mary Isabel Catherine Bernadette O'Brien) she joined her brother Tom in the folk trio The Springfields in 1960. She went solo in 1963 with the future classic 'I Only Want to Be With You', continuing with 'Wishin' and Hopin'' (1964) and the song for which she - and indeed, the decade - will be remembered, 'You Don't Have to Say You Love Me' (1966). She appealed both to dance-mad mods, and to a gay audience who appreciated her songs of hopeless devotion and lost love.

Springfield's image centred on her trademark make-up. 'I based it on models in French *Vogue* with black eyelids', she told the *Telegraph Magazine* in 1995. 'I thought, that's what I want to do. But I never did it right. I never knew how to blend it. I still don't.' Hers was not the boyish look of the Sixties models. 'I didn't know how to do that. They were too beautiful. My body was wrong, my face was wrong. I always had a very grown-up face. I didn't look like a singer or a model. Honest to God, the bigger the hair, the blacker the eyes, the more you can hide. I know that was most of it. So it all worked, but for the most insecure reasons.' The result was a Noh mask, a Sixties construct resembling a British version of a Warhol 'Marilyn'.

Disillusioned with the British scene, Springfield moved to Memphis, recording *Dusty in Memphis* (1968), her best work, and the single 'Son of a Preacher Man' which confirmed her ability to 'sound convincingly black'. Soulful, gutsy, truly iconic, she continued to release records with varying degrees of success until 1987, when the Pet Shop Boys recorded a duet with Springfield and Neil Tennant, 'What Have I Done to Deserve This?', firmly reinstating her in the pop public imagination, where she has remained, even after her tragic death in March 1999.

Dusty Springfield
1965

Dezo Hoffman

The 1970s brought a commercially-minded reaction against the seriousness of British rock, led by a slight figure, a Jewish London boy and ex-mod who moved out of a hippy-folk slipstream to seize his moment of pop fame. Marc Bolan (Mark Field) ushered in the glitter era when in 1971 his publicist, Cherita Secunda, wrapped a feather boa around his neck, swiped glitter under his eyes and sent him on *Top Of The Pops* singing 'Hot Love' and pouting outrageously. It was an amateur, unpremeditated affair; but it sparked an entire generation. 'There wasn't any grand plan to start glam rock', notes David Enthoven, his manager. 'All Marc really did was give pop some attitude. He made it glamorous, and he made it different'.

Bolan became the teeny bop idol for the new decade, an elfin jeepster making three minute pop records that sounded tinny, electric, ersatz, sexy and modern: the reaction became known as T.Rexstasy. 'I don't really care what people think', announced the twentieth-century boy. 'If the thing works, it works. Elvis Presley wore eye make-up for years. People thought he had dark sultry eyes. Mick Jagger has wonderful skin embellishment. People are really works of art, and if you have a nice face you might as well play about with it...' His *Top of the Pops* appearances were as flagrant and teasing as his hits: 'Ride A White Swan' (1970), 'Hot Love' and 'Get It On' (1971), 'Children of the Revolution', 'Metal Guru' and 'Telegram Sam' (1972). His dandy star would only be eclipsed by his friend, David Bowie, who took the glam image to new extremes, beyond Bolan's 'electric warrior', perennially-adolescent persona. Bolan himself might have faded into insignificance, had his purple mini not crashed into a tree on Barnes Common on 16 September 1977, and created glam rock's first martyr.

With a surprisingly long mod/folk/hippy history behind him, in 1972 David Bowie (David Jones - he acquired 'Bowie' for its glamorous American connotations) succeeded in reinventing himself - via a ground-breaking trip to New York which exposed him to the Warhol Factory scene and the music and looks of Lou Reed and Iggy Pop - as the alien face of the new rock. Totally artificial where all had been blue-denim earnestness, the monster that Bowie created was a puppet-robot, a mime actor playing the role of a rock star: the 'wild mutation' of Ziggy Stardust, the sexually amorphous Aladdin Sane, the cocaine-corrupted Thin White Duke - and all the permutations that followed. Bowie was the untouchable pop icon incarnate, existing as a (self) manufactured image of himself.

Perhaps most crucial in the formation of this image was Bowie's throwaway statement to the *Melody Maker* in January 1972, 'I'm gay and I always have been...' Whether in character or not, it was a ground-breaking 'confession' that immediately threw him into the media spotlight; although there was a degree of ambivalence even about his words, as the journalist who reported them, Michael Watts, noted, 'David's present image is to come on like a swishy queen... But there's a sly jollity about him as he says it, a secret smile at the corners of his mouth. He knows that in these times it's permissible to act like a male tart, and that to shock and outrage, which pop has always striven to do throughout its history, is a ball-breaking business.'

Controversy continued to rage around the prettiest star. In 1973 Simon Frith wrote: 'Bowie constructs his music around an image rather than a sound or a style and it's this that disturbs rock purists. I mean, what a cheek, deciding to be a star before he'd even got a fan. But it isn't a con trick. Ziggy Stardust is the loving creation of a genuine rock addict and the purpose of the Bowie show isn't to give pop a falsely glamorous glow but to point up the reality of the continuing star/audience relationship.'

Mick Rock's photographs appeared first on the reissued Space Oddity sleeve, from which session this picture comes. It was made in March 1972 at Haddon Hall, the Victorian mansion in Beckenham rented by David and Angie Bowie, and which they ran as a semi-commune, filling it with their circle of friends and creators - including the designer Freddi Burretti who set up shop there, making their clothes. The photograph was taken 'in the baby's bedroom - Zowie's bedroom - which was painted pink', recalls Rock. 'Even the baby was very camp. David's holding the original artwork for *Hunky Dory*' (which had been photographed by Brian Duffy).

Rock's photograph marks a pivotal point in the formation of the modern pop world: 'I was the man who framed Ziggy Stardust, and who, one singular afternoon...realised that, in the end, Ziggy Stardust had framed me.' Through the camera lens Bowie's new image came into focus, the crucial shift from hippie to spaceman: the red patent, black wedge boots, the flimsy woman's blouse, the tight, almost skinhead trousers: this was the year after the release of Stanley Kubrick's film *A Clockwork Orange*. 'It was a dada thing', said Bowie later, 'this extreme ultraviolence in Liberty fabrics.' Bowie cut and dyed his hair as a reaction to the new decade, taking his style from a Kensai display Bowie saw in a New York department store in February 1971, where the designer had dressed his models in wigs based on kabuki lions.

Rock made a series of films for the star, 'all shot for a ridiculously small amount of money because no-one saw any commercial potential in them'. Pre-empting Bowie's later movie role, principally as himself, in *The Man Who Fell to Earth* (1976), the brittle decadence of glitter rock was caught in Rock's work, especially in the 'Life On Mars' film (1973), for which Bowie was clad in an ice-blue satin suit designed by Burretti and 'exquisite' make-up by Pierre Laroche, the artist responsible for Bowie's *Aladdin Sane* thunderflash (1973), and the 'masks' on Bowie and 'Twig the Wonderkid' (Twiggy) on the Justin de Villeneuve-shot *Pin Ups* (1973). Given little exposure at the time, Rock's films nonetheless foresaw the use to which the video age would be put in the furtherance of the pop image.

Elton John
1975

Terry O'Neill

From Watford balladeer and bluesman to international superstar, Elton John rose on the back of glam rock to become one of pop's most prolific and celebrated, if unlikely icons. Having contrived his new name from two blues stars, (Elton Dean and Long John Baldry), the earnestness of his early work had already been subverted by the theatrical honky-tonk of *Don't Shoot Me, I'm Only the Piano Player* in 1973 when *Goodbye Yellow Brick Road* appeared later that year.

Drawing on the period's fascination with violence ('Saturday Night's Alright for Fighting') and nostalgic glamour ('Candle in the Wind'), the album even invented a Ziggy-like 'Bennie and the Jets'. Clad in rock's transforming lamé, John adopted the persona he had invented for himself wholeheartedly (and in a lifestyle which would provide its own melodramatic storyline), a ridiculous yet somehow glamorous figure in ever higher silver platforms and outlandish rhinestone spectacles. In the film *Tommy* (1975), he played the Pinball Wizard as himself, an exaggerated version of an already exaggerated stage presence, 'Perhaps the defining image of Elton's uber-man status during the mid-Seventies - maybe even the defining image of the entire decade...' wrote Phil Dellio and Scott Woods, 'a one-man Mount Rushmore of hyperbolic meaninglessness, a glittering tabula rasa for wayward pop dreamers...'

Beneath John's image lies an unsettling insecurity which is at least part of the reason for his longevity and his appeal. A vulnerable figure, his outrageousnes seems self-parodying. 'I'm not one for visual things', he declared in *Tantrums and Tiaras*, the revealing film made by his partner, David Furnish. 'I don't like doing videos. I don't like having my photo taken. It's probably because of the way I look, the way I think I look, the way I wished I looked. I'm not Madonna. I'm not someone who has a very strong visual image, so I don't feel that comfortable'. In recent years John has revamped his image, storing his costumes in a barn on his Windsor estate and assuming an ostensibly more tasteful, if not formal image both onstage and off. The established elder statesman of pop, his rewritten 'Candle In the Wind' in memory of his friend, Diana, Princess of Wales, is the best-selling single of all time.

Terry O'Neill has photographed Elton John throughout his career, in virtually every guise. 'He dresses quite straight now, but he always enjoyed dressing up.' O'Neill shot this photograph on the set of *Tommy*, wearing gigantic fibreglass boots. 'He took a while to get into them,' says O'Neill, 'but then, he has a personality even bigger than those boots.'

Roxy Music

1974

Brian Cooke

L to R

Phil Manzanera
Bryan Ferry
Andy McKay
Brian Eno
Rik Kenton
Paul Thompson

Roxy Music was the aural and visual expression of the obsessions of Geordie art school student and teacher Bryan Ferry and the avant-garde musicians he gathered around him in the early 1970s. Taking Billy Fury's lamé into the stratosphere, the band's 1972 *Top of the Pops* debut with the weird pop art allusion that was 'Virginia Plain' lodged them in the public consciousness, an image accented by Ferry's arched eyebrow above silver glitter lids and the posturing feather-surrounded Mekon head of the band's keyboardist, Brian Eno.

Here, almost for the first time, was a band whose very existence was predicated on their image - in their case, seemingly sourced from Weimar Berlin and 1950s America. Everything about them seemed to be a pose - from Ferry's curling camp sneer and blue-black neo-quiff (revolutionarily short for the time), to Eno's electronic blips and leopardskin lurex, and Andy MacKay's sinuous saxophone and Dan Dare boiler suit. The clothes, made by a girlfriend of Eno's, Caroline McNichol, and the influential designer, Anthony Price, had tuned into what a 1971 *Vogue* saw as a new 'fashion anarchy'. 'Our costumes were quite deliberate takes on those Fifties versions of space nobility - the masters of the Galactic Parliament and so on', recalled Eno.

The first two albums - *Roxy Music* (1972) and *For Your Pleasure* (1973) ('the only truly timeless rock music ever recorded', according to Tony Parsons and Julie Burchill) - were both intensely art-directed by Nick de Ville, dressed by Price, coiffeured by Keith at Smile, narrated by Simon Puxley and personified by glamorous models. The results - more expensive to produce than the actual music itself - looked like pages out of *Harpers & Queen* rather than *Melody Maker*, and set new standards in the medium of sleeve art. As the visual competition between Ferry and Eno intensified, the latter departed, leaving Roxy Music to streamline their sound into the realms of art-pop sophistication - although the image perhaps reached its peak with Ferry's solo albums, *These Foolish Things* (1973) and *Another Time, Another Place* (1974), in which Ferry presented himself as a transatlantic crooner caught somewhere between Noël Coward and Elvis Presley. Eno, meanwhile, became the *eminence grise* of avant-garde pop and influential producer.

Brian Cooke's photograph was taken at the Royal College of Art during the making of Roxy Music's first promotional film, for the album track 'Re-Make, Re-Model'. Cooke had already shot the first press photo-session of the band at his home studio in Blenheim Crescent (his wife remembers Bryan Ferry putting on his make-up in her kitchen), and would photograph them on their first official live performance at the Lincoln Festival - where the band had to perform in their glam outfits in broad daylight and pouring rain.

Together with Doug Smith, Cooke used an improvised studio at the RCA, and then state-of-the-art video techniques (which had to be transferred onto film). 'It was all very modern and electronic to reflect the group', remembers Cooke, 'done against a bland black set so that we could use the effects against it - solarisation, strong, bright colours'. Simon Puxley recalls that the film was done purely for its own sake, with 'the band miming, electronic keyboards, and psychedelic effects. It was pretty rough-edged, but that's part of its charm'. For Cooke, the band were easy enough to work with - 'they were all polite, well-educated university boys' - but he saw little evidence of the omniscient art direction later exerted by Ferry in pursuit of his pop art dream. His dark, glamorous photograph is one of the very few of the early line-up of the band not to be taken in some incongruous setting (backstage at a students' union, or lined up in an office): a reminder of how pioneering Roxy Music were in their consummate assumption of pop artifice.

'Rod the Mod', lead singer of The Faces, broke off to start a solo career which, in the early Seventies, defined a heterosexual side to glam rock: tight suits, rooster haircuts, roistering, blues-influenced songs, and a number one album, *Every Picture Tells A Story* in 1971. But as Stewart achieved even greater success with *Atlantic Crossing* (1975) (which produced 'Sailing') and *A Night on the Town* (1976) the image went into overdrive: he had become, in John Walsh's words, 'a cocktail roustabout; a conceited, jet-setting crumpet-chaser, who got off with an annoyingly large number of attractive women...' Brian Aris's picture, taken under the clear light of California at Stewart's Beverley Hills home (where he was living with Britt Ekland) marks the transition from the 'one-of-the-lads' Stewart to his leopardskin-lycra period. Floppy, fey and quintessentially Seventies, there's a pronounced femininity to his image which only a man so sure of his own sexuality could get away with.

In contrast to his current LA lifestyle, Stewart was born in North London (his father was Scottish) and first sang in public on 'Ban the Bomb' marches. 'I was a real little Red when I was 19. I was your actual beatnik, mate. Your actual Jack Kerouac. Barnet right down to here. Ban the bomb. You name it, we ban it. Anti-apartheid. Save cats. Save dogs. Shag in tents. Aldermaston Marches. What a life. What a life.' Now aged fifty-five, Stewart's superstar profile seems far removed from the raucousness of his roots. He owns a Beverley Hills mansion with a collection of Pre-Raphaelite art to rival Lord Lloyd Webber's, and has sold all his future royalites to a Wall Street firm. He recently recorded an album of cover versions, including songs by Primal Scream and Oasis, the latter returning the compliment - and reflecting a symbiosis of image - by singing Stewart's praises as the prototype lad.

Queen

1974

Mick Rock

clockwise from top left

Roger Taylor
Brian May
John Deacon
Freddie Mercury

Mick Rock's hold on the glamorous side of Seventies rock was consolidated with his work with Queen, the late-glam band fronted by Freddie Mercury, who was fond of quoting Oscar Wilde, 'Often, that which today is considered pretentious is tomorrow considered state of the art' - although in their case, perhaps the reverse was true: 'The important thing is to be considered'. A outrageous as their Zanzibar-born vocalist was, the band appealed to a remarkably straight audience. 'His queerness, like the name of the band, was so in-your-face that no-one even noticed it', writes Barney Hoskyns in *Glam!*. Queen bridged heavy metal and pop, and their adept manipulation of their image drew on the lessons of the glam rock era, moving between heavy rock and high camp, as well as referencing pre-war glamour. As Freddie Mercury said of their single, 'Killer Queen' (1974): 'People are used to hard-rock, energy music from Queen, yet this single, you almost expect Noël Coward to sing it. It's one of those bowler-hat, black-suspender-belt numbers'.

The group's ground-breaking video for 'Bohemian Rhapsody' helped keep the single at number one for nine consecutive weeks from November 1975 to January 1976, an extraordinary feat for the time. Mick Rock's photograph is a reflected image from the video, as well as being a tribute to Freddie Mercury's impersonation of Marlene Dietrich and her insistence on always having an overhead light to highlight her cheekbones. "'Glam' was rampant and that was what Queen wanted to project above all', wrote Rock. 'Glamorous, androgynous, provocative "and unforgettable," said Freddie.'

When Rock shot this, the session for the album cover for *Queen II*, he had just become friendly with John Kobal, the famous Canadian collector of vintage film stills. Kobal sent Rock prints of Marlene Dietrich in *Shanghai Express*: 'Her arms were folded and she was wearing black against a black background, and was exquisitely lit. Her tilted head and hands seemed to be floating. I saw the connection immediately... Glamorous, mysterious and classic. I would transpose it into a four-headed monster. They had to go for it. So I went to Freddie... He loved it immediately... "I shall be Marlene," he laughed, "what a delicious thought!"'

Peter Vernon

Deep in the bleak Seventies, with three-day weeks, power cuts and industrial unrest, pop, bored of glitter and prog-rock, needed a new messiah. It didn't expect the Sex Pistols. Born out of dole-queue boredom, incubated in Malcom McLaren's shop SEX, and fostered by the New York punk of Richard Hell (whom McLaren had first seen sporting chopped up hair and safety pins), the Pistols exploded the indifference of the post-glam rock era by shock tactics: none more shocking (or calculated, in hindsight) than their appearance - along with the Bromley Contingent and a youthful Siouxsie Sioux - on Bill Grundy's 'Today' programme. Having released 'Anarchy in the UK' on 26 November 1976, the promoter Eric Hall booked the band onto the show on 1 December. Invading the quiet local London news backwater, this extraordinary collection of Dickensian sci-fi misfits were encouraged by Grundy to 'say something outrageous'- and duly obliged. The next day this photograph appeared on the front of the *Daily Mirror* under the headline, 'The Filth and the Fury', along with reports that one angered viewer had actually kicked in the screen of his £380 colour TV.

The image was not that easily shattered. It would take the short shelf-life of McLaren's enthusiastic, cynical exploitation (best before 1977) to do that. Emblems of a new generation, vitriol and lager spewing from their gobs, legs shackled by McLaren-Westwood bondage and mouthing McLaren's Situationist slogans, in 1977 the Pistols released a series of definitive punk singles ('Anarchy', 'Pretty Vacant', and 'God Save The Queen') and one of the great debut albums (*Never Mind The Bollocks*), then fizzled out. There were other punk groups, some of them more musically proficent and many more long-lasting, but none could rival the sheer amphetamine offensive of the Pistols' visceral but suprisingly poppy onslaught. They were figureheads for an entire culture in which the image of the group performing was symbiotically that of its audience; a far cry from the distanced, manufactured pop culture which had gone before. Pop had been reinvented as audience participation: DIY music, fashion and literature (the fanzine *Sniffin' Glue* printed a diagram of three guitar chords with the instruction, 'Now form a band') were stamped with a radical message - albeit a nihilistic one - unheard since the Sixties.

In her book of photographs of EMI acts during the Fifties and Sixties, *The End of Innocence*, Liz Jobey notes: 'Even the Sex Pistols were photographed signing their EMI contracts in 1976 in exactly the same way that Pink Floyd had been photographed signing theirs almost ten years before'. Shortly after the band had signed, photographer Peter Vernon was asked by EMI press officer Tom Nolan to do another session with the Pistols. Vernon took this picture at the entrance to the basement car park below EMI's offices in Manchester Square. 'They were drinking lager - it's a great advert for Carlsberg - and I asked them to burst through the door and open the car. I was ready - and luckily it worked.' The door, however, was wrenched off its hinges. The photograph's spontaneous exhibition of punk manners coincided with the next step in the Pistols career: the Bill Grundy escapade, 'and suddenly, wallop! The group were being banned around the country.' Vernon's picture - until now uncredited - was also used on the Pistols' bootleg, *The Filth and the Fury*, widely circulated before the release of *Never Mind the Bollocks*.

Glen Matlock
Paul Cook
Johnny Rotten
Steve Jones

Kate Bush

1978

Gered Mankowitz

Kate Bush, a doctor's daughter from Welling, seemed to come out of nowhere with the release of 'Wuthering Heights' in January 1978, and appeared to be a step back into glam with her theatrical, studied performance. But she had already written two hundred songs by the age of sixteen, and had spent the past two years being prepared by her record company for this moment. Pink Floyd's Dave Gilmour brought her to EMI's attention, who gave her a £3,500 advance to enable her to develop her career in music. Like her hero, David Bowie, she was introduced to the mime artist Lindsay Kemp, an experience which inspired her performance. EMI's modest but remarkably patient investment paid dividends: Bush, with her four-octave voice and quirky glamour, became a major star with the release of 'Wuthering Heights' and the album, *The Kick Inside* (1978).

Early attempts to capture her eccentric image did not always please Bush. She disliked the overt sexuality of the 'dancewear' sessions done with Mankowitz in 1978 which revealed her nipples through a pink vest. She succeeded in vetoing the photograph on the single sleeve, but EMI used it in a major ad campaign, including on the front of London buses. 'There were stories of buses being delayed because the queues were shuffling round the front to look at the picture', recalls Mankowitz. Like her airwave-grabbing record, Bush caught the attention of the public. Mankowitz commented, 'I knew that if people saw her once, they'd want to see her again.'

What they got was another side of the mirror. This is a more gothic portrait, showing the darker side of Bush's work, an occasional preoccupation with death and interest in the supernatural - whilst still addressing her sexual appeal. Its glossy, glamorous quality is belied by that somewhat tremulous sexuality, giving the picture its edge. Bush's work often seemed to dwell on the dividing line between sanity and madness, a sensibility Mankowitz's portrait projects: Bush's elusive qualities, her body-consciousness, a sense of both innocence and experience; the potentially banal subverted by lush sexuality and an acute, almost painful self-awareness which has resulted in her withdrawal from the examining public eye.

As stylized as any of their peers (the first division punk groups of the late Seventies: the Pistols, The Damned, The Stranglers and The Jam), The Clash presented a united front of socialist causes and screen-printed shirts as tight as the zips on their combat pants. The band formed when art students Mick Jones and Paul Simenon met up with diplomat's son Joe Strummer (Joseph Mellor), but again it was a manager - Bernie Rhodes - who directed their visual assault (inspired by a military book from the local library) in a similar manner to Malcolm McLaren. But where their rivals, the Pistols, imploded, The Clash went on to become one of the most solidly-successful bands of the era.

The ethos was radical West London boho (ostensibly working-class but with a hint of trustafarianism yet to come) and, despite the whiteness of the band members, multi-racial: their reggae covers did much to popularise the genre beyond the arcane world of pre-releases. A classic boys' band, Strummer's hoarse-voiced holler and the guitar-hero posturing of Mick Jones and Paul Simenon were channelled by producers Sandy Pearlman, on Give 'em Enough Rope (1978) and Guy Stevens (London Calling, 1979), shaping but not compromising their energy.

In the same way, a refined version of street-credible photography was crucial to the band's image. It was the responsibility of one photographer. 'I specialize in rogues and vagabonds', says Pennie Smith, who shot all but one of The Clash's album sleeves. Displaying the group in their anarcho-military gear - stagewear as streetwear - this was an early session, shot in 1976 in a flat belonging to the music journalist Caroline Coon, another early punk propagandist. 'That's a poster she had on the wall. Personally, I clicked with them', remembers Smith, 'they started throwing the right shapes. We knew what we were doing from that moment on.' Smith's shots of the group - including her famous live shot of Mick Jones smashing his guitar on stage as used on the Elvis Presley-pastiche cover of London Calling - were collected in her book, The Clash: Before and After which helped instil the image of the band as a supergroup of the punk generation.

L to R

Nicky 'Topper' Headon
Mick Jones
Joe Strummer
Paul Simonon

Pennie Smith

Of all the female icons thrown up by punk (from The Slits and The Raincoats to Toyah and Hazel O'Connor), Siouxsie Sioux (Susan Dallion) seemed the least compromised and her band, The Banshees, the most credible in what the artist-performer Linder calls 'the Punk War'. As the Bromley Contingent, Siouxsie (described by Julie Burchill as a Sex Pistols 'go go dancer') and Steve Severin melded Bowie/Roxy glam with Velvet Underground/Stooges punk to produce a strident image that, as extreme as it seemed, nonetheless ensured the band's success for the next fifteen years. Siouxsie's sexually-provocative, decadent warrior queen was supported by the first (recording) Banshees line-up: the peroxide glam Severin, the pallid urchinlike Kenny Morris (a male version of Siouxsie), and John Mackay, a dark-eyed fugitive from a Fritz Lang movie.

Perennially clad in black, between them they 'taught a whole generation to pose without humour', according to Mary Harron. The singalong quality of their first single, 'Hong Kong Garden' (1978) was deceptive: their early music was as harsh as their song titles - 'Metal', 'Suburban Relapse', 'Premature Burial' - drawing on horror movies and homocide. They would be seen as progenitors of the Goth movement, although as Budgie (Peter Clark), the group's later drummer, noted, 'I blame Robert Smith. He took Siouxsie's look and ran off with it. He took backcombing to its ultimate, and we got all the blame for goth.'

'NME, doorway in Tottenham Court Road' rattles out Pennie Smith, who found the notoriously frosty ice maiden of punk (as the music press liked to call her) 'a bit precious... I got the feeling that she was fragile - that she might fall to pieces at any minute...' This iconic shot of the group reflects some of their inner tensions (Morris and McKay would walk out dramatically in 1979), as well as the dark, threatening aspect of their image - the flailing limbs and barely-repressed violence of Siouxsie's stage persona. Smith's photograph encapsulates the band at the time of a concerted graffitti campaign to 'Sign The Banshees'. Polydor duly obliged, and thus began one of the longest and most successful punk-germinated careers with singles such as 'Happy House', 'Dear Prudence' (1982) and albums from *The Scream* (1978) to *Kaleidoscope* (1980), *Ju Ju* (1981) and *A Kiss In The Dreamhouse* (1982) and beyond. After numerous personnel changes, Siouxsie and husband Budgie splintered into The Creatures, and The Banshees only split up in 1996 in a statement perceived to be a reaction to the reformation of the Sex Pistols that year.

L to R

Siouxsie Sioux
Kenny Morris
John McKay
Steve Severin

As sombre an image as ever came out of the gothic North, Joy Division formed after the Sex Pistols' famous Lesser Free Trade Hall concert as Warsaw, taking their name from a track on Bowie's electronic *Low* album. Their radically stripped-down, clinical sound was reflected in the urban alienated, low-key look of the group themselves. Together with Tony Wilson's independent label, Factory Records, they projected an obscure gloom that drew on the post-industrial surroundings of their environment, apparently authoritarian allusions (the name came from concentration camp brothels for Nazi troops), Wilson's intellectual Situationist fixation, and Peter Saville's influential graphics and typography.

The echoing, cavernous soundscapes of *Unknown Pleasures* (1979) and the single, 'Transmission' were complemented by an avowedly European, not American, image. Sporting disco-boy, barber-shop short-back-and-sides haircuts, tonic shirts and army surplus raincoats down to their shins, they appeared to play with issues as dark as Ian Curtis's soul: his frenetic, magnetic stage performances combined Jim Morrison with St Vitus's Dance, and often ended in epileptic fits. Curtis's suicide, on the morning of 18 May 1980, ensured that the romantic heart of the group's darkness would remain unsullied (just as Kurt Cobain's suicide in 1994 cryogenically preserved Nirvana). 'Love Will Tear Us Apart', released after Curtis's death, was a classic pop song in which Curtis almost managed to sound like Frank Sinatra. A funereal second album, Closer, seemed a soundtrack to the depths which Curtis's depression had taken him, swirling with his demons and the helicoptors from Francis Ford Coppola's *Apocalypse Now*; the end, indeed. To dispel the deathly gloom, the band reinvented themselves as New Order, and recorded 'Blue Monday', the best-selling twelve inch single (it spent 130 weeks in the British chart), although its UK profits were virtually wiped out by the expense of producing its 'floppy disc' sleeve, an acknowledgement of impending computer culture. Highly influential in both their incarnations, the band are still playing and recording.

Kevin Cummins' portrait of Ian Curtis was taken on 19 August 1979 at T.J. Davidson's rehearsal rooms in central Manchester, behind Deansgate station - the same room used for the 'Love Will Tear Us Apart' video. Salford-born photographer Cummins used no lighting - 'just whatever was creeping through the dirty windows' - and in two afternoons produced some of the most iconic images of the band. 'Every time I meet Peter Hook he says "You made more out of Joy Division than we ever did"', reports Cummins.

He finds the 'dead soul' image of Curtis deceptive. 'People didn't want Ian Curtis smiling - they wanted him looking mysterious. But he liked a pint you know - he wasn't just sitting on the bus reading Sartre'. In the same way, Cummins' version of the gloomy Manchester image is rather more pragmatic. The 'long grey overcoat look' (an exampe of which is hanging behind Curtis) was 'a myth really - the weather was so bloody awful and there were no studios to use so we'd be shooting outside all the time. It was cold and wet and you had to wear them...' Cummins adds that 'a lot of the reason why photos were dark and mysterious is because the bands were all signing on and didn't want to be recognised by the DHSS. So they were shot in profile or silhouette - they didn't want people to know who they were.' For all such practicalities, Joy Division wove a legend of dark gothic-industrial romance in which Cummins' photograph, and its subject, seems complicit.

Cybernetically created out of experimental electro from a Kraftwerk mould and presciently computer-conscious, The Human League began life in 1977 with Martyn Ware and Ian Craig Marsh twiddling knobs on early synthesizers to obscure lyrics sung by ex-hospital porter Phil Oakey ('the only reason I'm a singer is because I'm tall') and slides projected by film student/ice cream salesman Adrian Wright. The name came from a sci-fi board game called Starforce. In 1978 The League (the ironic possessive employed by the cognescenti) released the anti-silkworm abuse protest 'Being Boiled' on Bob Last's indie label, Fast Products, generating (along with fellow Sheffield industrialists, Cabaret Voltaire and Vice Versa, later ABC) a new era of electronic music.

Vexed by Gary Numan's usurpation of their techno-pop masterplan, the group split in 1980, Ware and Craig Marsh departing to form B.E.F./Heaven 17, leaving Oakey and Wright musicianless. But the schism enabled The Human League to restructure along more blatantly pop lines. Desperately seeking new personnel for a forthcoming tour, Oakey recruited two schoolgirls spotted by his girlfriend at the local disco: Joanne Catherall and Suzanne Sulley, electro/New Romantic fans. 'We had to go round to their parents to reassure them, let them see we were normal people', Wright told *The Face*'s Steve Taylor in 1981 - shortly after Oakey had shown Taylor his pierced nipples.

The girls' contribution - not immediately obvious to hardcore League fans who at first pelted them with beer cans on stage - was crucial: they gave The League its glam pop edge: 'They were the same as the people we were trying to sell it to', recalled Oakey. Recreating Sheffield as a post-modern Motown, their sexually-updated, provincially-empowered, synthesised Spectoresque made them logical heirs to Roxy Music's crown. The inclusion of Catherall and Sulley plugged perfectly into the Zeitgeist, an ironic gloss on an upwardly-mobile, shifting decade, summed up in a line from their Christmas number one, 'Don't You Want Me' (1981): 'You were working as a waitress in a cocktail bar...'

The girls' disco outfits, eyelined and pursed-lips faces, Oakey's asymmetrical haircut and ambisexuality created a potent triangle (counterbalanced by new boys Ian Burden and ex-Rezillo Jo Callis) for a sequence of hits that defined a key moment in Eighties pop. 'Love Action (I Believe In Love)' (inspired by the love affair between Oakey and Catherall) and 'Open Your Heart' from *Dare* (1981), the glossy, Brian Aris-photographed, *Vogue*-parody-sleeved (in the same way that Roxy Music's album *Country Life* had parodied that magazine), which sold five million copies worldwide. At their height, The Human League represented chart-friendly, art-credible electro-pop, a vision most completely realised in their movie pastiche videos. The group, once again stripped down to the Oakey/Catherall/Sulley nucleus, remain resolutely in Sheffield, where they continue to record.

Interviewing The Human League in their later stages of celebrity, Dave Hill wrote that 'in the field of what the experts call post-modernist pop, it is always hard to draw a line between irony and innocence...' To Hill, The League were an example of how 'everyone born after 1955 is pop culture-literate to some extent, because no-one under the age of 30 can possibly have experienced a time before Elvis Presley. Baby, we've been soused in pulp, free-enterprise culture since birth. No wonder the children of Punk compulsively re-cycle it in their own image. What splits the smart from the stupid is that while some milk the whole farce for every miserable cent, others - more sussed, step back - they do it as serious pleasure, but also they know what it's worth. I think the League are the latter, no matter which way you cut it. Unlike an increasing number of people, they still understand celebrity is daft..."We never pretended that was true," [Oakey] insists. "We pretended ever such a lot of things, but they were simply lies. We did that right from the start. It doesn't matter how much you try and demystify something. Even saying it is another myth, another lie. We're nothing to do with ordinary people."'

In the late Seventies a new pop hybrid evolved, its foundation in punk/new wave, but also in mod, and the ska/blue beat scene. The Special AKA - the Coventry band led by Terry Hall and Jerry Dammers - paved the way with 'Gangsters'(1979), released on their own label. Two-Tone had a vividly recognisable graphic - the black and white check which symbolised its multi-cultural ethos - and an even more recognisable sound: The Selecter, The Bodysnatchers and The Beat all recorded on the label. The Specials would go on to record 'Ghost Town' (1981) and the great anti-Apartheid protest 'Nelson Mandela' in 1984, but above all it was the Nutty Boys from Camden, Madness, who became Two Tone's greatest commercial success. The title track from *One Step Beyond* began a line of sixteen hits, accompanied by cartoon-style videos that endeared the group to a wide audience. Their liberated skinhead look - sharp suits, flight jackets amnd DMs - was street-articulate, their pure pop reprised in the band's Finsbury Park reunions in 1992 and 1998.

Jill Furmanovsky accompanied the group to New York in 1980. 'They were going to see their record company, and they all piled into this lift and exploded out at the top, where there the company logo was woven into the carpet - they knelt down and began worshipping it! We did a lot of photos outside - performing pyramids, stuff like that. They were great fun.'

L to R

Mark Bedford
Daniel 'Woody' Woodgate
Christoper Foreman
Suggs (Graham McPherson)
Chas Smash
Mike Barson
Lee Thompson

L to R

Merrick (Chris Hughes)
Terry Lee Miall
Adam Ant (Stuart Goddard)
Gary Tibbs
Marco Pirroni

Adam and the Ants

1981

Alan Ballard

Alan Ballard photographed the band for four of their album covers; this shot was taken during the filming of the 'Prince Charming' video (which featured a cameo by Diana Dors as the fairy godmother) at Shepperton Studios. Ballard set up a makeshift photographic studio onsite. 'Adam was a very determined, very positive, strong person', recalls the photographer. 'We worked together for three years at the height of his career. It was all of an era - it wasn't fashion, it was something he created himself. I knew the image he was trying to create, what he was trying to put over, and we worked on it together.' The result was yet another image in the parade of pop guises, quickly outmoded by virtue of its fantastic nature. 'A lot of pop is to do with myth and image. It's very fickle, transient - you get success for a certain time, then...'

A late Seventies glam-punk band with a heavy accent on *Rocky Horror* S&M, the early Ants were managed by Jordan, the shockingly-dressed shop girl at McLaren/Westwood's renamed 'Seditionaries'. But Adam Ant (Stuart Goddard), a product of Hornsey Art College, escaped the clutches of Malcolm McLaren (who stole the rest of the original Ants to form the rival BowWowWow) to take the pirate look one step over the top into glam and, in the person of his dandy punk highwayman, hold up the charts with *Kings of the Wild Frontier* (1980). The image - hussars' bum-freezer, braided hair, tribal swipe across the nose - was the Gary Glitter end of the New Romantics, cleverly propagated in boys-own swashbuckling videos; the music, as catchy as anything written by Chinn and Chapman in the Seventies, relied on Burundi drum-beats, Native American chants and Marco Pirroni's twanging bass to instil comic-book hero bravery on the dance floor. 'I began to feel an obligation to produce massive videos, whole wardrobes for people to wear, something for them to live for', Adam told Elissa von Poznak in 1984. Antmusic represented the highpoint of early Eighties video pop, all brocade and furbelows, unashamedly escapist. As Adam sang in 'Prince Charming' (1981), 'Ridicule is nothing to be scared of'.

The Police

1983

Terry O'Neill

The Police - Geordie son of a milkman and former teacher Sting (Gordon Sumner), CIA officer's son Stewart Copeland and 'brilliant technician' Andy Summers - surfed the new wave of the late Seventies with a punk-derived look (the band were peroxided for a 1979 Wrigley's gum TV ad, and, liking the result, kept it) and a new pop invention, white reggae, given a raucous sexy edge by Sting's almost hoarse vocals. The result was a remarkable run of singles including 'Roxanne' (1978), 'Can't Stand Losing You', 'Message in a Bottle' (1979), 'Don't Stand So Close To Me' (1980), 'Every Little Thing She Does Is Magic' (1982) and 'Every Breath You Take' (1983).

Terry O'Neill's photograph was taken in 1983. Two years later Sting was already pursuing a solo career, releasing the album, *The Dream of The Blue Turtles*, and the single 'If You Love Somebody Set Them Free', branching out into acting and the support of good causes (memorably the stretched-lipped Yanamani tribe of Brazil). O'Neill's powerful image predicts the imminent separation of the band; he found it difficult to photograph three people, and naturally concentrated on the lead singer. To O'Neill, Sting had 'true charisma. Like David Bowie, he brought something to it - you could feel there was a lot there...'

Sting has since become known as a gentleman of pop, his high-profile glamour image contributed to by his marriage to model and actress, Trudi Styler, and country squire life in his Wiltshire Jacobean manor. Stewart Copeland went on to write successful movie soundtracks (including *Rumblefish*) and operas; Summers pursued photography and continued recording.

L to R

Roger Taylor
John Taylor
Simon Le Bon
Andy Taylor
Nick Rhodes

Duran Duran

1981

Andy Earl

Birmingham-born progeny of the New Romantic movement and the Rum Runners club, Duran Duran took their name from an angel in the sci-fi movie, *Barbarella*, and their look from a cult of fancy dresss that had sprung up in the immediate post-punk era. The New Romantics affected a riotous rag-bag of historically-referential imagery that ran the gamut from the Westwood-McLaren pirate look to the bazaar pantomime of its more amateur versions. Duran Duran tended towards the latter (sneered Blitz Kid metropolitan sophisticates, whose allegiance lay with the just as preposterously costumed, caped and kilted Spandau Ballet), but had their revenge in the pop charts: they were all millionaires by their mid-twenties. Coinciding with the rise of the MTV generation, they made adept use of the new medium of video (famously the Russell Mulachey-directed, Sri Lanka-set 'Hungry Like A Wolf' and yacht-borne 'Rio' films) to promote their rocky-pop vision, an increasingly aspirational tale of glamorous models and international lifestyle well attuned to the culture of the Eighties.

Having watched the band 'do a score or more' of photo-sessions, Dave Rimmer, in a piece on Duran Duran written for *The Face* in 1985, noted, 'Duran take both fashion and photography deadly seriously... It's something they see as absolutely basic to their work. That...is one of the reasons why so many of Duran go out with models: they actually have a lot in common.' The band had become the image that they projected, a provincial fantasy which achieved fruition in a new glamocracy of style, propagated largely by gossip columns and, latterly, the pages of *Hello!*.

It is fitting that Andy Earl's photograph should have been taken at Milton Keynes. The new town bright, anonymous blandness provides the perfect setting for Duran Duran's Eighties futurist image, caught somewhere between sophistication and naïveté. Earl received a call from the marketing manager at EMI. 'He said they're a pretty rough-looking lot from Birmingham - see what you can make of them. We shot it at Milton Keynes because they wanted to look electronic. I was interested in modern architecture as well and Milton Keynes was being built at that time. This is the early Eighties and there was this wonderful glass sewage works where it's actually photographed. We shot it at night and it kind of looked all zappy and fun.'

1982

Of all the pop creations of the early Eighties, Wham! appeared the most egregiously artificial, most brazenly pop. Basically the child of soul boy George Michael, in visual, if not creative partnership with Andrew Ridgeley, Wham!'s unashamedly poppy playboy-next-door buoyancy would lay the way open for the boy-bands of the Nineties. But the rebel image - James Dean via the Home Counties, it seemed, was not just a put-on. Michael (Georgios Panayiotou), in an interview with Tony Parsons in 1985, claimed that they were reacting to *Saturday Night Fever* in the same way as the previous generation reacted to the Sex Pistols. Malcolm McLaren commented, 'The strange thing about those pop icons of the Eighties was they were part of a legion of disaffected youth that left home at the end of the Seventies and wanted to go back home by the middle of the Eighties. They wanted to sit down with mum and dad and tell them how they'd become successful'. Stuart Maconie recently contended in *Q* magazine that '"Wham Rap" is a pithier comment on The Thatcher Years than any number of earnest diatribes by polytechnic students on Rough Trade...'

Brian Aris's image of Wham! confirms their status in the new pop aristocracy of the time - specifically a glamour beyond rock, which the pair professed to despise (despite their assumption of that perennial symbol of rock rebellion, the biker's jacket). George Michael's bouffant hair-do even seemed to reference the image of a yet more famous Eighties icon. 'The hair-dryer was working overtime', says Michael in *Bare*. 'Some days I made the covers of the tabloids. Some days Princess Di made the covers of the tabloids. Some days I think they just got us mixed up.' Commenting on the group's less sophisticated, shuttlecocks, singlets and shorts look, Michael told Michael Parkinson, 'We must have been really annoying to all the other bands around who thought we were for real. But we thought it was funny.' Elsewhere, he added, 'Did we look stupid? Yes we did. Did we know we looked stupid? Yes we did. I rest my case.'

Michael's appearance on the *Parkinson Show* seems to have drawn a line under his career, and the ghost of Wham!, his outspokeness marking a sea-change in what a pop icon can be, or say: the pop idol as pop philosopher, determining a new morality; a new Establishment represented not by *Tatler*, but *Hello!* It is perhaps no coincidence that both band and magazine punctuated their titles with exclaimation marks. The assumption was further confirmed, in both Michael's and Elton John's cases, by their connexion with the greatest non-pop pop icon of the age, Diana. As much as anyone, George Michael represents both the legacy of the Eighties, and its continung influence.

ABC

1981

Gered Mankowitz

With the renewed focus on pop in the post-punk era, bands began to evolve knowing, artfully-contrived versions that seemed to catch up entire eras of pop culture and re-present them in a tongue-in-chic manner which was, and is, a purely English characteristic. Roxy Music had done it in 1972; ten years later ABC took up the lamé mantle.

As Vice Versa, the band were part of the electronic Sheffield scene which had produced techno-ironists The Human League; and like them, they moved out of experimental obscurity into a pop sensibility. Loudly trumpeted by their media champion Paul Morley, the advent of ABC was deftly manipulated and publicised, yet credible: their fans, the *Face* generation, appreciated both the irony, and the quality of the music: polished retro-pop with a post-modern edge. ABC were able to match style with substance, producing some of the most sucessful, pop songs of the period: 'The Look of Love', their biggest hit; 'All of My Heart', 'Poison Arrow', and the defining album, *Lexicon of Love* (all 1982).

It was telling that the best photographs of the band were produced by Gered Mankowitz, who had been successful shooting glam rock groups. 'A great band to work with', said Mankowitz, 'very serious, very concerned with detail. Every session I've done with them has produced a picture I'm really happy about.' The ABC sessions recalled Mankowitz's glitter period, as well as harking back even further - the group's lead singer Martin Fry had inherited Billy Fury's gold suit which, as Michael Bracewell notes, had already passed through the hands of Malcolm McDowall in *O Lucky Man!* (1973) and would end up on the back of Morrissey in 1992.

clockwise from top left

Mark Lickley
Martin Fry
Mark White
Stephen Singleton
David Robinson

The Smiths

1983

Kevin Cummins

L to R

Andy Rourke
Morrisey
Johnny Marr
Mike Joyce

One bleak day in 1982 (it may have been raining; if it wasn't, it should have been), Johnny Marr, his hair in a 'massive quiff', knocked on the door of the suburban house in Kings Road, Manchester where New York Dolls fanatic and Manchunian 'minor local legend', Steven Patrick Morrissey lived. Marr invited Morrissey (a Warholian contraction) to form The Smiths, and the result was the most important independent British band of the decade.

Morrissey was made for Marr, and vice versa: 'He was my biggest fan', says Marr. Taking elements of pop history - Billy Fury, Dusty Springfield, Sandie Shaw, David Bowie and Marc Bolan - and charging them through a Northern reaction to the prevailing synth(ethic) pop, The Smiths produced a completely individual sound that burred with worrisome, neurotic energy. Marr's querulous guitar was the perfect foil for Morrissey's yearning, emotion-catching vocals; Andy Rourke and Mike Joyce provided the faintly anonymous, solid rhymn section: here was a band that could be Britain's Velvet Underground with a pop sensibility. As Paul Morley wrote of 'This Charming Man' (1983), 'This group understands that casual is not enough'. 'I really do think that what we do is of tremendous value', Morrissey modestly told *Smash Hits* in 1984. 'I think people need a different voice and we supply it. The face of pop music has become a little too grim, too clean and safe and tidy. I couldn't imagine how things would be if we weren't here.'

Their song titles are enough to conjure the Smiths ethos: 'Heaven Knows I'm Miserable Now', 'What Difference Does It Make?' (1984), 'The Boy With The Thorn In His Side' (1986), 'Girlfriend In A Coma' (1987); mournful, soaring wallows in self-pity given an ambisexual duotone by a succession of sleeve icons: Truman Capote, Terence Stamp, Joe Dellasandro, Jean Marais and Edith Sitwell. The image was elaborated upon by Morrisey's careering stage persona: his polyester women's blouses, vintage Levis, gladioli, hearing aid and National Health specs gave him the appearance of a cross between his heroes Oscar Wilde, James Dean and Johnny Ray. Morrissey had become a role model for a generation of misfits and sufferers from unrequited love, a Shelleyan romantic stranded in a 1960s brutalist film.

Kevin Cummins' picture was taken in September 1983 at Tatton Park, Cheshire 'on the way to the M6'. 'It was going to be a cover but the features editor decided the Smiths would never be big enough to go on the front of the *NME*'. The picture makes subtle reference to their song, 'Reel Around the Fountain'. Cummins 'loved them. I really liked Johnny Marr. Morrissey was infuriating to work with - he's such a difficult bastard.'

The band split with Marr's departure in 1987. Morrissey's solo career further mined the genius, with attendant controversy, such as his Union Jack-waving when, clad in gold lamé, he supported Madness in Finsbury Park in 1992. Morrissey was accused of right-wing nationalism, although a year later the Union Jack was reprised as a pop graphic by BritPop - an example of the cyclical, genealogical nature of pop iconography. Both Morrissey and Marr have proved themselves as crucial links in the pop chain: besides his ongoing inspiration to indie bands of the Nineties, Marr's partnership with New Order's Bernard Sumner as Electronic has produced the sort of sublime pop one would expect from a marriage of the two bands.

Bay Hippisley

Bananarama was created by punk fans Siobhan Fahey, Keren Woodward and Sarah Dallin who rehearsed with ex-Pistols Steve Jones and Paul Cook in the rooms used by the group in Denmark Street. They released the Africanesque 'Aie-A-Nwana' in 1981, and when ex-Specials Terry Hall saw them in *The Face*, he invited them to join the Fun Boy Three, with whom they made their Top of the Pops debut with 'It Ain't What You Do' (1982). Their style was specifically early Eighties - moccasins and root perms, sportswear and braces - and was copied by thousands of girls of their generation and younger, new female role models. Part of their charm, and the accessibility of their image, was the fact they did not behave like pop stars, but truant schoolgirls. They may have made it to TOTPs, 'but we were still on the dole and very recognisable - we had to don headscarves to go and sign on'.

Malcolm McLaren expressed an interest and delivered an ultimatium: 'Do you wanna be like The Slits or Bucks Fizz?' 'They weren't very attractive', he said, 'they almost looked like boys.' That was the point, of course; they were stroppy girls, recalled London Records' Colin Bell: 'They always picked the worst photographs from the session. They were never prepared to be styled, to be told what to do. They came out of the DIY punk ethos and were very much determined to keep control of what they did'. Producers Jolley and Swain defined them as 'singalong with attitude'. Then came Stock, Aitken and Waterman; Bananarama took on the HiNRG sound wholeheartedly, 'adding campness to campness' in the 'Venus' video (1986). 'We did it all for our own amusement', said Keren Woodward.

Bay Hippisley's photograph, taken for the group's first album, *Deep Sea Skiving*, was made on an elaborate set designed to divert the group with their notoriously low boredom threshold. During the shoot - for which his assistant dressed as a frogman - the girls did indeed grow restive, and began breaking the suspended glass balls for fun.

Ian Dury

1984

Steve Pyke

Ian Dury and The Blockheads' 1978 album *New Boots and Panties!* and singles such as 'Sex and Drugs and Rock'n'Roll' (1977), 'Hit Me With Your Rhythm Stick' (1978) and 'Reasons To Be Cheerful' (1979) gave the new wave backbone, a sound shaped with Chas Jankel, leader of the Blockheads (Julie Burchill called Dury and Jankel 'the Taylor and Burton of rock'n'roll'). Former artist and art college lecturer, Dury, his arm and leg withered from a childhood attack of polio, resembled like a Mervyn Peake character crossed with his rock'n'roll hero, Gene

Vincent. His tongue-twisting, lascivious lyrics combined with a baroque stage presence to create something almost music hall, and peculiarly English.

Dury's style drew on the area where he grew up. 'I was always attracted to the sartorial low life of the Dagenham area', he told the *Sunday Times's* Bryan Appleyard. 'If I'd had enough allowance, I'd have had a velvet collar. My first Italian-style moddy suit was from a tailor in Romford marker - I had two pairs of trousers, one with 15 inch bottoms and one with 16 inch. The styles

crept down from Canning Town and all along the District Line. It was smart, glamorous.' From art school in Walthamstow Dury moved to the Royal College of Art, painting under the influence of his friend, Peter Blake. But he turned to music and after a period busking, he and Humphrey Ocean formed Kilburn and the High Roads, an unashamed celebration of outer London life: 'I remember one big rock star saying, "Who the hell wants to write about Watford?" and I thought, I do.'

Paul Weller
1984

Eric Watson

In 1976, The Jam, with their black mohair suits and black and white winkle-pickers, were a sharp contrast to the ripped t-shirts and safety-pins with which they shared the black hole that was The Roxy nightclub. Where their peers were urban anarchists in paint-splattered rags, The Jam - from Woking, Surrey - were smart suburban boys. Paul Weller was the style leader, a man seemingly obsessed with sartorial details, especially those of the Sixties. Listening to early Who and Kinks tracks 'was all new to me', he told Gary Crowley in 1980. 'I got into the clothes...I used to get the piss taken out of me a lot.' 'I don't know why people get so het up about it', he added. It's just fashion.' It may have been just fashion, but it garnered Weller dedicated disciples for whom the new mod became just as much a way of life as the original movement had been.

After chart success with fiercely polemic, angst-ridden urban anthems ('In the City', 1977, 'Down in the Tube Station at Midnight', 1978, 'The Eton Rifles', 1979, and 'Going Underground' 1980') Weller - already deified as a style god by *The Face* (whose founding editor, Nick Logan, had been an Essex mod) - left the band in 1982 to form the jazz-influenced The Style Council. He then pursued a solo career in which Sixties influences were evident in both image and sound, from early mod/Who look to Kinks paisley and *Sgt Pepper* psychedelia. A boys' guitar hero, his perservance paid off: a new generation would hold albums like *This Is The Modern World* (1977) as points of inspiration. 'Indeed, the reverence afforded him by the BritPop bunch took Weller's reputation to its highest point since The Jam's glory days', notes the *Guinness Rockopedia*. 'The angry young man had become a grumpy elder statesman'.

'I think style's important', Weller told *Smash Hits* in March 1983, 'more important than fashion. Everyone's got their own perception of it. I want to try and create this one image, one style, one direction...' Eric Watson, who contributed heavily to *Smash Hits* throughout the 1980s, was asked to take this shot of Weller for the last issue of 1983, 'so we gave him *1984* to read'. (The following year he photographed Morrissey holding the Weller cover and a copy of Anthony Burgess' *1985*). Watson points out that Weller's artfully-place handkerchief serves as a red focus 'in the same way that Renaissance painters always included something red to draw the eye'.

Band Aid (over)

1984

Brian Aris

In the middle of the 1980s, pop's aristocracy were assembled - photographed here like an Edwardian country house party - to record one of the biggest hits of the decade. The Bob Geldof-Midge Ure written 'Do They Know It's Christmas?' by Band Aid ('the plaster on the world's wounds') was conceived to alleviate the terrible Ethiopian famine of 1984, and Geldof summoned the volunteering stars to Sarm West studios to perform it. The line-up gives an accurate glimpse of high Eighties pop style: the jewel-coloured Katherine Hamnett silk shirts, the Yohji Yamamoto suits, the Western consumption that contrasted with the charitable intent of the project. It was a new phenomenon (although a 'Save the Children' album had previously made use of pop personalites in the Sixties): the use of pop celebrity to make serious world issues sexy, and thereby grab the attention of a pop-conscious population.

And it worked: the session was spread across the front page of the *Daily Mirror*, filmed and shown on *Whistle Test* and *The Tube*, and a week after its release - 3 December - the single had sold 600,000, becoming the fastest-selling in British pop history, and paving the way for the pan-global extravaganza that was the Live Aid concert of 1985, as well as a whole series of celebrity-conscious charity projects which allied (sometimes uneasily) fame and philanthropy. It made Geldof famous (again), most especially for two pronouncements: that it had made 'compasssion fashionable', and his exhortation to millions of viewers on live TV, 'Give us your fookin' money'. It was as simple as that.

Brian Aris had been photographing the famine in Ethiopia (and at one point had to be rescued by a national newspaper). Back in London, he got the same urgent call Geldof was putting through to tens of other friends and celebrities. 'I knew Bob, and it was in his mind that I'd been there. He called up and said, "I want you here next Sunday".' Aris recalls that because many of the pop stars had never actually met each other before, when he took the first Polaroid, he realised they were all busy chatting to each other. That, and the presence of film crews, made it a difficult session, even above and beyond the sheer logistics of photographing thirty-six pop musicians and one pop artist - Peter Blake, creator of the *Sgt Pepper* collage, who designed the single sleeve.

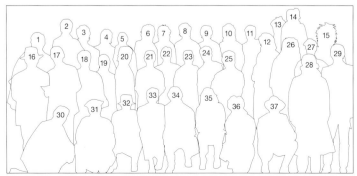

1	Adam Clayton (U2)				
2	Phil Collins	16	Bono (U2)		
3	Bob Geldof	17	Paul Weller		
4	Steve Norman (Spandau Ballet)	18	James Taylor		
5	Chris Cross (Ultravox)	19	Peter Blake		
6	John Taylor (Duran Duran)	20	George Michael		
7	Paul Young	21	Midge Ure (Ultravox)		
8	Tony Hadley (Spandau Ballet)	22	Martin Ware (Heaven 17)	30	Robert 'Kool' Bell (Kool and the Gang)
9	Glen Gregory (Heaven 17)	23	John Keeble (Spandau Ballet)	31	Dennis Thomas (Kool and the Gang)
10	Simon Le Bon (Duran Duran)	24	Gary Kemp (Spandau Ballet)	32	Andy Taylor (Duran Duran)
11	Simon Crowe (Boomtown Rats)	25	Roger Taylor (Duran Duran)	33	Jon Moss (Culture Club)
12	Marilyn	26	Sarah Dallin (Bananarama)	34	Sting
13	Keren Woodward (Bananarama)	27	Siobhan Fahey (Bananarama)	35	Rick Parfitt (Status Quo)
14	Martin Kemp (Spandau Ballet)	28	Peter Briquette (Boomtown Rats)	36	Nick Rhodes (Duran Duran)
15	Jody Watley (ex Shalamar)	29	Francis Rossi (Status Quo)	37	Johnny Fingers (Boomtown Rats)

Eurythmics

Eric Watson

Annie Lennox
Dave Stewart

1983

Annie Lennox was working as a waitress in a restaurant and running a secondhand clothes stall when she met Dave Stewart in 1976. They formed The Tourists, relying heavily on Lennox's flamboyant centre-staging, with Stewart's image less defined ('I suppose I used to look like a clown most of the time', he told Ian Birch in 1984). Soon after their biggest hit with the Dusty Springfield classic, 'I Only Want to Be With You' (1979), The Tourists split and Lennox and Stewart returned with the sharper, more sophisticated upgrade that was Eurythmics, creating massive hits 'Sweet Dreams (Are Made of This)' (1983), 'Here Comes the Rain Again',and 'Who's That Girl' (1983), for the video of which Lennox became a drag king, posing as 'Earl', a swarthy rocker, much to the confusion of their American audience at the Grammy Awards in 1984. 'We wanted to go as Eurythmics per se, not "carrot-topped" Annie Lennox.'

Tailored to the video age, Lennox's red-crop and fine bone structure, recalled a female version of David Bowie (indeed, Lennox's solo appearance with Bowie for the 1988 Nelson Mandela tribute at Wembley, wearing a ballgown and a *Bladerunner* swipe across her eyes, was a stylistic highpoint.) 'I think the papers want me to be the equivalent of Boy George' (with whom she shared a *Newsweek* cover, photographed by Jamie Morgan, in 1984), Lennox told Max Bell. 'I don't fit that bill. The only contrivance is that you have to stick to an image or you confuse the public. Dave helped me realise that. I don't use clothes as escapism. I've never wanted to represent myself as one thing: more a bit of this and a bit of that. If I want to don a wig and wear a mini I don't see why not.' Asked in 1984, 'Do you think that your face will be remembered as an Icon of the Eighties?', Lennox demurred, 'I don't think I'm that famous - if I disappear tomorrow not many people would remember me.' Her solo career disproved this in a spectacular fashion.

After the separation of Eurythmics in 1989, Lennox's solo debut, *Diva* (1990) produced six hits and sold five million copies worldwide. Her visual/video work continued, notably appearing with a Claire Eastman-choreographed troupe of male ballet-dancing 'swans' for 'No More "I Love You's"'(1994). Dave Stewart went on to develop a catholic variety of projects, including a record label, Anxious, and helped launch Shakespear's Sister, the band formed by ex-Bananarama Siobhan Fahey - whom Stewart subsequently married.

Eric Watson's photograph was inspired by the paintings of Thomas Eakins and John Singer Sargent: the formality of nineteenth-century portraiture reproduced in an tableau of a 1980s pop group. Specifically, Watson drew on James McNeill Whistler's famous composition of his mother, using a similar north light to get the effect. Lennox and Stewart arrived in the clothes in which they were photographed; no stylist was employed. Watson's background assumes an importance of its own and reflects back that highly considered space on his subjects. The picture also includes a trademark spot of colour (Lennox's red gloves), another Renaissance reference which, as Watson observes, turns a largely monochrome photograph into a colour one, the saturated pigment almost bleeding into the rest of the composition.

and the indie jazz revival of bands like Weekend, Sade (Helen Folasade Adu) was the glamorous, half-Nigerian fashion student figurehead of the scene, possessed of both a sublime voice and sultry model looks. Cool, haughty, and aware of her own talent, at the time, she was ultimately credible (not least because of her ethnicity and position as darling of *The Face*), a fact which the subsequent assimilation of her records into the MOR mainstream - the background to countless Eighties wine-bar seductions - has tended to obscure. The album *Diamond Life* (1984) spent 99 weeks in the charts and did as well in the USA, where her first album sold 1.5 million, and Sade was featured on the cover of *Time* magazine.

'To get noticed you have to play on anything you've got going for you', she told Lesley White in 1984. 'That's why we didn't object to being called a trendy group...We are. You have to be aware of how record companies and the press work. I don't totally disrespect the media - though it can be fickle and mean. They're got to have something to write about. I get a lot of press personally because I look different from other women, that's all.' It was a quality of which Sade was all too aware: as a line on her 1986 *Promise* had it, 'Don't blame her for her beauty'.

Sheila Rock, a major contributor to *The Face* during the Eighties, was impressed with Sade when she photographed her in 1984. 'I thought she was more beautiful without make-up. She was this beautiful black girl with freckles, very quiet, very shy.' Shortly after the session came Sade's success, 'and everyone wanted the photographs because she wasn't doing any more.' Sade had already entered the ranks of rarefied, untouchable stardom.

Culture Club

Eric Watson

1983

L to R

Roy Hay
Mikey Craig
Boy George
Jon Moss

Out of punk and New Romanticism, Boy George (George O'Dowd) emerged from Eltham via his Warren Street squat (shared with his best friend Marilyn) to become the mascara'd star of the 'second Golden Age of British Pop', leading a band whose second album, *Colour By Numbers* (1983), produced no less than five global hit singles. It was no fairy story, however: 'I could have ended up in suburbia, you know', said George. 'No one came down the chimney and said, you may go to the ball. I went myself and made the fucking clothes to go in.'

Having briefly fronted Malcolm McLaren's Bow Wow Wow as 'Lieutenant Lush', George assembled a representative section of pop's human race, put them in Sue Clowes' Judeo-Catholic-mystic outfits and sailed into the British pop charts with 'Do You Really Want to Hurt Me?' (1982) and 'Karma Chameleon' (1983). 'I didn't know everyone was going to go mad over me', said George. 'I thought we'd have a full-on freak following - freaky girls and boys - that was our audience. Then overnight, after being on TV, we became pop pin-ups... That's not what I expected, or planned'.

Nonetheless, George took full advantage of it, branding himself as the image of the band. Jon Moss, drummer and businessman of the group, recalls that 'he even had a shape...George was like a living logo'. Cross-gender, cross-generational, he was dubbed 'the Queen Mum of Pop' - although Princess Margaret thought him 'an over-made up tart'. Culture Club's unadulerated pop was eminently ready for mediation: the camera loved George almost as much as the tabloids did. Anodyne but with a hint of teenage subversion in his pantomime dame asexuality, George was acceptable to middle-aged women who longed to cuddle him and didn't quite believe that he really preferred a nice cup of tea to sex. Not everyone approved: to Phil Oakey of The Human League, 'Boy George killed pop music. He took the bizarre visuals that had been carried right through from The Beatles, David Bowie, Lou Reed and Roxy Music and he allied them with music even Marjorie Proops found attractive. Until then, if someone looked outrageous you could rely on them making weird music your parents would absolutely hate. Instead everyone thought: Ahh, isn't he sweet. He was the end of rebellion because mums and dads started telling their children that pop music was a respectable career.'

Nonetheless, George became a pop hero. Even the subsequently well-publicised fact that George was actually having an affair with his drummer contributed to rather than dispelled the group's allure, in which the musical contribution of guitarist Roy Hay and bassist Mikey Craig is often thrown into shadow by their 'living logo'. A great survivor, George came out of the band's destruction and his heroin addiction, becoming a DJ, and reviving Culture Club for their 1998/9 reformation tour with ABC - and The Human League.

Eric Watson's lustrous photograph was taken in 1982 for *Smash Hits*: spare and minimal as the rest of Watson's work, it displays the band's line-up (wearing Sue Clowes' clothes) without the usual prominence given to Boy George.

John Stoddart

In the same way that Culture Club seemed to be a bubblegum card collection of early Eighties types, so Frankie Goes To Hollywood (they took their name from a US movie magazine which referred to Frank Sinatra's move to Los Angeles) offered a newly gay-aware audience a band of three Liverpudlian scallies fronted by a pair of gay would-be icons: the clonish Paul Rutherford and the charismatic Holly Johnson. Both had served time in cult Liverpool bands: Johnson - like Morrissey, a local punk legend - had played bass in the self-consciously legendary Big in Japan, taking his name from the lyric of Lou Reed's 'A Walk On the Wild Side'; while Rutherford had appeared with the Spitfire Boys. Openly gay, their subversive style combined perfectly with the laddish appeal of ex-labourers Mark O'Toole, his brother Ged (later to be replaced by their cousin, Brian 'Nasher' Nash), and Ped (Peter Gill).

Frankie may have been Holly Johnson's creaton, but it was only the potent force of their record label ZTT - formed by the producer Trevor Horn, his wife Jill Sinclair, and cult Eighties journalist Paul Morley - which would disseminate the band's raucous, sexy, outrageous image and harness their music. Whilst Horn's state-of-the-art production shaped the sound, Morley's post-modern 'marketing and conceptualising' mediated the band by sharpening the appetites of a sensation-hungry public. They were the subjects of a sophisicated campaign, but it was old-fashioned sensation that sold Frankie.

L to R

Ged (Gerard) O' Toole
Paul Rutherford
Holly (William) Johnson
Ped (Peter Gill)
Mark O' Toole

The banning of 'Relax' (1985), with its blatantly sexual lyrics, and the accompanying video by Bernard Rose depicting the band, their camp followers and a tiger cub in a decadent nightclub, perfectly chimed with the perceived excess of the times. Morley's further coup was a clever piece of direct marketing: the best-selling 'Frankie Says' t-shirts (after designs by Katherine Hamnett) which sold alongside their twelve inches in record shops and took the band's image out of the racks, off the TV screens, and into street fashion. Suddenly everyone could look as cool, and pervy, as Frankie, the band's name writ large in condensed typeface across their chests.

These photographs, from Frankie's first photo-session, were taken before their record deal and were a crucial part of the campaign to get them signed. John Stoddart had covered the band's outrageous performance at a music festival in Sefton Park in July 1982. 'It was all a giggle and very tacky', he remembered. Soon after, a session based on the show was arranged. 'Paul and Holly turned up in leather gear heavily influenced by Mad Max,' recalled Stoddart. 'They had an idea that they wanted Mapplethorpe-type photographs. They had a good image. I just pointed the camera. It was great fun. They were very much at their ease - and though the lads weren't particularly into the ideas, they didn't seem to be that bothered.' Stoddart's pictures were circulated in the press to entice record company interest, but the overtly gay image of the band had the opposite effect. Chris Blackwell of Island Records, sent a promo video of the group in performance, declared, 'Not the sort of image for my company', only to sign a distribution deal with ZTT and thereby help launch Frankie Goes To Hollywood on the world.

In the early Eighties the exploration of crossover electronic dance music in Britain was epitomised by New Order's ground-breaking 'Blue Monday' single (1983). Hearing the track made Neil Tennant and Chris Lowe's hearts sink: it was exactly the sound they were intent on producing: a mixture of the gay disco being played in New York or Chicago nightclubs, and a yearning, classically English pop sensibility.

Having met in a shop in London, journalist Tennant and architect Lowe formed the Pet Shop Boys (the name sounded sufficiently urban-tribal, but came from friends who actually did work in a pet shop). After a fitful start - the pair were looked upon with some suspicion as being products of both Tennant's insider knowledge as former assistant editor of *Smash Hits*, and manager Tom Watkins' fervent manipulation - came a glorious run of hit singles. The drum machine beats, addictive melodies, lush arrangements and restrainedly emotional vocals of 'West End Girls' (1984, re-released 1986), 'Opportunities (Let's Make Lots of Money)' (1985, re-released 1986), and 'It's A Sin' (1987) commented on and helped to define mid-Eighties British pop.

The cool, often static image they projected - seen by some irritated (and perhaps envious) rock journalists as cynical and ironic - was in fact born of an appreciation of fashion and pop culture (Newcastle-born Tennant had been a glam rock fan, and Lowe, from Blackpool, a disco boy), combined with a degree of reticence, intelligence and objectivity which their late start in pop gave them. Their strength derived from the fact that they were not a band, but a duo; that they didn't deal in rock cliches; and that they seemed in control of their own destinies where others before them had been controlled.

The monetarist sardony of 'Opportunities' ('You've got the brains/ I've got the looks/ Let's make lots of money') encapsulated the image in cartoon terms: Tennant, tall dark and handsome in smart suits, the intellectual mastermind; Lowe, the keyboard *wunderkind* and sullen, cheeky, laddish half of the deal. The group's sharp grasp of cultural and social issues emerged in exquisitely-shaped pop songs unafraid of delving into the emotional states they apparently mask. Their famously uncompromising attention to detail (witness the intricately conceived stage shows of the 1989 tour, *Performance* in 1992, and *Somewhere*, 1998) presents one of the most honed images of any modern pop group.

Shot by Eric Watson in a studio in Farm Lane, Fulham, this session produced the sleeve of the 1986 single, 'Suburbia'. Watson recalls that Chris Lowe had just returned from Japan with clothes from a shop called Posh Boy, in which Watson shot him alone, adding Neil Tennant to produce press shots. The daylight effect was achieved with hall lighting, and Watson built a cone around the subjects through which he made a hole for his camera to prevent his own reflection. The sleeve - designed by Mark Farrow - subsequently won a DNDA award.

The Stone Roses

Pennie Smith

1988

In the late Eighties musical and cultural re-alignment sparked off by the 'second Summer of Love', The Stone Roses reinvented British rock. Melding rave with psychedlia, they were the focus - along with Happy Mondays - of the Madchester/Baggy scene, re-establishing the city's pop cultural hold and continuing a tradition (New Order and A Certain Ratio via Northern Soul) a white boys' hybrid of dance and rock. 'Manchester's best-kept secret', The Stone Roses influenced a generation and brought flares back onto Deansgate.

As cocky working-class Northerners, sprawling and shambolic, their 1989 album, *The Stone Roses* and the single, 'Fool's Gold', marked their overground peak, its signature the intricate guitar figures of John Squire (whose artwork also appeared on the band's covers, following in the art school/pop tradition). In recent times lead singer-gone-solo Ian Brown's increasingly erratic pronouncements and gestures have resulted in his incarceration at Her Majesty's pleasure. Now released, he is back in the charts with Unkle.

Pennie Smith's photograph was taken whilst she was covering The Stone Roses' European tour in 1988. She and the band were driving up to a roundabout in Belgium, recalls Smith. 'John Squire insisted on screeching to a halt and seeing this fighter plane stuck on the roundabout.' Smith's composition addresses the united front, brothers-against-the world stance, evident elsewhere in Jill Furmanovsky's photographs of Oasis and Chris Floyd's photographs of The Verve.

L to R

Mani (Gary Mountfield)
Ian Brown
Reni (Alan Wren)
John Squire

Shock troops in a Nineties resurgence of Welsh pop, Manic Street Preachers grew up in Blackwood, Gwent, and formed around bassist Nicky Wire (whose predeliction for make-up earned him the nickname 'Shirley' at school), James Dean Bradfield and Sean Moore. Like other bands of their generation, they were heavily influenced bythe events of 1976-7. 'A big moment was on the tenth anniversary of punk', recalled Wire. 'The Clash were on a compilation of that Tony Wilson programme *So It Goes*, doing 'Garageland' and 'What's My Name'. That was the catalyst to us forming a band. We thought we could look like that, walk like that. Although we couldn't play...'

The addition of Richey Edwards brought punk's nihilism: 'We are the suicide of a non-generation', he declared. Literate (their sleeve notes quoted from Primo Levi and Jackson Pollock), nationalistic and working-class, the Manics looked like a Nineties version of The New York Dolls. And like both the Sex Pistols (Edwards' followed a tradition of onstage self-mutilation begun by Iggy Pop and continued by Sid Vicious) and Joy Division, the group lost a crucial member when Edwards - whose anorexia, depression and other symptoms of dis-ease had become painful public property - disappeared in February 1995 on the eve of an American tour. His fate locked into rock myth; but ironically, only then, with the band's first release as a three-piece, *Everything Must Go* (which incorporated lyrics by Edwards), did the Manics turn their anarchy into mainstream popularity, toning down their image in the process. 'On the surface, we're not as sexy as we were when Richey was here', Wire told *Q* magazine in 1998. 'But it's all still there. It's all on the record.'

Kevin Cummins' photograph was shot at Holborn Studios, Back Hill, for an *NME* cover. The gold cloth and composition was influenced by Gustav Klimt, 'we just wanted that lushness', recalls Cummins. 'I thought it went with their tacky image. They took the idea very seriously - they wanted to exaggerate the trashiness. They went out the night before and got love bites from strangers to exaggerate the look. Then Richey got out this school compass and scratched "HIV" on his neck. He thought it would piss off everyone in the world. The trouble was, he'd done it in the mirror, so it said "VIH" when you looked at it.'

'We took a gamble putting these two on the cover and not the singer. But they had the look and that was the image of the Manics at the time', says Cummins. 'I like the power of a picture like that. Within the music industry it becomes iconic because people remember that shot. You feel you're helping to shape their look... At the *NME* we really helped to develop bands' looks - we were encouraged to use ideas on sessions. We could control it more - nowadays the PR wants to control it all the way.'

Blur

1994

L to R

Graham Coxon
Damon Albarn
Dave Rowntree
Alex James

Cocksure and confident, Blur's image has shifted from early Nineties slacker (their first single, 'She's So High', 1991, bore the influence of The Stone Roses) to smartened-up neo-Mod with *Modern Life is Rubbish* (1993), Paul Weller's favourite album of the year. *Parklife* (1994), with its snapshots of British life, evolved the mod connexion with the appearance of *Quadrophenia* star Phil Daniels. Sampling Sixties and Seventies British pop with a Nineties aesthetic, Damon Albarn's sarcastic Mockney voice was a cynical critique of suburbia ('everything we do has a subtle jibe at that suburban way of thinking', said Albarn), and of the subordination of British culture by the USA. Blur finally achieved mainstream success with the 'Club 18-30' satire 'Girls and Boys' from *Parklife* in 1994, which had the targets of their irony singing along to a song which parodied themselves.

Blur's success ensured that they and their contemporaries - Suede, Pulp, Elastica - became the public face of the phenomenon that came to be known as BritPop - a ubiquitous, media-invented term for the musical reaction against dance/rave culture. Albarn's boyish good looks, and his relationship with Elastica's Justine Frischmann, established the group on the frontline of the media frenzy, forced to do battle with their chart challengers Oasis in a stage-managed fight for number one with Blur's 'Country House' and Oasis's 'Roll With It' in the summer of 1995 - a competition which nonetheless put pop on the *Nine O'Clock News*.

The band have since subverted the BritPop tag with the grungey Americanism of 'Song 2' - an about-turn on their anti-USA stance, and publicising the latest, more introspective album '13', Albarn specified that he would only be photographed unshaven, claiming his boyish looks militate against him. Like Bowie before him, his not-so-secret ambition is to act, a theatricality traceable in his lyrics. Blur have grown up, no longer the young lads of the early Nineties, depicted here by photographer Harry Borden.

Shot in a lean-to at the end of an alleyway off Beaufort Street, Chelsea, Borden found the group 'weren't particularly easy to work with. They were all quite young - the same age as me - and they tend to gang up on you. It was quite confrontational - I suppose that's was makes it a strong photograph. They'd had a long time in the indie wilderness, and they'd just made it big.' The edginess is apparent in the hands-in-pockets, elbows-on-knees stance; they look like a gang of graffiti-writers caught on a suburban railway station. But the look - student/mod/art school - is as knowing as their clever brand of Nineties pop.

L to R

Paul 'Guigsy' McGuigan
Noel Gallagher
Liam Gallagher
Alan White
Paul 'Bonehead' Arthurs

Oasis

1995

Jill Furmanovsky

Antidote to the faceless and sometimes souless hegemony of the dance scene, Oasis revived British pop culture with their brand of laddish, anthemic rock in the mid-Nineties. They cited The Beatles as their gods, but were the legatees of the continuing Manchunian revolution begun by The Stone Roses and Happy Mondays. Product of a Northern love of clothes which traces back to Billy Fury and beyond, theirs was a logical evolution of the Baggy look: the trademark anorak, shaggy haircut and hunched-shoulder, hands-in-pockets swagger-slouch affected by would-be Manchunians well below the Watford Gap. The arrogance was justified by the *Definitely Maybe* (1994) and *(Whats the Story?) Morning Glory* (1995) albums and singles 'Cigarettes and Alcohol' (1994), 'Roll With It', and 'Wonderwall' (1995).

Powerfully underpinned by overt hedonism and turbulent private lives which become public expressions of the group's ethos, Oasis were readily assimilated into the late-BritPop, media-created world of 'Cool Britannia'. The image of Liam and Patsy Gallagher, as photographed by Lorenzo Aguis on a Union Jack-covered bed for the cover of *Vanity Fair* in 1997, was an iconic/ironic highpoint of the phenomenon, closely followed by news footage of Noel and Meg Gallagher drinking champage at 10 Downing Street. That year the album *Be Here Now* sold a record-breaking 696,000 copies in its first week of release, but the band appeared to be already past their peak. 'I know where we lost it', said Noel Gallagher recently, 'Down the drug dealers.'

To the public at large, the Oasis image is the Gallagher brothers, and their love-hate relationship. It is characteristic that, as Jill Furmanovsky comments, this photo session was preceded by a violent row between the brothers: the photograph is charged with their tempestuous relationship. In the catalogue to her exhibition of Oasis photographs, 'Was There Then' (1997) Furmanovsky writes 'I haven't ever seen them actually fighting, but when I did these pictures of Liam and Noel in Paris, I really thought that at any moment something would spark off... You didn't need to have them actually scrapping, but you can see - the body language is all there. It's like war photography. The interesting thing was that I kept it going and they let it happen and they let the pictures go out. It really should've been cancelled'.

What Helen Shapiro began in the Sixties, and Bananarama continued in the Eighties, The Spice Girls completed in the Nineties. Taking up Madonna's provocative cue, yet remaining somehow innocuous, The Spice Girls rode on a triumphant slogan of 'Girl Power', but were easily assimilated into the sexual stereotyping of their media image. They were a paradox: an assembled, pre-packaged retort to the sway of the boy bands and the fastest selling new act since The Beatles, yet a strong, identified female image (what Boy George refers to as 'council estate glamour') which symbolised a new empowerment of women in pop - although it was immense success which gave them that power.

With names invented by *Top of the Pops* magazine, 'Ginger Spice', Geri (Estelle Halliwell) 'Sporty Spice', Mel C (Melanie Jayne Chisholm), 'Scary Spice' Mel B (Melanie Janine Brown), 'Baby Spice', Emma (Lee Bunton), and 'Posh Spice' Victoria (Adams) all ready for bedroom pin-ups, the group cut through social barriers in the meritocracy of the Nineties: witness their global centrestaging with Nelson Mandela, flirtation with the heir to the throne - and declaration of war on Oasis. 'If Oasis are bigger than God', said Mel C, 'what does that make us? Bigger than Buddha? Because we are a darn sight bigger than Oasis.' Comic-strip characters neatly self-parodied in their box-office success, *Spiceworld* (1997), their staying power helped transcend the Barbie Doll image, along with the pop survival gene that enabled them to reposition after adversity. A perfect example of the lowering of pop's age of consent, The Spice Girls fan base begins at around the age of five, and continues well into the first generation of pop.

Lorenzo Aguis' photograph - commissioned for *Spiceworld* - is full of pop cultural references, from the pneumatic Vargas girl looks, to Dezo Hoffman's *Twist and Shout* jumping Beatles, via Philippe Halsmann's famous 1959 *Jump* series of leaping mid-century celebrities. Aguis - who also shot the portraits for the *Trainspotting* poster - used a trampoline in a studio in Islington, taking just eight frames per Spice. Other action shots used on the video sleeve were taken on running machines which were subsequently digitally removed.

L to R

Emma Bunton (Baby)
Victoria Adams (Posh)
Melanie Brown (Scary)
Melanie Chisholm (Sporty)
Geri Halliwell (Ginger)

Jarvis Cocker (Pulp)

1995

Barry Marsden

Pulp, like their fellow BritPopsters Blur, had been around for some time before achieving chart success and public celebrity - most notably with the single 'Common People' and an establishing appearance at Glastonbury in 1995 which showcased both Jarvis Cocker's sardonic stage repartee and camp posturing, and - paradoxically - the band's somewhat elusive image. 'We try as hard as we can to avoid being too clearly defined,' says Cocker, 'because once people think they know exactly what niche to fit you into, you lose a lot of your power.'

Nonetheless, their stance is defined here by Cocker - Sheffield-born fish-cleaner and St Martin's School of Art student - whose dead-pan humour and mannered charity-shop chic is a remarkable pop creation. A transgenic cross between Andy Warhol, Kenneth Williams, Morrissey and Bryan Ferry, Cocker and Pulp expanded on the sort of pop cultural sampling which fellow Sheffielders ABC and The Human League had explored a decade before. 'Most people are quite conservative', says Cocker. 'They assume that because we're bothered about what we wear, we have no emotional depth.' Drug controvesy fed the release of 'Sorts For E's and Whizz' (1995), when the group made the front page of the Daily Mirror, but with his stage invasion during Michael Jackson's hyperbolic appearance at the BRIT Awards in February 1996, Cocker truly endeared himself to the discerning British public.

Photographer Barry Marsden recalls that the portrait was taken 'at the very end of the shoot, in the last ten minutes. I hadn't shot any black and white and I took Jarvis aside - and got the two best shots of the day. He's an absolute star - just point the camera and he does it.' Asked to bring props to the session, Cocker produced a Seventies Thimble advert of a woman's waist cinched with a tape-measure belt, and a copy of the art book, The Body. While both were abandoned for the last few frames, they appeared to have informed Cocker's pose: it tilts at the fashion- and body-consciousness of his media. The shape is Madonnaesque (in her 'vogeuing' phase) via Fifties kitsch, rendered in the clean, clear lines of a Richard Avedon portrait; Marsden saw in the picture a comment on the vogue for ultra-thin models. 'The pose was carefully worked out between us' he notes, a complicity apparent from Cocker's louche stare, an irony shared between him, Marsden, the viewer, and the image itself. In seeking to avoid definition, Pulp subvert the entire process of the creation of a pop icon.

The Verve

1997

Chris Floyd

The Verve (the definitive article was added after a legal injection from Verve Records) appeared in the slipstream of Oasis (although the Manchunians had supported them in 1994),the Stones to the latter's Beatles, led by a virtually mystic, acid-taking frontman and drawing on influences as diverse as Can, William Blake, Northern Soul and Iggy Pop. Best known for their 'Bitter-Sweet Symphony' (1997), the song contained more than a clue to their stylistic influences, sampling as it did the orchestral version of the Rolling Stones' 'Last Time' arranged by Andrew Loog Oldham; much was made of the resemblance between Richard Ashcroft and Mick Jagger. Wigan-born Ashcroft was an adolescent style experimenter, dyeing his hair every shade from peroxide through purple-black to a footballer's perm before arriving at his shaggy cut (with a nod towards *Performance*, the 1970 film whose decadent spirit the band also seemed to reflect).

Chris Floyd photographed the group throughout 1997, taking this shot in Richmond Park while the band were recording the *Urban Hymns* album at a studio in Chiswick. Floyd echoed the title by positioning the band on a hill with a view of London in the distance (the setting and styling seem to reference Mankowitz's 1967 Stones portrait for *Between the Buttons*, taken at dawn on Primrose Hill). The group assumed the 'flying V' formation, which Floyd had seen used by Iggy Pop and the Stooges. 'They're in a "get on with it" mood: "We're doing this because we have to, we're not enjoying it." They didn't like having their picture taken.' Floyd shot just two rolls of 24 exposures film. 'You concentrate in situations like that. It's about engineering a moment with what you want it to be.' Floyd was aware of the group's almost fetishistic eye for clothes. 'They are all pretty stylish people. A lot of thought has gone into what they're wearing. It doesn't look like it - that's the point.'

L to R

Peter Salisbury
Simon Jones
Richard Ashcroft
Nick McCabe
Simon Tong

Steve Gullick

As a satellite zone of London, Essex had ever been a fertile breeding ground for pop culture from its keen mod following, to the Canvey Island Forties revival of the Seventies, Ian Dury's paeans to the area, and Depeche Mode's techno-pop. It was a place ready to take up the dance revolution of the late Eighties. Like the Kent-grown Orbital, The Prodigy were a prime product of that movement, which took the DIY attitude of punk, some of the social exclusion of the convoy people, and much of the homegrown black dance music which was itself a product of a multicultural country. The result was the 'Second Summer of Love'. Liam Howlett, living in Braintree, Essex, had been steeped in ska, punk and hip-hop when he was introduced to the phenomenon at a rave in The Barn in Braintree. 'I thought it was the bollocks, such a different experience from what I had become used to. Hip-hop was such an exclusivist, pretentious scene, and to a certain extent, it always excluded white blokes. Then to experience something like that first night at the Barn was such a stark contrast, I really liked the music and the whole vibe. I had never been into dancing that much, but it didn't matter, because you could enjoy it, you didn't have to dance properly.'

Out of this experience, Howlett created The Prodigy (later to dump the definitive article), with long-haired Led Zep fan Keith Flint, 6'5"dancer Leeroy Thornhill, and vocalist Maxim Reality (Keith Palmer). They produced commercial hits like 'Charly' (1991), yet remained largely underground. Then Flint got multi-pierced, cut and dyed his hair (the look seemed to derive directly from the punk sub-heroine and Sex Pistols' *Anarchy in the UK* fanzine cover star, Sue Catwoman) and sang 'Firestarter' (1996), appearing in its video (the group refused to perform live on *Top of the Pops*) as a arsonist demon in a sewage pipe. The image was as extreme as the music - especially on stage, with Flint's caricature punk partnered by Maxim Reality in metal teeth, satin kilt and nail varnish: 'Once I'm ready, I've got my kilt on and the mic in my hand and my gauntlet on, I feel like a bigger person', he told *Vox* in 1997. 'I feel like a warrior. I'm going out there to conqueror something'. Prodigy had overstepped the boundaries of techno, hip-hop, pop and even heavy metal ('Breathe' was voted single of the year by the readers of *Kerrang* magazine in 1996).

As pop icons, Prodigy derived their strength by that very transition, from the alternative into the mainstream, although the banning of the predictably controversial 'Smack My Bitch Up' seemed to be as cynical a ploy as the gender-reversing video which accompanied the single. The now-iconic Flint - his image already parodied in advertisements - rehabilitated the group in PC eyes with his recent decision to have 'Dump the Debt' tattooed on his back in the Band Aid-like campaign against the collection of interest on Third World loans.

Steve Gullick accompanied the band to the Lebanon on assignment for the *NME* in 1997. It was a very hostile environment, he recalls: the band are posing on a bunker where the government buildings had stood, and they were on the verge of pulling out from the gig they were due to play that night. Guarded by government security, they were told by the British Embassy that if they didn't play, their security might turn on them; they played, and the concert drew its energy from the tenseness of their situation. Highly aware of their image, the band sanctioned Gullick as the only photographer with whom they will work.

clockwise from top left

Keith Flint
Maxim Reality
Leeroy Thornhill
Liam Howlett

The Welsh pop renaissance - Manic Street Preachers, Super Furry Animals, 60 ft Dolls, Stereophonics - has reached a peak with the recent successes of Catatonia. Founded in 1992 when Colwyn Bay-born Mark Roberts found former council rubbish collector and doctor's daughter Cerys Matthews busking Jefferson Airplane songs outside Debenhams in her native Cardifff, and joined by Mark Roberts, Owen Powell, Paul Jones and Aled Richards, they released three singles for the Welsh independent Crai. In 1995 they were signed by far-sighted Rough Trade boss Geoff Travis to Blanco Y Negro, recording the *Way Beyond Blue* (1996) and *International Velvet* (1998) albums. 'Road Rage' earned them a 1998 Brit Awards nomination, but it was 'Mulder and Scully' (1998), a witty tribute to *The X-Files*, that established them for the public, additionally alerted to Cerys Matthews' sassy looks and strong voice by her duet with Tommy Scott from Space, 'The Ballad of Tom Jones' (1998).

In the modern high-turnover, artificial pop world, Catatonia's is not a manufactured image: Cerys Matthews' is a thrown-together look, part early Madonna, part Bet Lynch, laden with junk shop costume jewellery. She cites her influences as Tom Jones and Judy Garland, and her growling Celtic vowels and hippie chic have made her a modern pop icon, not least amongst her male fans. But the appeal appears to be transgenerational. 'Children like it because it's honest, Matthews told the *NME* in 1998. 'And they like my jewellery. It's not got pretensions, that's all, and there's a lot of pretensions around at the moment...We are a natural band, you know, nobody comes and says, 'This is your look". So we veer on the edge of disasters all the time. But that makes us more normal.' 'And ultimately this is what makes Catatonia so cherishable', noted their interviewer, Stephen Dalton, 'the bruised, lived-in quality of their anthemic pop stompers. There is always a sting to their tales, a sour dash of grubby realism and genuine heartbreak beneath the skin of deep glamour.'

Klanger and Boink's specially commissioned photograph, entitled 'Portrait of a Girl with a Lovely Voice' was based on a 1940s photograph of Jack Kerouac in his National Coastguard uniform smoking a cigarette, and Vermeer's 'The Girl with the Pearl Earring'. The photographers note: 'The word "Caption" on the hatband is obviously a pun on words with "captain", but more important than that it is a photographic device to point out the triangular relationship between the word "caption", the title of the image, and the fact that visually the "lovely voice" is replaced by the soft blow of smoke. Above all, though, it is a portrait of an enigmatic lovely, sexy sailor girl!!'

KODAK TX 6043

110

British pop's newest star, Robbie Williams is a little boy showing off, a cheeky chappie in music hall mode not averse to charlestoning on stage. Out of the prototype - and immensely successful - Nineties boy band Take That, which he left in 1995, Williams emerged, via a queasy indie drugs-and-drink phase, as a true star, merging rock and pop in a cabaret manner; people's pop via the working mens' club.

The image is laddish couture with a touch of Lancastrian camp; a series of tabloid-advertised romances lending the air of a Northern Nineties sub-James Bond (an image caricatured by Williams in the award-winning video for 'Millenium', 1998). His signature tune is the rousing anthem 'Let Me Entertain You' (1998), parodic and sincere at one and the same time, whilst the preceding hit, the ballad 'Angels'(1997) is proof of a sweeter soul. 'I'd like to be a cross between Tom Jones, John Lennon, Chuck D and Gene Kelly', he has declared. A classic showman for Blairite Britain, Williams has become the acceptable face of pop, characterised by his professionalism. 'If I'm going to do this entertaining thing, I might as well be good at it'.

Hamish Brown's photograph is an attempt to contain Williams' energies and expressions; stilled here, amongst the mayhem backstage at *Top of the Pops* (for 'Let Me Entertain You'). Brown had to stand on a pool table for the fifteen-minute session, during which he shot three rolls of black and white film and two rolls of colour. 'He's fantastic to work with - he gives you everything', enthuses his 'official' photographer. Witty, energetic, stylish, Williams' enthusiasm for his art sums up five decades of British pop culture.

Selected Bibliography

Ash, Russell & Crampton, Luke, with Lazell, Barry,
The Top 10 of Music, Headline 1993

Bowie, Angie with Carr, Patrick, *Backstage Passes*, Orion 1993

Braun, Michael, *Love Me Do*, Penguin 1964

Burchill, Julie, and Parsons, Tony, *The Boy Looked at Johnny*, Pluto 1978

Cann, Kevin & Mayes, Sean
Kate Bush: A Visual Documentary, Omnibus 1988

Cass, Caroline, *Elton John's Flower Fantasies*, Weidenfeld & Nicolson 1997

Cranna, Ian, *Rock Year Book Vol VI*

Davies, Ray, *X-Rayed*, Viking 1994

Du Noyer, Pauk (ed), *Encyclopaedia of Singles*

Faith, Adam, *Act of Faith*, Bantam 1996

Fletcher, Tony, *Dear Boy: The Life of Keith Moon*, 1998

Furmanovsky, Jill,
The Moment: 25 Years of Rock Photography, Paper Tiger 1995

Hammond, Harry & Mankowitz, Gered, *Hit Parade*, Plexus 1984

Heatley, Michael,
Manic Street Preachers: In Their Own Words, Omnibus 1998

Heatley, Michael, *The Encyclopaedia of Rock*, Grange Books 1997

Hoskyns, Barney, *Glam!*, Faber & Faber 1998

Jobey, Liz, *The End of Innocence*, Scalo 1997

Larkin, Colin, *Virgin All-time Top 1000 Albums*, Virgin 1998

Lazell, Barry & Rees, Dafydd, *Bryan Ferry & Roxy Music*, Proteus 1982

Michael, George, with Tony Parsons, *Bare*, Michael Joseph 1990

Paytress, Mark,
Twentieth Century Boy: The Marc Bolan Story, Sidgwick & Jackson 1992

Rock, Mick, *A Photographic Record, 1916-1980*, Century 22 1998

Roberts, David (ed), *Guinness Rockopedia*, Guinness Publishing 1998

Savage, Jon, *England's Dreaming*, Faber & Faber 1990

Shaw, Sandie, *The World At My Feet*, HarperCollins 1991

Smash Hits Yearbook 1983-1990

Stump, Paul,
Unknown Pleasures: A Cultural Biography of Roxy Music, Quartet 1998

Vermorel, Fred & Judy, *Sex Pistols: The Inside Story*, Omnibus 1987

Waller, Johnny & Rapport, Steve, *Eurythmics: Sweet Dreams*, Virgin 1985

Wedgbury, David & Tracy, John, *As Years Go By*, Pavilion 1993

Newspapers and Magazines:
Selected issues of *NME, Melody Maker, Sounds
Let It Rock, ZigZag, Sniffin' Glue, The Face, iD, New Sounds, New Styles, Blitz, Smash Hits, Vox, Q Dazed & Confused, Sleazenation*

National newspapers, including:
The Times, The Independent, The Observer, The Telegraph, The Sun, Daily Mirror

Television:
Young Guns, BBC TV series, 1998
BBC documentary, *Robbie Williams*, 1998
BBC Omnibus, *Billy Fury*, 1998

Acknowledgements

Firstly we would like to thank all the photographers who have made this book, and exhibition, possible by giving their time, and vital information on their lives and the circumstances of the photographs.

Eric Watson may be justly credited with inspiring *Icons of Pop* through his generous donation of many of his key colour and black and white photographs from the visually important years 1981 - 6 spent at *Smash Hits*. This inspired us to research further the fuller context and look both backwards and forwards at pop iconography. His generosity has been matched by the photographers represented here, many of whom have made works available to us which will form a permanent, and expanding record of pop history at the National Portrait Gallery.

We would also like to thank:

Mark Ashurst, Vonetta Baldwin and Lorraine Griffin (Public), Michael Bracewell, Murray Chalmers, Rosalind Crowe, Paul Davies (Q Magazine), Norman Davies (Scope Features), Emily Dowler, Claire Eastman, Robert Ellis, E P Trust, Alix Holden, Michael Holden, Rob Holden, Jez (Terry O'Neill Archive), Virginia Lohte (Star File), Janet Lord and John Mouzouros (EMI Archive),Yumi Matote, Neil McKenna, Glenn Marks and Sasha Tanyar (Rex Features), Theresa Moore, Philip Nevitski, Alexander Proud, Simon Puxley (Roxy Music Archive), Terry Rawlings (Wedgbury Archive), Gina Spencer (Mercury), Neil Tennant, Vicki Wickham, John Ross, Tomoko Okano, Aska, Riki

We would finally like to thank all those from within the National Portrait Gallery who helped with the project by giving their support, encouragement and enthusiasm.

Neil Tennant
Neil Tennant is one half of the pop duo Pet Shop Boys

Philip Hoare
Philip Hoare has written books on Stephen Tennant and Noël Coward, and claims to be Southampton's first punk.

Terence Pepper
'Sergeant' (Terence) Pepper split with his eponymous Band to become Curator of Photographs at the NPG in the late 1970s but still regularly visits Planet Pop.

Susan Bright
After teaching English in Mongolia Susan joined the NPG in 1998. She is currently coming to terms with her ra-ra skirt.